THE OLDEST
GAY COUPLE
IN AMERICA

THE OLDEST
GAY COUPLE
IN AMERICA

A Seventy-Year Journey
Through Same-Sex America

GEAN HARWOOD

A Birch Lane Press Book
Published by Carol Publishing Group

A Birch Lane Press Book
Published by Carol Publishing Group
Birch Lane Press is a registered trademark of Carol Communications, Inc.

Editorial, sales and distribution, rights and permissions inquiries should be addressed
to Carol Publishing Group, 120 Enterprise Avenue, Secaucus, N.J. 07094

In Canada: Canadian Manda Group, One Atlantic Avenue, Suite 105, Toronto,
Ontario, M6K 3E7

Carol Publishing Group books may be purchased in bulk at special discounts for sales
promotion, fund-raising, or educational purposes. Special editions can be created to
specifications. For details, contact Special Sales Department, Carol Publishing Group,
120 Enterprise Avenue, Secaucus, N.J. 07094.

Manufactured in the United States of America
10 9 8 7 6 5 4 3 2 1

Library of Congress Cataloging-in-Publication Data

Harwood, Gean.
    The oldest gay couple in America : a seventy-year journey through
same-sex America / Gean Harwood.
        p. cm.
    Includes index.
    ISBN 1-55972-426-9
    1. Gay male couples—United States.   2. Gay men—United States—
Family relationships.   3. Aged gay men—United States.
4. Interpersonal relations—United States.   I. Title.
HQ76.3.U5H37   1997
305.38'9664'0973—dc21   97-16955
                                                                        CIP

To my life-partner, Bruhs Mero, who lived the dream with me and made my life a grand, creative adventure.

And to my son, Richard Harwood Brown, whose steadfast devotion transposed the dream to reality through the pages of this book.

Contents

Foreword

It has never seemed to me that longevity is the hallmark of lives or relationships. A person can live a very long life indeed, sucking up the world's energy and not leaving a trace of good works or deeds behind. On the other hand, at this moment in time, many of our friends are dying young and some of them leave us with sparkling legacies.

Likewise, some relationships are beautiful and brief, ended by death or by choice, while others may endure for decades propped up on mutually destructive fears, bad habits, or just plain languor.

Why, then, is the story of Gean Harwood and Bruhs Mero so compelling beyond the fact of its longevity? The answer is in this book. It's about years, yes, more than sixty of them, but moreover it's about trust, devotion, courage, and, of course, love. And, my personal favorite, it's about the ability to change.

Gean and Bruhs met at a time, 1929, when there was a considerably gay community in New York, but no public discussion, no legal protection, and very little social support. Gean and Bruhs made their own way. Cautiously but determinedly, they lived as a couple. Often they were lonely and, with good reason, frightened. After World War II and into the McCarthy era, life for lesbians and gay men became ever more dangerous and fraught with challenges.

Gean and Bruhs barely related to the events surrounding the Stonewall rebellion in 1969. Gean reports that as they grew older they became more isolated. So their enormously public coming out in the 1980s, when both men were in their seventies, is an inspiring story for us all.

We no longer have to accept, "he's too old to come out" or "she's from an earlier generation" as complete explanations of behavior. It's demeaning to old people to suggest that they're stuck, that they can't change, just because they're old.

My lover and I have been together a mere twenty-one years and we're often asked, "What's your secret?" Gean and Bruhs were asked this same question by friends, by strangers, and by television, radio, and newspaper interviewers.

There's no secret. Gean Harwood's autobiography, *The Oldest Gay Couple In America,* is not a self-help book and not a text. To my way of thinking, it's better. It's the intimate, day-to-day, year-to-year recollections of a man who loved another man, and still does.

That this love happened to span more than sixty years is our good fortune as well as Gean's and Bruhs's. It provided the stuff for a book, this book.

Tom Wilson Weinberg
Composer of *Sixty Years with Bruhs and Gean*
Philadelphia, June 1995

Preface

When the documentary, *Silent Pioneers,* about elderly homosexuals was shown June 25, 1985, on WNET-TV, the *New York Times* television review by Walter Goodman said in part:

> Perhaps the most moving moment of the half hour comes when a man named Gean...reminisces about his lifetime romance with Bruhs. "After 54 years we're still in love," he says, and chucks his friend under the chin. He recalls how handsome he always thought Bruhs was, and Bruhs sings to him, "If you hear me calling, it's only my heart."*

The film turned a brief spotlight on the lives of two men who lived a different love story. This book tells how Gean met Bruhs, and how they shared their life and dreams for more than sixty years. It will show that despite all sorts of social and personal obstacles, such continuity is possible for those striving together for a life of dignity and purpose. Telling this story of "a love that dared not speak its name" but nonetheless prevailed, some stereotypes may be shattered and those who need it enlightened.

The term *gay* has been adopted by almost everyone, including the *New York Times*. The expression *gay* is in such common use today that it is difficult to always place in its proper time frame, and its use here in the earlier parts of the book is perhaps anachronistic. It was a term used privately, if flippantly, for years prior to the gay Stonewall uprising of 1969. Only after Stonewall and the emergence of gay liberation did it come into general use. Nonetheless, throughout this narrative the term *gay* is used purposely. It is not perfect, for it fails to adequately describe preponderantly sober-minded, totally re-

---

*"It's Only My Heart," lyrics by Bruhs Mero, music by Gean Harwood (see page 183).

sponsible homosexual men and women. Nevertheless, *gay* is vastly preferable to *homosexual,* which places an undue emphasis on sexuality.

Most gay people would be quite content to be treated as people, in all the complexity and fullness of their lives, as fellow human beings, engaged like everyone else in living and loving. Yet for most of their lives as gay men, Bruhs and Gean have traveled in a corridor of fear. Those who are gay know the route only too well. For too long and without reason, gay people have been subjected by bigots to vile epithets, snide innuendo, sneering contempt. At the hands of such homophobes, gays and lesbians have been victims of all manner of quite legal but discriminatory maneuvers and of senseless acts of barbarity.

Therefore, this narrative respects the anonymity of many who, for reasons of their own, are still held hostage in that corridor of fear. But in mentioning the openly gay activists, their own names have been used, with pride in their achievements for gay liberation and with admiration for their inexhaustible dedication to the cause of gay rights.

Yet many of the people who had a vital impact on the lives of Bruhs and Gean may be totally unknown to present-day readers. Buildings that held so many memories and helped shape their lives are gone, victims of New York City's ubiquitous "demolition derby" and high-rise-construction frenzy. But though people and buildings may have vanished, the memory still remains of the richness and color they brought to these two lives.

On July 13, 1993, the documentary *For Better or for Worse,* begun in 1989, was finally shown on the New York Public Broadcasting System. In a review in the *New York Times,* Walter Goodman wrote:

> Five love stories are told in *For Better or for Worse.* Three of the couples, all of whom have been together for more than half a century, are white and heterosexual, one is black, and one is homosexual. Yet these ten people are very much alike in their feelings for the person who is never referred to as the "significant other" as the camera catches hints of their class, their milieus...and their quirks, [as] they talk about their lives—how they have managed to stay together all these years.
>
> High points: The homosexual couple is seen being

celebrated in a New York City gay pride parade as "The Two Oldest Gay Men in America."

The hour, which has lots of tunes in it, ends on a perfect note with Billie Holiday's delivery of "Our Love Is Here to Stay."

In 1980, the film *Cruising* so grossly misrepresented gay lifestyles that it evoked mass picketing by the gay community. More recently, in *Basic Instinct* a heartless killer was portrayed as lesbian. In *Silence of the Lambs*, the killer is a gay man, and in *JFK,* a group of gay men are conspirators in the assassination of Kennedy. Even in the 1990s, gay people are made to appear threatening and a menace to society.

In March of 1993, *For Better or for Worse* was nominated for an Academy Award. It did not win an Oscar. Could the reason the Academy rejected it have been that the producer equated a gay relationship with those of straights?

The homophobic bias of Hollywood (and mainstream America) is to still picture gays either as sinners against God and nature, as a corrupting influence on society, or as bizarre subhumans, whose commitment to each other, regardless of its depth, somehow lacks validity. It is not surprising that two fine recent films, which portrayed gay men as caring human beings, *The Wedding Banquet* and *Farewell My Concubine,* were passed over by the Academy. It is to the Academy's credit that they at least gave Tom Hanks a Best Actor Award for his role in *Philadelphia,* in spite of its gay theme, which was possibly Jonathan Demme's conscious act of atonement for his denigrating treatment of gays in *Silence of the Lambs*.

In writing *The Oldest Gay Couple in America,* my hope is that it will add strength to the struggle to liberate gay people from the burden of false judgment and malicious ill will they have endured over the years.

Acknowledgments

Rita Addessa, for her gracious hospitality in Philadelphia and for introducing us to a TV appearance on *Horizon*.

Chris Almvig, for her friendship and support.

Nancy Andrews, for including the touching portrait of us in her book *Family: A Portrait of Gay and Lesbian America* (Harper San Francisco, 1994) and for her warm support and belief in my book.

Richard Harwood Brown, for his inexhaustible efforts on my behalf, and for his enveloping love and assistance.

William Brown Jr., M.D., for his abiding interest and affection.

George Chauncey, for including us in his extraordinary book *Gay New York*.

Mark Dunn, playwright, for his encouragement and friendship.

Ken Dawson, whose loving interest at SAGE made us gay activists and introduced Gean and Bruhs to the public.

Jim Ellison, author/editor, and Steven Schragis, publisher, and all the many hardworking hands at Carol Publishing Group.

Richard E. Feldman, Esq., of Sonnenschein Sherman & Deutsch, for over a decade of loving interest and advice.

Milton Goldman, whose gracious help was extended on countless occasions and whose words of encouragement started my work on this book.

Harold Gomeau and John Harbster, for their support and encouragement.

Thomas Keith, actor/playwright, for early assistance with the manuscript and unflagging encouragement and support.

Egbert Knight, for his loving friendship and unflagging loyalty.

Arlene Kochman, for her loving support and assistance at a most critical time in my life.

Jed Mattes, whose bleak appraisal of my literary ability doubled my determination to get my story to its readers.

Carolyn Micklas, for her patience and skill in preparing the manuscript.
Matthew Moross, for loving interest and thoughtful cooperation.
Thomas Nuendel, poet and musician, for his efforts in distributing the CD and finding a publisher.
David Powell and Tom Pileggi, for their early support and generous assistance.
Luis Rey, for his friendly strong support.
Vito Russo, for including us in his history-making book *The Cellulloid Closet.*
Wayne Steinman and Sal Iacullo, for loving support.
Danny Toma and Vincent Colavito, at Omni-Tech of Albany Inc., for their technical assistance with the CD.
Gene Tunezi, for his support and generous guidance.
Laurie Wagner, Stephanie Rausser, and David Collier, for *Living Happily Ever After* (Chronicle Books, 1996).
Carl Watkins, for spiritual guidance and inspiration.
Tom Wilson Weinberg, composer/playwright, for warm assistance and especially for his touching musical portrait, *Sixty Years With Bruhs and Gean.*
Malcolm Willison, for his patience, perception and editing skill.

THE OLDEST
GAY COUPLE
IN AMERICA

1

Recharged Memories

It was Friday evening, June 25, 1982; Bruhs and I were watching our accustomed television. We had become the hermits of Third Avenue; death or relocation had taken away practically all our friends. Bruhs and I had been together since 1930 in a relationship that had spanned fifty-two years. We felt the need to communicate our lifestyle to others, yet our isolation seemed to grow more acute with each passing day.

Suddenly we were startled by the phone. It was Milton Goldman, one of our few remaining friends.

"I'm at Kennedy for a flight to London tonight," he said. "I've made arrangements with Ken Dawson, the executive director of SAGE, to pick you up tomorrow at 1 P.M. He'll take you to the gay synagogue, to be honored by a luncheon for your fiftieth anniversary. That is a milestone in gay relationships. It rates a celebration and, short of a mention in the *Guinness Book of World Records,* I'm seeing to it the event is properly covered. I have arranged with Arthur Bell to interview you for the *Village Voice.* Congratulations! Enjoy! Bye."

Bruhs and I looked at each other. There was no time to decide whether we would choose to have a "coming out" party. For us the die had already been cast.

Saturday, June 26, dawned bright and clear. There was no flash of lightning, no rumble of thunder, no shaking of the earth as Bruhs and I emerged from the closet. Ken met us at our door with a bouquet of roses. After a fast trip to the Village by cab, we were ushered through the door at SAGE (Senior Action in a Gay Environment) into the embrace of a most loving group of people. We had been transported into the middle of the gay community!

We didn't have the heart to tell anyone the golden anniversary

3

party was two years late. When we cut the spectacular cake provided by our friend Milton, the flashbulbs popped, and we were hugged by lesbian friends whom we hadn't seen for years. Tears of joy streamed down their faces.

We were asked to speak. Bruhs, too overcome by this outpouring of affection to marshal his thoughts, handed me the microphone to answer the questions being thrown us by the crowd:

"How'd you make it to the fiftieth?" "What's your magic formula?" "How did you face the straights' hostility all those years?"

I was as bewildered as Bruhs, but I managed to express our appreciation for this beautiful reception, and to acknowledge that we had no magic formula beyond establishing as our priority our being together. I stressed the need for compromise, without sacrificing one's individuality. Sometimes that is a large order, but the guests seemed to accept it. Men and women came up afterward to embrace us and wish us well.

From the luncheon table we moved to the dance floor, where we were invited to lead the dancers in the "Anniversary Waltz." Bruhs had been a professional dancer and I was always his accompanist on the piano, but we had not danced together since the 1940s. I felt completely disorganized and could hardly put one foot before the other. Bruhs, on the other hand, was completely self-assured and was fully in command. He counted in my ear and skillfully manipulated me to make it appear that I was actually waltzing!

We left the dance floor to be interviewed in another room by Arthur Bell, a name well known to us because we had read his articles. He often dipped his pen in acid, and his wit crackled across the page. He could devastate pompous personalities and had a sixth sense in uncovering the phony, yet he could be passionate and eloquent in defense of those people and causes dear to his heart. Knowing his mercurial nature, we were unprepared for the supremely beneficent manner he exhibited toward us; it was as if he had adopted us. He continued his friendship until his early death in 1984.

Arthur had set up a tape recorder to get our story. Turning to me, he started with, "How did you two meet?"

Bruhs seemed to hesitate, so, oblivious to the presence of Arthur's brother at the table, I began:

One evening late in 1929, a mutual friend brought a charming, handsome young man, Bruhs Mero, to the apartment that I shared with three other gay young men on Hudson Street. As he walked in, our eyes met for a moment, and an unspoken understanding passed between us. A surge of warmth filled my body and I caught my breath. This unaccountable depth of feeling on a first meeting was a rare experience for me, but I was careful to conceal it, for fear it was not reciprocated.

Although he was visiting a gay household, by his attitude this visitor appeared uninterested in an amorous experience with another male. I eventually learned that he was engaged to a young woman who was making plans for their marriage. So I had been wise to conceal my attraction to him. However, he did seem inclined to expand our platonic relationship, and we met occasionally for lunch.

Several months later, one of the young men with whom I shared the apartment, returning from a cocktail party, stopped in a subway station men's room. In those days, vice-squad detectives concealed themselves in public toilets. If his quota of arrests fell below expectations, the detective would actively entice the unwary into a compromising situation and then, in a show of "moral" indignation, collar the unsuspecting participant. The hapless roommate, his judgment impaired by alcohol, was the victim of entrapment and taken into custody.

The police contacted the landlord, who notified the superintendent. That very day we were served with an eviction order to vacate the premises within forty-eight hours. When we protested on the grounds of our lease, we were told that it was automatically canceled and the owner was within his rights to deny housing to "fags."

This action against those with absolutely no connection to their roommate's difficulties brought me face-to-face with the homophobic climate of the 1920s and 1930s and showed me just how much justice gay people could expect. I had been introduced to the "corridor of fear" and would travel its dreary length for years to come.

The other two roommates scattered, and I, in a panic, found a studio listed in the Sunday *New York Times*. Without thinking, I put a nonreturnable deposit on it. Repenting at leisure, I called Bruhs to tell him of the first crisis in my independent life. He joined me to look at the place I had rented and made the horrifying discovery that, in addition to its being just slightly larger than a closet, it had no radiator. "How are you going to survive the winter without a radiator?" he asked.

I had recently started work at Paramount Pictures, handling transportation for their stars and executives. I was earning a magnificent $20 per week, so every penny counted. At this point, the man whom I would know as Bruhs for sixty-five years came to my rescue, as he was to do many times throughout our lives. He suggested we take a larger studio together in the same building, thus saving my precious nonrefundable deposit. The building into which fate had thrust us was the Vanderbilt Studios on East 38th Street. It housed musicians and vocal students and provided an appropriate setting for an alliance that was soon to go from warm friendship to a tender and enveloping romance.

Our close proximity living in one room posed a problem for me. I felt myself more and more attracted to him and yet respected the connection he had with straight life. I was not about to interfere in his relationship with his girlfriend and had no wish to unduly influence the direction his love interest had taken.

The Vanderbilt Studios was a rare example in New York City of mid-Victorian architecture, with mahogany balustrades on winding staircases that would have made an ideal setting for an Agatha Christie mystery. The talented people who lived at the Studios were highly diverting.

Our floor boasted a famous tenant, the character actress Alison Skipworth. She was making films at the old Famous Players–Lasky Studio in Astoria, Queens, and had rented her studio to be near her protégé, Daniel Wolf. The Vanderbilt Studios had no elevator, which meant Skipworth had to climb four long flights of stairs each day. The first time we heard her climbing the stairs, panting and wheezing, we looked out our door and called down:

"Can we help you, Miss Skipworth? Are you all right?"

Between gasps she airily replied, "Oh, I'm just fine, dear."

We made friends easily at the Studios. Daniel Wolf invited us to evening musicales in his studio. Jeanne Palmer Soudeikine, soprano at the Metropolitan Opera, was a frequent visitor there and stirred us all with her "Ho Jo to Ho's" from Wagner's *Die Walküre*. Daniel himself was not only a composer but a fine pianist, and he frequently entertained us with brilliant renditions of Chopin.

Through Daniel, I became familiar with much of the great piano literature and finally decided I must have a piano of my own. With the financial help of a gay friend I knew at work, I bought a lovely little Fischer baby grand piano. Because nothing that large would fit through our dormer windows, it was carried up four flights of winding stairs to our fifth-floor studio apartment. After my piano came, Bruhs, who loved to sing, would sit beside me for many happy hours. I began to try composing melodies to which he fashioned lyrics. We became known as budding composers at the Studios, and Daniel affectionately dubbed us "Bach and Beethoven."

There is a chemistry at work in all relationships. Who is to say at what moment the emotional balance tipped in my favor and this attractive man began to feel that I was more than a friend? Ever so gradually, he felt free to express his own emotions, and to release those feelings with affection. Who knows how it happened? Some force, stronger than either of us realized, was beginning to shape our destiny.

When the lease at Vanderbilt Studios expired, we were ready to embark on a truly shared life together in another apartment on West 37th Street— At this point Arthur Bell interrupted my reminiscence in a mock tone of admonishment:

"We are not doing *Gone With the Wind* here, you know! My column has limits, and we have to start condensing a little! I can't get a whole issue at the *Voice* for this story." Though his tone was commanding, I could see he was enjoying the interview and he devoted that whole column to us.

As we left the SAGE anniversary gathering at the gay synagogue, three of the lesbian friends with whom we had been reunited that day invited us for dinner at Fedora's Restaurant. A Greenwich Village bistro with Fedora and her husband Henry's own added warmth of welcome, for years it had been a favorite with gay people where they felt at home and could be themselves.

That evening at dinner was filled with reminiscences, but the fast wrap-up for Arthur had left me with memories still spinning in my mind. It is one thing to remember events of fifty years ago, but quite another to recapture their mood. Memories may crowd the mind, but to organize them into some semblance of order is, at my age, a challenge. I couldn't stop. I had to relive our life together and reassemble its pieces like a gigantic scrambled picture puzzle.

2

Love and Separation

The apartment we rented together on West 37th Street, in 1930, was ordinary, with none of the picturesque quality of the Vanderbilt Studios. It did have a separate bedroom, however, which would later give us a chance to add to our income when we became financially hard-pressed.

My sister Marie visited us several times. She frequently made the six-hour trip from Auburn to New York City in her own car. Once when she and I were driving on the West Side Highway, she discovered to her dismay that she was headed in the wrong direction. With the utmost confidence in her judgment, she made a U-turn (on the West Side Highway!) and continued undaunted on her merry way.

The stock market crash of 1929 had already sent shock waves through the economy, warning signs of more economic hard times to come. Bruhs had left his position as assistant to the advertising manager at Arnold Constable to assume greater responsibilities at Gimbels. His salary increased, and his career in advertising appeared to be going nicely.

I had settled into the work at Paramount Pictures and became accustomed to handling celebrities and dealing with their whims and temper tantrums. Unfortunately, details of transportation, passports, and the like are the things that stars and company executives care the least about, and so it was not surprising that many were unappreciative and even uncooperative.

I remember meeting Marlene Dietrich when she arrived on the *Bremen*. She was fresh from her European triumph, *The Blue Angel*, and had not yet become the legendary star that Josef von Sternberg created. I was struck by the simple and wistful charm she possessed,

8

but I was totally taken aback when I learned that she traveled with fifty-four pieces of baggage, mostly trunks! It crossed my mind, what could one person possibly have in all those trunks? I never found out, but I had the responsibility of getting all that baggage to and from the West Coast, and back and forth to Europe, on her many trips.

On one of them to Hollywood, I had arranged for fresh flowers in Ms. Dietrich's drawing room aboard the Twentieth Century Limited. I had turned over to her the many transportation and baggage claim checks and was standing not three feet away. Just as the "All aboard" was heard, she turned to a publicity department representative and, nodding toward me, said to him in her husky voice, "Tell the young man I thank him for everything."

I was too tired to respond appropriately to her thanks.

In the twenty years that I labored in the Paramount vineyard, the whole roster of stars—Gary Cooper, Cary Grant, Claudette Colbert, Maurice Chevalier, Jeanette MacDonald, Bing Crosby, Bob Hope, Jack Benny, the Marx Brothers, Kitty Carlisle, Loretta Young, Charles Laughton, Ethel Merman, Mae West, Gloria Swanson— passed through my hands. My disillusion with "stars" and "stardom" became almost complete. Some of the *Hollywood Variety* stars felt it accentuated their importance to be difficult in any dealings with the motion picture company. Their behavior would not have advanced their popularity if their fans had witnessed it. Those who seemed really to appreciate or acknowledge our efforts on their behalf were shockingly few.

Fortunately for me, there were some exceptions to salvage my morale. Some stars, mostly from the stage, who felt secure in their positions in the theatrical firmament were gracious and treated us humanely. Kitty Carlisle and Gladys Swarthout were both charming. The day I delivered Ethel Merman's transportation receipts to her, she welcomed me into her suite with her great booming voice and insisted that I have coffee and chat with her.

The most notable example of gracious behavior was that of Helen Hayes. When she signed to do *A Farewell to Arms*, the shooting schedule compelled her to leave for Hollywood in the midst of a summer heat wave. When I met her at Grand Central to escort her to the train, the terminal was stifling. I handed her transportation papers over to her and started to take her through the train gate. She turned to me and placed a hand on my arm, and with the most winning smile I have ever seen, she said, "No, young man, you go somewhere and get cool. I'll manage very well by myself."

I seemed to fare better with male than with female stars. By and large they were easier, and I enjoyed my encounters with Brian Aherne, Henry Wilcoxson, Ray Milland, and Regis Toomey, to name a few. The day that Oscar Levant embarked for his first picture at Paramount, he paced back and forth in great agitation and said a cup of coffee would help. When I got him some and assured him that an unlimited supply was available for the trip to the Coast, he became quite affable and gave me a big smile. If troublesome stars could only have been so easily satisfied by a cup of coffee!

Often after an exhausting day with some difficult star, I played hookey and stole away to the Museum of Modern Art on West 53rd Street. Every afternoon they screened films from their enormous collection of film classics. I spent many an hour watching again the films that had enriched my growing up. Before the controversy that surrounds the film today, I was stirred by the dramatic sweep of D. W. Griffith's *The Birth of a Nation* and the brilliant performances of Lillian Gish, Mae Marsh, and Wallace Reid. I was enthralled by the sexual dynamism of Gloria Swanson and Thomas Meighan in *Male and Female* and lost in the exquisite beauty of *Broken Blossoms*—the sheer poetry that Lillian Gish and Richard Barthelmess evoked together has never been equaled. I went back again and again to see Douglas Fairbanks's ebullient personality and athletic prowess displayed so effectively in *The Thief of Bagdad* and *The Black Pirate*. To me these actors represented the true essence of film greatness. As Norma Desmond, the silent star portrayed so brilliantly by Gloria Swanson in *Sunset Boulevard,* said, "Who needs voices! In those days we had faces!"

In 1932, we met Howard Sosnicki, who is presently my oldest living friend, at a Sunday afternoon tea party (cookies included). These rather strange affairs were attended by a diverse group, both gay and straight. Their patronage helped our host, who occupied a spacious apartment on Central Park West, to pay his rent. It was a novel, but effective, way to meet his living expenses. It also provided a meeting place for friendships to develop. I distinctly remember that the cost of admission was twenty-five cents.

The economic crisis continued to deepen; we were all sinking into the Great Depression. Taking a cut in salary, I had to be thankful that I still had a job. Bruhs was not so fortunate. He was an early victim of a retrenchment that spread like wildfire through advertising. He looked for related work but found nothing, given the severity of the Depression.

We found it necessary to rent our bedroom to supplement our income. We had frequently eaten dinner out. A complete delicious dinner at Ruth Garner's Little Tavern on West 47th Street cost seventy-five cents! Another restaurant frequented by gay men was Madge Surtee's Better 'Ole. Madge, once a British actress and married to a bisexual man, always visited the tables of her gay patrons, where, wreathed in smiles, she would inquire in her British accent, "Are you enjoying your dinner? How is your meat? Is it warm?"

There was an unspoken acceptance at these restaurants, and the gay clientele, always welcome, never violated the rules of proper decorum. But soon, even these restaurant outings had to be curtailed, and we found ourselves preparing our evening meal in a little kitchen we improvised at one end of the bathroom. It was impossible to save anything from my meager salary, and Bruhs, who had enjoyed a much better income than mine, finally used up what little savings he had.

At this point, Fate smiled again, albeit a bit wryly. Bruhs was offered a job with his brother, Gilbert. Gil had assumed control of a small vegetable farming interest in Bradenton, Florida. He wanted someone with him whom he could trust implicitly.

This was a difficult step, for it meant that we would be parted indefinitely, after only two years into a relationship that grew more meaningful each day. After many tearful discussions we decided that the Florida job with Gil was a life preserver. In a mood of resignation, Bruhs packed for the trip. That last night neither of us slept and we held each other close to ease the pain of the impending separation.

That was the first time I had really been totally by myself. Without him I felt indescribably empty, and waves of abject loneliness washed over me. Only his blithe spirit could fill the void that engulfed me; only his warmth could abate the chill that crept into every corner of my life.

The first night he was away, I tossed and turned in my bed, hoping that sleep would come. Near dawn, I lapsed into a fitful slumber and I relived, as in a dream, the events of New Year's Eve, 1930....

Unaccountably, Bruhs had no date that night with his fiancée, so he and I spent it together at a party at Daniel Wolf's, downstairs from our place in the Vanderbilt Studios. The champagne flowed freely, due no doubt to Alison Skipworth's largesse. But shortly after midnight, he and I climbed the stairs to our studio on the fifth floor. We were both giddy from the wine, and I was ecstatic from spending an evening with someone who had become very dear to me.

Ever since we had begun living together we had each had our own bed, but on this night I could not bear the thought of sleeping alone. I had often seen him undressed, and he always reminded me of Michelangelo's *David*. Now his tantalizing nearness seemed to demand that I share the warmth of this rare human being.

We began to take off our clothes for bed, and we both sat on the edge of my bed. I helped him out of his last bit of clothing, and as he stretched out full length, he closed his eyes. I looked at his lovely frame and caught my breath. How I wanted to worship at the shrine of this diminutive alabaster god!

I took him in my arms. There was no resistance. My lips brushed his cheek and he did not recoil. Our lips met, and there was only a childlike acceptance of my embrace.

There was no turning back now. We were starting down a quickening descent. There was no time to question my action—no thought of trying to stop. Somewhere along the steepening slope he must have felt any resistance melt, for he gave himself completely in total surrender to my passionate pursuit.

It was an unbelievable outcome, a consummation of months of repressed longing. I knew that nothing would be the same for either of us from that night on....

Now that he was gone, there was no one I cared to turn to for companionship, though he and I had made many friends. One day, one of these friends approached me with what I felt was an unusual request. He had just met a young man about whom he knew very little. He politely asked me to speak to his new friend. "You are discreet and never give the impression you are prying. I want to know if he is a c.s."

I viewed the whole thing as a rather quaint way of phrasing a gay persuasion. It certainly avoided a vulgar expression and, slightly amused, I agreed to speak to his friend. A few days later, having observed the friend's mannerisms, I reported that I was sure the acquaintance was a c.s., to which he replied, "How can you be sure?"

I smiled and said, "It takes one to know one."

At that he blushed and stammered, "Oh, I guess I didn't make myself clear...I wanted to know his religious persuasion—if he was a Christian Scientist."!

Every one of our friends traveled in the same corridor of fear that we did—fear of parents finding out, fear of the ever-present and painful rejections associated with being a "known homosexual." There was fear of being ostracized by straight peers who might totally misunderstand our sexual preference. With employers there was an even greater risk, with economic repercussions too dreadful to contemplate. To exist at all, we felt we had to conform. Most gay people were forced to lead double lives, never daring to reveal their true selves, or their deepest feelings. Because of what society demanded of us, we felt we both had to avoid men who were effeminate and women who were too obviously masculine, because associating with them would reveal too much about us to the straight world.

But when Bruhs arrived in the small Florida community of Bradenton, his situation became even more difficult. He was thrust into a totally new and narrow environment, and he quickly learned that Southerners just didn't trust Northerners. But besides feeling like a foreigner in a strange land, he had his own personal loneliness to deal with. He spent long hours by himself on the beach, and from the depths of this emotion came the lyrics for a lovely song:

COME AND TAKE MY HAND

Lyrics by Bruhs Mero; music by Gean Harwood

Somewhere, in the far away,
A voice whispers, "Come and take my hand"—
Parting cry of a soul forlorn
Wafted 'cross the shifting sand.
Time tho' fleet as a winged bird
Cannot still the echoes of thy voice—
Visions wakened at dawning
Fill this heart with a longing
For a voice from the far away
Whispering low, "Come and take my hand."
Far away on a misty shore
Where the waves break high upon the land—

> Someone, standing patiently,
> Waits for me to take his hand.
> When the moon casts its path of light
> Shining far across the deep blue sea—
> Voices telling their story
> Echo love's own great glory
> But one voice calling plaintively
> Whispers low, "Come and take my hand."

How many months he spent in Florida, I do not remember. I only know that the days seemed interminable. But again by some twist of fate, we were to be reunited.

I learned from Bruhs's sister Anne that there was to be a World Peace Festival with Walter Damrosch conducting the New York Symphony at the old Madison Square Garden in January 1933. The featured work was to be the "Ode to Joy" from Beethoven's Ninth Symphony; Irma Duncan, Isadora Duncan's adopted daughter, was to do the choreography. Anne's daughter, Jean, aged twelve, had studied the Duncan technique at Irma's studio. One day when Bruhs had visited his niece there, he had joined a class and begun to move with the youngsters. Impressed by his natural flair for movement, and now needing male dancers for the Madison Square Garden performance with Damrosch, Irma remembered him and persuaded Anne to contact him to ask him to come back to New York City for rehearsals as quickly as possible.

The venture with his brother, started with high hopes, had gone steadily downhill, and Bruhs was overjoyed at the opportunity to return to the city and to me. He managed to scrape together bus fare, and thirty-six grueling hours later, I took him in my arms. The part of me that was an empty shell without him was now filled, and I felt complete. We both were ready to trust in our destiny and face each tomorrow together.

3

The Dance

When Bruhs started dance rehearsals with Irma Duncan, a door opened on a different world for him—the world of dance. At first, everything felt awkward and strange to him, but as he began with the other dancers, he became aware of what this change meant to his inner being. Gradually he realized that dance supplied an element in his life that had been missing—an outlet for creativity that was an undiscovered part of him, waiting for expression.

Irma Duncan's need for male dancers also prompted her to contact Denishawn House. There she was able to recruit several young men from a group that also functioned as a part of Ruth St. Denis's ballet company. Through the cooperation of Miss Ruth, as her group always called her, Irma could also use the capacious rehearsal space at Denishawn.

After the first day of rehearsals there, a group of the dancers came back to our West 37th Street apartment and clustered around the phonograph. As the "Ode to Joy" rose from a well-worn record, they listened intently for the musical cue to their entrance, to set it firmly in their minds.

Each day brought my partner new experience as the rehearsals took shape. They were days of physical exhaustion for him, but the undercurrent of exhilaration sustained him. At last he seemed to be doing what he was destined to do, and above all something that he liked.

At Denishawn, a young man named Harry Losée had become Ruth St. Denis's partner and principal dancer. He replaced the cofounder Ted Shawn, who decided to concentrate his artistic efforts on an all-male group and severed all connections with Denishawn House and Ruth St. Denis. Losée frequently watched the Duncan rehearsals; he observed an attractive youth moving with the others and was struck by his innate talent and natural grace. As I was to learn later, he was quite smitten by Bruhs's physical appeal. Losée's willingness to take Bruhs under his wing and devote many hours to instruction and guidance was not wholly without ulterior motives.

Like it or not, there seems to be an unwritten law that would-be professionals must learn to live with. They must early on accept that progress in any theatrical endeavor is dependent on trade-offs. By now everyone in the theater knows that there is a price on every-thing—call it "the casting-couch syndrome." They also know that payment will be exacted in whatever way the recipient of favors can deliver. This is true whether the "desirable one" is gay or straight, and the person who has the power to grant the favors can, as well, swing any way that his or her libido dictates.

After weeks of preparation, Bruhs made his dancing debut at Madison Square Garden. As the dancers took their places on the double stage, designed by Joseph Urban to fill one end of the cavernous old Garden, I looked for one in particular. As Walter Damrosch led the two-hundred-piece orchestra and the thousand-member chorus into the opening bars of the "Ode," the dancers cast a glance at the audience of twelve thousand people and, for a moment, must have felt overwhelmed by the sheer magnitude of the event and awed by the realization that they were a part of it. Caught up by the magic of the moment, Bruhs danced with fanatical energy and fire right up to the last bar of the triumphant score.

The Madison Square Garden performance quickened the pace of his career. His second public appearance was to be in a February Carnegie Hall concert with the St. Denis company in which Harry Losée offered him a part. For his appearance with the Ruth St. Denis company at Carnegie Hall, Losée coached Bruhs daily in intensive dance training. As Harry was Miss Ruth's principal dancer and director and took charge of most of the rehearsals, he easily arranged for Bruhs to be a member of the ensemble. This became a foundation in dance movement that was to shape his entire approach to the dance and the development of his individual style.

Losée had worked extensively with the celebrated German Dr. Bess Mensendieck, who had demonstrated her unique muscle-control technique to many groups, including the physical education department of the New York public school system. Dr. Mensendieck, who had done valuable work with war-injured veterans, hoped to bring her system of muscular control to American youngsters to replace the sterile and ineffectual practices still in use. However, her methods were considered too complicated for youngsters, and her ideas were accepted only in limited ways by some physical education personnel as well as by only some dancers. However, Losée incorporated many of her methods in his exercise classes and adapted them to dance movement. His personal style was greatly influenced by Mensendieck, and so Harry's student absorbed these basic ideas of controlled movement.

Eventually, as Bruhs spent more and more time away from me in pursuit of his career, I began to feel deprived and jealous. Although I realized the value of this instruction to him and tried to put it in perspective, this assuaged me only up to a point. I didn't want to stand in the way of his progress, but night after night alone made me feel our relationship was doomed.

At this stage of our lives, we did not have clear communication; that came much later. Unfortunately, at this time my way of handling difficult situations and feelings of hurt was to clam up. I gave Bruhs the silent treatment; but instead of easing the problem, this only made things worse.

Bruhs stood it as long as he could, but finally one day he put his arms around me and held me close. His voice was earnest and tender.

"What is happening to us? I know you're hurt, but we have to talk about it. I am doing what I'm doing because I see no other way to go on with my dancing. You are the only one who means anything to me. Anyone I see, or even sleep with, means nothing. Nothing can change or affect what we have together. Don't you know that?" He could tell by the tears that welled up in my eyes that I believed him, but I still could not voice my fears. Although reassured by his words, the next night that he was away from me, all the old doubts surfaced, and I was again filled with frustration.

The Carnegie Hall experience gave Bruhs a stronger feeling for performing before an audience, and he welcomed the opportunity to continue with Miss Ruth and Harry when they did a week's performances at the Mansfield Theatre in April 1933. While there, he moved up to a duet with Jack Cole, as part of Harry's placing him in more prominent spots. Jack Cole, who later capped a brilliant career with dazzling choreography for *Man of La Mancha,* was far from happy at sharing the stage with a brash young novice. He considered himself a seasoned performer, having had a close association with Denishawn

House. It really rankled to be asked to forgo a solo and to accept a beginner as a partner. Because of this, the atmosphere was frigid between them, but eventually Jack warmed up a bit, and by the end of the engagement he and Bruhs were friends.

Sunday evening, April 30, 1933, was the closing performance of the Mansfield Theatre engagement. The final portion of the program was an elaborate allegorical dance-drama entitled *The Prophetess*. Miss Ruth danced the title role, and the stage was filled with dancing figures representing all kinds of human activity—workers, soldiers, artists, mothers.

Many dancers frequently defer their meal until after a performance; they feel they can work better on an empty stomach. As Miss Ruth moved among the dancers, they became aware that she was having some flatulence. An old English limerick flashed through Bruhs's mind:

> I sat by the Duchess for tea.
> I knew just how it would be.
> Her rumblings abdominal,
> Were something phenomenal,
> And everyone thought it was *me!*

For the finale, the dancers formed a mound of humanity over which Miss Ruth did a spectacular back-bend. As the strains of Gustav Holst's *The Planets* suite soared forth, it happened. Miss Ruth could contain herself no longer and delivered her own resounding fusillade. The huddled dancers under her were convulsed, and they started to giggle and shake. This "mountain of humanity" was rocked by a mirthful earthquake. It was good to know that Miss Ruth, who so often personified an ethereal goddess in white jade, was as fundamentally human as the rest of us. In 1969, when we went backstage to congratulate Jack Cole for his work with *Man of La Mancha*, Bruhs reminisced about the old days when they had worked together, and how Miss Ruth's unexpected "jet propulsion" had shaken the mound of dancers.

In 1934, Harry Losée introduced Bruhs to Gluck-Sandor and Felicia Sorel, who were doing presentations at the Barbizon Plaza Concert Hall. They were interested in expanding their company and eager to offer a showcase for young talent.

This meant a preliminary "audition" for Bruhs, which involved spending the night with both Sandor and Sorel in their suite at the Barbizon. It was most embarrassing for him: they were both attracted to him, and he literally didn't know which way to turn. It must have been frustrating for everyone, and ultimately little more than affectionate fondling occurred.

Important as such encounters were to him, they represented time and attention he was devoting to others rather than to me, and I was perturbed by the infringement of these bizarre episodes on our life together. But I could do little beyond handwringing and praying that somehow our fragile craft would ride out the storms.

Whatever disappointment Sandor and Sorel may have felt from Bruhs's "audition," they exhibited only the utmost cordiality as they welcomed him into their company, the Dance Center. Among the modern ballets they performed during their season were *Salomé* from Richard Strauss's opera and *El Amor Brujo* to the music of Manuel de Falla.

Gluck-Sandor was a fascinating choreographer/performer whose flashes of theatrical genius dominated his work. At times he bordered on the psychotic in his movements, best illustrated in a brilliant piece entitled *Phobias.* He provided consistently interesting pictorial effects, and Bruhs relished every opportunity to expand his performing experience in working with this extraordinarily talented man.

In addition to performing with the company at the Dance Center, Bruhs gave classes in the Mensendieck exercise method. One day in his class a brash young dancer showed up who had adopted the name Robin Gerald. After class he had everyone in stitches with his deft imitation of some typical Sandor movements. This talented young man was destined to reach the very zenith of the dance world as America's top choreographer, Jerome Robbins.

The closing performance of the Dance Center season was a repeat of the popular *El Amor Brujo.* José Limon had performed the leading role in previous performances, but at the last moment, he was unable to appear for the season finale. Sandor, on the edge of panic, appealed to Bruhs to take over the role. Without rehearsal, and in a last-minute rush before curtain time, he had to improvise a suitable costume and get into makeup.

As he struggled with these details, a smiling, friendly face showed up at the dressing room door. It was Robert Lewis, known to his friends and associates at the Group Theatre as Bobby. He quickly sensed how tense Bruhs was, and seeing him striving to get the effect of high cheekbones with makeup, Bobby proceeded to do a ten-second demonstration of the art of makeup that was to stay with Bruhs throughout his career.

He danced the leading role and did it with uncommon authority. Every movement was strong and secure. He was lyrical when the part demanded it, and passionate and fiery in his breathtaking changes of pace. I sat with Bobby Lewis in the audience, and we were both thrilled to see how beautifully Bruhs had risen to the occasion.

Bobby was so impressed by that performance that he kept in touch afterward and introduced Bruhs to several members of the Group Theatre, including Sanford Meisner and Elia "Gadge" Kazan. This legendary assemblage of talent in all phases of the theater went on to make theater history with an imaginative and innovative playwright, Clifford Odets.

With dance activity in the city on the wane for the summer, Harry Losée decided to take a group of dancers to Pawling, New York. An estate at Duell Hollow was at his disposal, with room for sixteen dancers. In June, Bruhs went off with the group to work on Harry's ambitious project, *The Passion of St. Sebastian,* set to the Debussy score *The Martyrdom of St. Sebastian.* If all went well, Harry hoped to interest John Murray Anderson, one of Broadway's busiest impresarios, in getting it produced at the Metropolitan Opera House in 1934.

Meanwhile, the lease on our West 37th Street apartment was expiring, so before Bruhs left for the country, we scouted the city for new quarters. We found a charming place in Chelsea with a living room that featured floor-to-ceiling windows with a pier glass mirror between. The room also boasted a white marble, working fireplace. To one side of the living room, a tiny staircase led to a balcony that could accommodate a small bed. There was also a bedroom off the living room. The kitchen consisted of an alcove with a small gas stove and an old-fashioned icebox. Even though these facilities would not lend themselves to large-scale meals, we knew they would do for our limited entertaining. The best part was that all this was available at $35 a month.

Transferring our belongings to the new apartment could not take place until after Bruhs left, and I missed his strong supervisory hand. However, I had the help of a young man of about twenty, named Charlie. He had come to our door one day looking for the young actor who rented our spare room. They had met when Charlie ushered at a theater in Paterson, New Jersey. Charlie knew no one in New York, was coming out of the closet, and gratefully turned to us for guidance and companionship in finding himself. Charlie had entered a new world and needed the advice of those whom he thought knew the ropes.

The day before the move took place, Charlie and I visited the new apartment and were horrified to find an army of roaches wandering across the living room floor. My heart sank--why had we ever rented this place? I might have known there had to be a catch! It was my first experience with the oldest inhabitant of New York, the ultimate survivor—the cockroach. Fortunately, Charlie's resourceful-ness came to the rescue, and he battled the invaders with an effective spray. By the time the movers arrived the following day, no roaches were to be seen. After a minimum of settling in and putting some things away, I dropped into a chair to catch my breath. The big jobs simply would have to wait for Bruhs's return. He was the homemaker in our partnership, and I bowed to his superior know-how in putting on the finishing touches that would turn mere living quarters into a home.

I tried to forget the long summer months that lay ahead and the time that I would have to spend alone. For the moment, I was content that we had a new roof over our heads and would be together in September. I did not reckon on the changes that were waiting in the wings.

4

Work and Crisis

My days were filled with the problems surrounding my duties at Paramount. The Marx Brothers had been signed for a picture, and I started planning the details for transporting them to Hollywood. The four brothers were married and, with their wives and children, would require two Pullman cars for the trip. To accommodate stars I frequently arranged to have the railway cars transferred from the Twentieth Century Limited at the La Salle Station, Chicago, to the Santa Fe Chief, which departed from Dearborn Station. This allowed our privileged passengers to remain in their railway car and made baggage transfers between stations unnecessary. This operation required tricky switching maneuvers across the city. Naturally, once the railroads had set it up, they expected the date to be firm and that the film company, for whom the favor was being done, would follow through as scheduled.

I completed all arrangements, and with their tickets in hand, I went out to the Brooklyn Paramount Theatre where the Marx Brothers were doing a stage show. I waited in their dressing room. As Groucho came through the door, I stepped up to him and said, "Mr. Marx, I want to give you your transportation for the trip to Hollywood."

With no change of expression, he said in a flat voice, "We're not going."

I looked at him dumbfounded, speechless. I saw days of dickering with the railroads going down the drain. Finally I asked shakily, "What am I supposed to do with these tickets?"

It was a mark of restraint that Groucho didn't tell me what I could do with them, but in the same expressionless voice he replied, "I don't care what you do with them. We're not going."

Talk about being in the dumps! Back at the office, the production manager tried to explain that there had been contract snags with the Marx Brothers, so their departure date was indefinite. My only reply was, "Why couldn't someone have told me?"

Of course the Marx Brothers did go to Hollywood, and I did the entire rigmarole all over again.

To get away from the stress of the job, I often visited some friends' rambling fieldstone house near Woodstock, New York. I had known the Anderson brothers since 1928 when they occupied a duplex in Washington Mews, off lower Fifth Avenue. Albert, the younger, was a fine organist and teacher. He was in his late forties, and gay, though he never pressed on me any sexual relations. He expanded my musical education beyond the classical areas introduced by Daniel Wolf and made me aware of a whole new world of composers such as Delius, Poulenc, and Prokofiev. The older brother, Adolph, a dentist, had been left a very wealthy widower. Having built this lovely house in the country, Happy Brooks, the Anderson brothers entertained many well-known musicians and a host of other friends.

One weekend, I came up to Happy Brooks and was surprised to find only two other guests. One of these was a tall, personable young man named Gene Hollister, who had been brought to Happy Brooks by Tom Mairs, a sweet person. An old friend of Albert Anderson's, Tom and Albert had probably had an affair, but they were so discreet and so fearful of being found out that this must have frustrated any deep expression of their affection.

In any case, the sleeping arrangements at Happy Brooks were interesting. There was a sleeping porch with four single beds. On this occasion, Albert occupied the end bed; next to him was Tom; I was next; and Gene had been assigned the other end bed. When the lights were out, it was dark on the porch and difficult to see. I was astonished when I found Gene in my bed. I had not even been sure that he was gay. He held me close for only a few moments, then with a good-night kiss silently left my bed for his own.

Sunday evening Gene returned to New York City with me on the train. He talked freely about himself, and of wishing to continue his education in something practical, such as business management. He was ushering part-time at the Roxy Theatre to pay his way. When we left the station, Gene shook my hand, and he said he would call. He was a likable fellow, but I was sure I would never hear from him again. I was wrong; he called me every day thereafter.

Because Bruhs was away and I had nothing else to occupy my leisure, I began to see more and more of Gene, first for dinner. When he was working the door of the Roxy, he often passed me in to see the show. When he worked late, I frequently waited for him and then went on to his place to spend the night. It somehow didn't occur to me where this was leading. We were both lonely, and we found each other's company congenial and comforting. At times a show of affection would lead to sex, but there seemed to be no complete desire on my part, or Gene's, to accentuate the physical aspect of the friendship. I never pretended to be a single on the loose, and I made a point of telling Gene about my partner and how much he meant to me. I felt that Bruhs and I were as close as ever, and that he, with his philosophy about spiritual fidelity, would understand. It is a measure of my naïveté that I believed Gene's understanding would match my partner's.

The day that Bruhs returned from Pawling, I called Gene to tell him I could not see him that evening, and that we would have to rearrange the times we might spend together. I could sense that he did not accept this change of plans and he said rather abruptly, "I'll meet you after work at your office, and we'll talk."

When I saw Gene in the lobby of the Paramount Building, I was shocked by his appearance. His face was white as a sheet and he hustled me into a coffee shop without a word. We were scarcely seated when he began to speak in a strange, tense way that was totally unlike him.

"Gean, you can't do this to me! You can't shut me out of your life! We have meant too much to each other—at least, I thought we did! It just can't happen this way. It was so right! We were meant for each other. You can't turn your back on something that is true and real."

I was totally unprepared for this turn of events, and my consternation showed. "Gene, wait a minute, you have everything twisted around. I have never misled you into believing we have any commitment to each other. I have never pretended I was in love with you, and I never expected any such declaration from you. I'm sorry if you assumed otherwise."

Gene shook his head and tears came into his eyes, but he went on, "You have to choose between us, Bruhs and me. You have to consider how beautiful our existence has been together, yours and mine—what we can do for each other. You need me, Gean, and I need you. You can't deny what is true."

I could see that our talk was getting nowhere, and my only thought was to get away, to give myself an opportunity to think clearly. As long as I looked at his distraught face, I felt only shame and guilt for my part in his bitter disillusionment.

I stood up, and as calmly as I could, I said, "Gene, please understand, I had no intention of hurting you and I am sorry, but we have to realize everything that's involved. We have to calmly reason it out, and we'll talk again when we're not so upset."

He grabbed my arm and held it in a viselike grip. "I'll never let you go, never. Never!" His words sounded grimly foreboding, and they echoed in my brain as I took the subway.

When I was able to speak to Bruhs about Gene, I approached him with many misgivings. I certainly did not feel good about myself, and I felt I had betrayed Bruhs in some irreparable fashion. As far as choosing between Bruhs and Gene, there was no contest, but I felt unworthy of the trust my partner had placed in me, and I despaired of communicating that to him.

When I started to explain the situation, he put his arms around me and drew me close to him. "It's all right, Gino. You got carried away because you were lonely. You don't need to beat yourself about it. You remember what we said before—what we have together can't be destroyed. You had to make a decision, and you decided to stick with me. We all learn our lessons the hard way. As far as I'm concerned, nothing has changed. We are still together, and that is all that matters. Okay?"

His words were warmly reassuring, and as far as he and I were concerned, the matter was closed. But not so for Gene. His ego had been badly bruised by my decision, and his disappointment and hurt had to find an outlet.

At Happy Brooks, Gene had learned that the Andersons were active in Christian Science, and as a beginner himself, he turned to them for help with his problem. It meant making disclosures about himself and me, and the whole matter proved an embarrassment for everyone concerned. Gene pursued the problem by consulting a Christian Science practitioner, but there was no resolution from that source, either. The friendship that I had enjoyed with the Andersons went into an eclipse. Albert Anderson was placed in the most difficult position of all, as he had no wish to reveal himself to his brother. He wrote long letters to me in an attempt to explain his position. His financial dependence on his brother complicated matters, but despite the dilemma Gene had injected into their lives, he assured me that his feelings for me were unchanged. Eventually, Gene and I resumed a less dramatic friendship.

Thus the first major cloud on the horizon of my life with Bruhs had been cleared away. Bruhs's steadfast common sense had made it possible for us to get on with our life together. I had learned a valuable lesson in human relations, one I hoped to retain.

5

Team Dancing

For Bruhs, the summer at Pawling had had many rewards. It gave him a solid background in movement work with Harry Losée. During the summer he was frequently paired with an uncommonly gifted young dancer named Miriam Louis. Because of their association with Losée, their approach to movement was strikingly similar; on their return to New York, they continued working together as a team. Dancers' lives are a struggle at best, so doing commercial work with her in theaters, clubs, summer resorts, and on cruise ships at least promised a better income and a means of survival in a fiercely competitive field.

It was a joy to see my partner and Miriam work together. Everything they did meshed into an exciting creation. Their unique, exotic style gave them an edge and moved them swiftly to a varied assortment of showcases. As "Mirienne and Mero" they launched their careers together.

The name, Bruhs Mero, which has always intrigued everyone (even pronouncing it has been a mystery), was adopted for his dancing career. His birth name was Emanuel Brown, and this was fine early on. But when he became a part of an exotic dance team, this was too prosaic for their style. The team originally started with the names Louis and Brown, which sounded like the closing act at the Palace.

We all agreed that some changes had to be made. Bruhs and I both greatly admired the celebrated pianist Yolanda Mero, so he borrowed her last name. And while he had always liked Bruce, he wanted an unusual spelling. So, with a little help from numerology on the significance of each letter, Emanuel Brown became Bruhs Mero legally, in 1934, and Eugene became Gean for its own unique spelling twist.

Bruhs and Miriam tried out their act at the Apollo in Harlem with a striking number set to Duke Ellington's "Sophisticated Lady," backed by Lionel Hampton and his band. At their opening they generated great enthusiasm. Bruhs revealed a compelling stage presence. Although it was a new experience to watch him with an audience, I realized that this wonderful talent was shared with me. But publicly he belonged to his audience, and only in private did we belong to each other. It would take some getting used to.

Mirienne and Mero were such a hit at the Apollo that they were held over for a second week. Their agent lost no time in booking them into the Metropolitan Theatre in Boston. There, their vibrant, sexy routine captivated the audience and garnered some great local press notices, plus a good review in *Variety,* the show-biz bible.

Even though I shared this rising star, I still had to meet the demands of the Paramount stars. It was a great surprise to finally meet Mae West at the Twentieth Century Limited as she left to make her first picture in Hollywood. She greeted me affably and I was struck by how totally unprepossessing she was in her attire and manner. She was notorious for her outspoken treatment of sex in her Broadway plays. She had even served a ten-day sentence in the workhouse for her lurid 1926 stage presentation, *Sex.* In 1928, her play *Pleasure Man* was closed by the police after the second perform-ance and the entire cast carted off in the paddy wagon. I felt sure that the public would remember Mae West's history and boycott any picture in which she appeared. Yet this rather dumpy figure was transformed by Paramount into a glamorous creature with her own unique style. The spicy dialogue she wrote for herself injected vitality into otherwise increasingly bland screen fare. Such lines as her greeting to Wallace Beery—"Hello, Wallace. Is that a gun in your pocket, or are you just glad to see me?"—caused some concern in the Hays office, whose head, Will Hays, was Hollywood's own "standards" czar. If they allowed it, they were uncertain how much further she might push the limits of acceptability.

It was a sign of her having arrived when raunchy stories began to circulate. One involved a Chinese laundry service she used. When her laundry was overdue, she called up: "Hop Sing? This is Mae West. You must be having a good time with my undies. You are three days late! Now get 'em over here right away, and lickety-split!" The laundryman's hasty reply: "Missy West, bring your stuff now, but I no lickety split!" She might have used that line if she could have gotten it past the Hays office.

Paramount's gamble with borderline raunch turned out to be a box-office bonanza. The public loved Mae West and virtually single-handedly she saved the company from bankruptcy. Its ordinary output had done so poorly the company was in deep trouble, but Mae West proved such a draw the box offices were swamped with patrons.

On their return to New York, Mirienne and Mero became headliners at the Tokay Club Restaurant on 52nd Street and Seventh Avenue, which featured Hungarian cuisine and entertainment. In keeping with the club's ethnic flavor, Bruhs and Miriam for their opening did a rousing number to Brahms's Hungarian Dance no. 5. In subsequent performances they built a solid repertoire of classic dance, including Ravel's *Bolero,* which had never before been performed in a club.

The Tokay engagement lasted several months and could have gone on. But for a change of pace, and to give themselves a vacation from the daily grind of club work, Bruhs and Miriam let their agent book them on a two-week cruise. This was a wonderfully inexpensive way to see the world, with the leisure of presenting only four performances during the entire cruise.

Most of these seagoing trips were smooth sailing, but once there was a storm off Venezuela and the seas were too rough for the ship to put into port. Miriam—Mim as we always called her—was feeling the effects of the ship's tossing. When the cruise director called for an extra performance to take the passengers' minds off the storm, Bruhs feared Mim would not be able to perform. He plied her with dry crackers and walked her around the decks until they were both exhausted. When showtime finally arrived, Mim pulled herself together and put on her makeup. The band struck up their number and they went on, like seasoned troupers, to give a full performance. Each time they lifted a foot, the deck came up to meet it! Their pluck won the admiration of the passengers, who crowded around them afterward to offer congratulations.

The Catskill Mountain region had many summer resort hotels featuring known and unknown talent. The busiest and most famous was Grossinger's, the best tryout spot for performers. When Bruhs and Miriam were first introduced to Jenny Grossinger by their agent, it was love at first sight. She adored their work, always made them feel at home the many times they performed there, and urged them to come back whenever they wanted. Bruhs showed me programs that gave top billing to Mirienne and Mero; far down on the list of entertainers was a beginner in show business, Danny Kaye.

When they were actually onstage, it was fun for Bruhs, but between performances was a lonely time for him. He was expected to play up to the women guests, but his heart was not in it, for his thoughts were with me, far from the Catskills. I never visited Grossinger's because the guests and their pastimes did not interest me. I also did not want to have to put on the face to the public that Bruhs did. With no chance there to be close to him or to show my feelings, it seemed pointless to spend time there.

While Bruhs was performing at Grossinger's in 1935, Albert Anderson, my music mentor, put me in touch with an old friend of his, Olivia Fay. She invited me to have dinner at her house. At her apartment on West 16th Street I was surprised to find a half dozen other guests—four women of various ages, one middle-aged man, and one young man in his twenties. I listened for last names, but as none bore the last name of Fay, it was impossible to determine if these people were part of her family or just friends.

The apartment was a rambling affair decorated in what can best be described as mid-Victorian taste. The centerpiece was an enormous dining table at which we were eventually seated. Olivia presided at the head of the table and served the guests with soup from a handsome ironstone tureen. I sat at Olivia's right and observed her as she skillfully performed her duties as hostess. *Performed* is the proper word; the setting was homey but she had an undeniable quality of performance. I watched Olivia's face and I speculated about her age. I assumed that she was in her late fifties or early sixties—obviously still an active, energetic woman.

During the meal Olivia indicated that the young man was an art student whom she had taken under her wing. She had gotten him part-time work as an elevator operator in her building; at the end of the meal he excused himself to go to his job. During the meal I had exchanged glances with him; we recognized that we had at least one thing in common: we both were gay. The younger women were also receiving Olivia's assistance in their careers. The middle-aged gentleman's relationship to the household was pointedly ignored.

Olivia knew that I had studied piano with Albert Anderson and learned I had written songs. She explained that Geraldine Farrar was a personal friend; she would like to have her listen to the songs. When I left that evening, I promised to have Olivia come to our studio to hear them. She greatly relished the role of patron, and I was curious to see what price she would exact.

The day Olivia came to the studio I had arranged for Jack Fuess, a music instructor who had helped notate the songs, to sing the lyrics. As we did the songs, I watched Olivia's face for reaction. She remained poker-faced until we had finished; only then did she say, beaming:

"They're lovely! Jack, do the song 'I'll Learn to Dream Again,' and do your own accompaniment on the piano."

When he had finished, she said, "Gean, you have written several lovely songs. They show great promise. But you play them badly. You punch and pound the keys and play in an utterly mechanical manner, absolutely devoid of feeling. When Jack played that one song, it was so full of meaning, like a caress, as it should be. Maybe if he works with you, we can eventually present them to Geraldine Farrar, but right now I wouldn't chance it."

That I was taken aback is putting it mildly. The full criticism took time to sink in. Unfortunately, it was a devastating blow to my ego and cast a shadow on my self-esteem impossible to forget. Over the years, again and again, "the Olivia Fay syndrome" comes back to haunt me, compounding my insecurities.

During the summer I saw Olivia many times. We had a picnic lunch in Riverside Park and listened to the carillon playing in Riverside Church. We attended many concerts together, and at one point she showed me a scarab that she wanted to have mounted as a ring for me. Much of her proprietary manner made me uncomfortable, but she obviously got great joy from doing things for people and I didn't wish to deprive her of that.

After Bruhs returned from his summer stint at Grossinger's, I wanted him to meet Olivia. We invited her to have dinner out with us and came back to the studio where Bruhs danced for her. She was gracious in her appraisal of his work, but I thought there was a hint of reservation, too.

Olivia next invited me to her home for the ring presentation. She did not include Bruhs. Dinner was a simple affair, just the two of us. Afterward she took both my hands in hers. "Gean," she said, "I have no wish to meddle in your private life. I admire you greatly and value your friendship. You have given me many moments of happiness just in spending time with me. I have your interests at heart so I must speak my mind. Frankly, I feel Bruhs is not a good influence in your life and you should find other interests on which you can focus your energy and attention. Watching Bruhs dance, he seemed to project a feminine quality I found distasteful. What you do with your life is your own business, but as a friend I offer this well-meaning advice—choose your friends wisely and carefully."

As she spoke, my resentment rose and I had difficulty restraining myself until she finished. Choking back harsh rejoinders, I was not sure how to control my voice and I sat silent for several minutes. I finally disengaged my hands from hers and stood up. This woman's price was now abundantly clear: the wish for total control. I struggled to keep anger out of my voice. My eyes filled with tears, I finally spoke:

"Olivia, you have been very frank, and I am both saddened and bewildered by what you have said. To say you're guilty of misjudging another human being only speaks to a fraction of the injustice. Bruhs is a man that I greatly admire. I am proud to have his friendship, his counsel and guidance, and my life would be wholly meaningless without it. I have chosen to spend the rest of my life with him, and there is no power great enough to convince me otherwise. The ring you are giving me seems to symbolize a hoped-for relationship between us that can't endure. I now see circumstances in quite a different light and I would wear it under false pretenses. I must ask you to take it back.

"I do thank you for all the many kind things you've done, and for your advice on choosing friends. But that only reinforces my belief that I have the ability to choose wisely and well, and I have done so."

Olivia grasped my hand and pressed it firmly, but after I returned the ring, we said nothing more to each other. We never saw each other again.

When Bruhs and Mim finished the first season at Grossinger's and returned to New York, he wanted a studio suitable for working out their dance routines. Fortunately, space at 66 Fifth Avenue was available. Since Martha Graham and several other dancers taught there, it seemed an ideal location. We moved from 22nd Street to lower Fifth Avenue and set up shop there in September of 1935.

We still had the little Fischer grand piano that we had acquired at the Vanderbilt Studios, but I felt we had outgrown the instrument. I went to the Aeolian people and had them exchange it for a six-foot Chickering grand. This more expressive piano inspired me to start practicing again.

The team of Mirienne and Mero had hit a slump, however. After several seasons of steady work, the agents simply were not able to come up with anything better than second-rate club dates. As an excuse for their inability to produce spots, they complained, among other things, that Mim lacked theatricality in her appearance at auditions. Mim was a sensational performer on the floor, but even Bruhs had been feeling for some time that something was lacking in how they presented themselves to agents in their offices. Finally, in desperation and with much soul-searching, Bruhs dissolved the partnership.

About that same time, an audition was called for the chorus of the Max Reinhardt production *The Eternal Road*. With nothing else on the horizon, Bruhs decided to answer it and was picked. Rehearsals started, and due to the enormous size of the production, they dragged on and on to the point where Bruhs dubbed it *The Eternal Rehearsal*.

Bruhs also found that, having made a name for himself as part of a team, he didn't fit in well with the chorus atmosphere. He objected strenuously to the effeminate characteristics of many of the chorus boys. Some had the limp-wrist syndrome or a too-sibilant *s* or a swishy way of walking. Bruhs thought this totally unnecessary; he himself neither practiced nor approved of this type of behavior.

In our life together he had always kept a watchful eye on me for those same telltale signs that would give outsiders a hint about our private lives. He always felt that what we did in the privacy of our own home was our business, and there was no purpose served in tipping off straight people by "campy" behavior or overt gestures. In traveling the corridor of fear, the more invisible we made ourselves, the safer we felt. This was a grim fact of life for us and we felt we had to abide by it to survive.

In any case, Bruhs met a young woman, Flora Osanna, who was also working in the chorus of *The Eternal Road*. The two of them were disgusted with the way rehearsals were going. They tried fooling around with dance movement during breaks and discovered that they seemed to hit it off as partners.

As the days wore on, both Bruhs and Flora felt more hopeless about their prospects with *The Eternal Road,* and before becoming completely demoralized by meager rehearsal pay, they decided to drop out. They started rehearsing as a team and worked on several of the routines that Bruhs had done with Mim, but Flora approached movement with a noticeable difference from Mim. She had never worked with Harry Losée as Mim had done, but she had flair and flash, and if she was not always completely secure, she covered it up beautifully. The agents loved her, and the new team of Mero and Zanna started working at many of the same spots that Mirienne and Mero had earlier.

Flora was an attractive and vibrant performer, but unlike Mim, who worked from the inside out, Flora's movements were on the surface. After finishing a performance, Bruhs would often feel the disappointment that comes when total perfection had eluded them. He would chide Flora about her role in this, but she would toss her head and flounce into the women's room, where she knew he couldn't follow, saying over her shoulder, "So what if it wasn't perfect! We got applause, didn't we?" Her response perfectly illustrated the wide gap between them, and the futility of trying to convince her that there was always room for improving any performance.

Little by little, any sense of accomplishment was lost in their work together. But unhappy as he was, Bruhs stuck it out, because no other path seemed open to him. At the start of the summer of 1936, Bruhs took off with Flora for White Roe, another Catskills resort. He felt that somehow, something had to happen to bring him out of the doldrums, or Mero and Zanna would break up. It also meant another summer away from me, and the changes that were to come had already begun to take shape.

6

Another Crisis

My duties at Paramount had made me rather blasé about the high-voltage personalities with whom I would come in contact. One assignment did, however, pique my curiosity. Cary Grant and his sidekick, Randolph Scott, had come East on their way to Europe. In those days U.S. passports were issued at the Customs House on Bowling Green, in lower Manhattan. Since the two stars had to go downtown to get their documents, they agreed to take the subway as the fastest way. In midmorning the three of us set off. We found the station and the cars virtually empty. No one recognized the two stars as they chatted with each other.

There are always rumors about the private lives of movie stars. I knew that Cary Grant and Randolph Scott shared living quarters, but anything else was sheer speculation. Straining my ears above the clatter of the subway car, I caught personal items in their conversation. Scattered through the mundane exchange on running their household was the definite picture of careful housekeeping and a division of labor that implied a deeper, ongoing relationship. The glances that passed between them left no doubt in my mind that they were more than "friends." Every gesture was made with great discretion, but to anyone who knew what to look for, the earmarks of a couple were unmistakable. Because they were so discreet and obviously feared the stigma attached to their real relationship, I never added any grist to the gossip about them.

One evening I headed home from the office to fix myself a bite and spend one of my evenings alone at the piano. The studio at 66 Fifth had a separate bedroom, which, to help defray costs, we had rented to a close friend of many years, René Ferraris. Sometimes René and I had dinner together, but it wasn't prearranged, and I was surprised to find him at home, talking with a friend. When he heard me come in, he brought his friend into the studio and introduced him. The young man was a bit taller than I and had deep-set brown eyes that seemed to look right through me. René gave me his friend's full name, but I was so puzzled by the intensity of his gaze that I only remembered the first name, John. I assumed that René had some sort of date with John, but that was not the case. René excused himself to keep another appointment and left John with me.

I felt slightly awkward in offering to share my meager supper with John, but he seemed only too happy to take potluck with me, and he gave me a hand in preparing the meal with far more expertise than I could manage. When we were seated at the table, he continued to subject me to unremitting scrutiny. I was startled when he said, "What do you do for fun?"

My stammered reply was itself another question: "What do you mean—'fun'?" rejecting his implied intimacy.

"I mean, what do you do for amusement? You seem to work all the time—at your job, at the piano. Don't you ever go out, go places, see people?"

His rephrasing of the question relieved me. I said, "Oh, Bruhs and I go to a party occasionally, but we have never been bar people. After all, we're not looking to pick up anybody, and if we want a drink, we like having it at home, together."

With his solemn gaze he said, "I think you should get out more and mingle. I'd like to show you New York."

I picked up on that and said, "Thanks, but I've seen the Statue of Liberty."

John smiled now and looked a little less intense. "I want to take you to the Monkey Bar in the Hotel Elysée. I'll bet you'll get a kick out of it. What do you say?"

His apparent interest and concern made me relent a little. "Well, we'll see."

When we finished the dishes, I sat down at the piano and played some things for him, which he seemed to enjoy. Later, at the door, saying good night, he put his arms around me, and again with that intense look, he said, "It was so good to spend this time with you, Gean. Thanks for letting me stay for dinner. It meant a great deal to me to meet you. I'm going to change your way of thinking about going out. You'll hear from me next week, for sure."

The following week, as promised, John called, and he began

seeing me regularly. I made it clear to him that, even though Bruhs was away from New York for the entire summer, I had a commitment to him, which did not include playing around. I wanted it clearly understood that Bruhs was the one man in my life. It seemed unnecessary to emphasize to John that there could not be a second, even if he was willing to fill a secondary place. I did enjoy John's company and conviviality and was content for the moment to postpone arguments with my conscience.

However, closeness leads to affection, and this, in turn, will inevitably lead to intimacy. When we did finally spend the night together, I was surprised by the depth of feeling John displayed. I was unprepared for my own sense of fulfillment and began to be uneasy about how deeply I had become involved. Unfortunately, most of the blame rested with me, for John had in all cases deferred to my wishes and, aside from a continuing show of interest, had never pressed me to give more than I was willing to. However, he had gradually insinuated himself into my life. With my inability ever to take a relationship lightly, I had again placed myself on the horns of a dilemma.

I didn't share these misgivings with John, but I did some agonized soul-searching. Had I gone too far to retrace my steps? By allowing this to happen with John, had I repudiated my commitment to Bruhs? I did not seem to deserve the love he had shown me over the years. Had I betrayed his trust a second time and destroyed the continuity of our relationship? I seemed to have a weakness for temptation. Last time it was Gene; this time it was John. Who would be the next man for whom I would fall! In all conscience, for the rest of my life, I would have to live my life on my own. This seemed the only honest thing to do in view of my emotional vagaries.

The lease at 66 Fifth was due to expire in September, and we were financially unable to consider a renewal. With the monthly rent in mind, and forgoing the luxury of studio space, I started looking for a small apartment. I particularly wanted something that I could pay for by myself, if necessary. With John's help I finally found a place in the West Seventies.

When Bruhs returned from his summer at White Roe, he had decided he could no longer continue dancing with Flora and told her that he would try something on his own again. He was already depressed when I told him that we had to talk. Considering how he felt, I was reluctant to add to his burdens. The longer I waited, however, the worse it would be, so I gave him an account of my time while he was away. I spared him no details. I ended saying that I was unworthy to continue with him and would go it alone.

Bruhs usually rallied to any occasion, but he seemed completely crushed, unable to express himself. He must have felt his world crumbling under his feet—his career in limbo, and now I was walking out of his life.

At that moment René called me from the other room, and I went to see what he wanted. We both heard the screech of a window suddenly being raised, and I dashed back into the studio to see Bruhs standing there before the open window. He was trembling, his face ashen. I rushed over to him and put my arms around him; we both started to cry. This episode, which could have ended so tragically, did nothing to assuage my guilt, but the tears did give Bruhs some momentary relief.

He finally spoke, so softly I could barely hear him. He nodded toward the open window. "I know that isn't the solution to anything. We've been through this before. After all, we have only been together six years. That's a drop in the bucket of time. If you want to be on your own, do what you have to do. For me, nothing will ever change what we have between us—and I'll be standing by."

The next few days were spent in packing for the move to 75th Street. There was one problem, which in my haste I had completely overlooked. The apartment was on the fourth floor of a walk-up building. My piano was a six-foot grand that, if hoisted, would not clear the small dormer windows in the new apartment. In panic, I approached the lady who occupied the third floor, whose windows were big enough, and appealed to her to let us take out one of her windows. This would permit the movers to hoist the piano to the third floor, take it through her apartment, and carry it up one flight to our apartment. She allowed us to do it! By the grace of God there was just room enough in the hallway to turn the big instrument and get it up the stairs. I realized with sickening dread that the same route in reverse would have to be followed when we moved out. All that year I fed the dear lady on the third floor weekly passes to the Paramount Theatre, to keep in her good graces.

The layout of the apartment was such that Bruhs and I each had separate rooms. Bruhs respected my wish to be on my own, and our comings and goings were done as individuals, not as a couple. When John stayed with me, it must have been difficult for Bruhs but he hid his unhappiness and never indicated how he may have been affected.

About this time, the federal government under Franklin D. Roosevelt began to address the desperate state of unemployment of people in the theater. Bruhs had been unable to make any progress with his dance career due to the severely depressed economy. He was in touch with Felicia Sorel, who was handling the choreography for the Opera Project, part of the Federal Theater Project, and she got Bruhs assigned to the Dance Unit of the Opera Project. He would draw a weekly stipend that would help to hold his life together.

Bruhs's joy at getting on the Opera Project was short-lived, for after only one performance of *The Tales of Hoffmann* the opera closed and the Dance Unit was suspended. Only the determined efforts of a few militants, who organized a sit-in hunger strike of the dancers, succeeded in winning transfers for them all from the Opera Project to a larger group designated the Dance Project. It marked a stormy beginning for Bruhs in the Federal Theater Project. He learned that one has to fight for crumbs, and the whole piece of cake is often a mirage just out of reach.

It was only a matter of a few weeks before John realized that I was steadily losing interest and his relationship with me was becoming a "lost cause." He stayed over one evening after we had celebrated a birthday. He had brought a bottle of brandy; we went to bed and between us drank the entire bottle. The next day, neither of us could get up. Among other things, I missed an important assignment at my office, but more important, I saw quite clearly I was headed nowhere with John. I shuddered as I realized how idiotically I had virtually abandoned the only worthwhile relationship in my life. Now I knew my foremost priority was restoring my life with Bruhs before it was too late. That he had chosen to stay under the same roof with me encouraged me to hope that a reconciliation was possible.

John and I parted without rancor, and we have remained good friends. I am grateful to him; I am more than grateful to Bruhs and his love. He believed in the strength of that love, a belief so strong that he could wait out my dalliance with another man with the assurance that we belonged together.

Back together, it was as though we had never been apart. His nearness was a comforting bulwark for me day after day and night after night.

7

Getting Through the Depression

The Dance Project occupied Bruhs throughout the balance of 1936 and well into 1937. Various dance productions enabled him to continue working in his chosen field. Most important was his weekly stipend as a member of the Federal Theater Project of the WPA (Works Progress Administration). F.D.R. had set up the WPA as a bold and innovative approach to unemployment. But these were difficult times for everyone. Although the Federal Theater Project brought hope to some of the most depressed theatrical occupations, it paid low wages and its bureaucratic atmosphere often stifled artistic expression.

Nevertheless, with the Depression clouding so many lives, Bruhs and I had to be grateful that our combined incomes allowed us to eat, buy clothes, and keep a roof over our heads. While the salary I received at Paramount Pictures was several notches above those of the Federal Theater Project, it was far from fair remuneration for the services I performed. Motion picture companies paid fat salaries only to stars and executives, while we working stiffs who kept the wheels of the industry turning were notoriously underpaid. Paramount was no exception; I was to play a role in changing this.

During this period we found ourselves frequently forsaking the dull area of the Seventies to spend time in Greenwich Village. Many of our friends were Villagers, and gay people felt a sense of belonging there unmatched anywhere else. We rarely visited the bars but often had dinner or Sunday brunch at one of the many Village restaurants.

One of the particularly appealing places was Alice McCollister's restaurant, a rambling affair on Eighth Street that occupied the ground floor of several adjacent buildings. Part of the natural brick-walled interior looked out on a garden full of vines and shrubs set off by a little fountain. It attracted all types of people, and many gay patrons relished the place.

The service at McCollister's was usually excellent, but we were sometimes treated with supreme indifference by certain waitresses. On one occasion I remarked with sarcasm to Bruhs, "She treats you like an equal." When he asked me to repeat it, he laughed, then said, "Oh, I thought you said she has features like a meatball." Either phrase applied.

We had never really felt at home in the 75th Street apartment. In fact, in those days the whole district lacked any distinctive character. The end of our lease was approaching and with relief we started packing our belongings to leave uptown. The Village was a magnet drawing us irresistibly. We finally found a basement studio right in the heart of the Village, at 23 Downing Street. The name of the street appealed to us, and, after all, No. 23 was only a bit removed from a famous address in London.

It was time to think about how to move the piano from our fourth-floor apartment on 75th Street. There was no other way out except the way it had come in. With my fingers crossed and a prayer on my lips, I approached our neighbor below us for her permission to take the piano through her window again, out this time. I had faithfully given her Paramount Theatre passes throughout the year. She once again allowed her apartment furnishings to be disrupted to bring our piano through her living room. When the piano was finally on the ground and loaded into the van, we heaved a sigh of relief.

Our relief was short-lived. When we arrived at Downing Street, we discovered that we had again miscalculated access for the piano into the building. The steep concrete steps leading down from the street were too close to the door for a six-foot grand to clear. We tried not to panic and huddled with the moving men. They agreed that if part of the steps were broken up, the piano could be maneuvered into the building. We could not leave the piano on the sidewalk, but knocking down some of the steps of course required the landlord's permission. We found the owners, a middle-aged Italian couple, who fortunately lived on the premises.

At first the husband hemmed and hawed, but his wife was more responsive to our agonizing dilemma and ultimately persuaded him. However, his permission was only given with the understanding that the stairs be replaced with new ones. Once again we seemed to have triumphed over adversity. But when the piano was inside and the solid steps replaced, we had a sinking feeling that we would have to stay at 23 Downing Street for the rest of our lives.

Bruhs's fortitude and patience had again bolstered my sagging spirits and assuaged my guilt. He seemed from the outset to accept that it was a question of "Love Gean, love his piano." He never asked, "Why do you have to have a six-foot grand that can never be fitted into any place we try to move to?" He knew I loved the Chickering and got so much pleasure from it that he never made an issue of my hanging on to it come hell or high water.

The year 1938 was important for us. It was good to be back in the Village; just being there made us more alive. We renewed old acquaintances and formed new friendships. Many of the dancers with whom Bruhs worked congregated at the Downing Street studio. The song, laughter, and camaraderie all helped us forget the hard times we were enduring together. Bruhs and I even revived our songwriting efforts and composed several ballads. Our lives expanded, and we shared new experiences and reached out for fresh means of expression.

An ambitious Federal Theater Project involving actors, dancers, and musicians had begun to take shape, to be known as *Sing for Your Supper*. Some very talented people had been enlisted to put it together. Almost simultaneously, after barely starting rehearsals for this, Bruhs was given the opportunity to choreograph and stage as well as dance the pirate captain's solo role in the Aeolian Choir production of *Drake's Drum* at Princeton. *Drake's Drum* was a musical extravaganza extolling the exploits of Sir Francis Drake, the first Englishman to circumnavigate the globe, and vice admiral of the fleet that destroyed the Spanish Armada in 1588. This would mean commuting at off hours to Trenton where *Drake's Drum* would be rehearsing. It was a backbreaking assignment for Bruhs as he had to work with complete amateurs in dancing, people who had beautiful voices, but not the foggiest idea of how to move their bodies. The double-duty activity at the Theater Project and in Trenton went on for weeks, and it was exhausting for Bruhs. I feared that he had taken on too much and would buckle under the strain.

For the opening performance of *Drake's Drum* I traveled to Trenton, and I was amazed at how successfully Bruhs had manipulated the singers' movements and given them the appearance of mobility, as they no longer appeared to be a static clump of humanity as at the start of rehearsals. And whatever movement the group may have lacked was forgotten completely when Bruhs took center stage in the spectacular *Carita Ballet* solo dance he had set for himself. His breathtaking leaps and turns generated such electricity that the whole performance lit up with excitement. It was amazing that he had this seemingly inexhaustible energy after weeks of pushing himself so hard.

Drake's Drum was a thrill, and Bruhs was overwhelmed by the audience reaction and the compliments from the Aeolian Choir. Bruhs had gotten a taste of being on his own, facing up to problems and surmounting them. A job well done made all the traveling and frantic schedule-juggling worthwhile.

For several years we had managed to time our vacations so we could take them together. This year, due to Bruhs's busy schedule, it was not possible. We usually spent two weeks together in Auburn, in upstate New York, where I had grown up. Although I had left for New York City at the age of 18 in 1927, I found myself going back there at least once every year. I was still attached to my mother by an invisible cord of indeterminate length. Every now and then, she would give it a tug and I would obediently come back to the nest. I never disclosed my sexual identity to anyone in the family, and though they knew that Bruhs was someone special to me, I am not sure exactly what they thought of our relationship.

On one of our vacations my brother, Norris, drove Bruhs and me into the country to meet an unusual man named Adrian Pisetta, who had come to this country before 1914 from his home in the Carpathian Mountains. A rugged man with big, rough hands, he had worked at his trade as a stonemason until World War I. He enlisted in the U.S. Army and served overseas until the end of the war, then returned to the United States and settled in a little village near Auburn.

The thing that made Adrian (or Andy, as we always called him) so unusual was his metaphysical knowledge. All sorts of people seemed to beat their way to his door to hear his quiet discussions on philosophy and the occult. He had a distinct accent, and it was often difficult to understand his English. But the knowledge he had was astounding. His big, rugged frame did not fit the picture of your average mystic, but his simple, direct way of imparting knowledge and his deep, compassionate understanding of every human problem won him the respect and admiration of all who visited him.

After the initial meeting, Bruhs and I visited Andy every time we came to Auburn, and we got to know him so well that we told him of our love for each other. One day I remarked to him that the world at large considered us "perverts." He smiled and, taking our hands in his, said quietly, "Perversion means merely a 'turning away.' Since the sex act has propagation as its primary purpose, then anyone who 'turns away' from that is a 'pervert.' By this token the world is full of 'perverts,' and who is qualified to ask of another why he has 'turned away' or to place a label of disapproval on him because of it?"

Andy guided us in understanding the laws of cause and effect, the truth of karmic justice, and the Hermetic axiom "As above, so below." He gave us the incentive to expand our thinking and to embark on studies in which such metaphysical concepts as reincarnation became part of the fabric of our lives.

Andy prepared a horoscope for Bruhs. He saw Bruhs's career in dance quite clearly and foretold much of the joy that Bruhs would derive from his creative expression. But then Andy stopped short, and his face clouded over. His voice grew hoarse and he said, "I have charted this to about age thirty-two, but I can't continue. From there on, everything looks cloudy and dark."

Years later I was to remember Andy's prophetic words. I have often pondered his mysterious gift of prophecy and his ability to expand our consciousness.

By now, Bruhs was too deep into rehearsals for *Sing for Your Supper* to take a vacation with me. Swallowing my disappointment, I planned to go with my sister, Marie, to visit my mother and brother, then living temporarily in Reno, Nevada. I set up our itinerary, partly by air and partly by train. It was fun to travel with my sister. We had always been close and had lots of common interests. She drove her car and came to New York City from Auburn each year and stayed with us, but only once did she make a U-turn on the West Side Highway.

We all caught up on shows offered at discount at Grey's Drug Store basement ticket counter. When Bruhs was free, he joined us in eating out and going to Jones Beach. Marie always accepted my relationship with Bruhs and asked no questions about it. Because of this, many times I wanted to tell my sister that I was gay, but something always prevented me. The trip West would have been an ideal time, but I always waited for the right time, and the right time never seemed to come.

The Western train journey went smoothly and it was interesting to see the country through which I had routed others for so long. Reno was then the gambling capital of the United States, but it held little interest for me. One day of Reno would have been enough. I was impatient to get to San Francisco. I finally persuaded Marie Wilbur, the wife of my brother's boss, who planned to take us in her car to San Francisco, to start a few days early. My mother, sister, brother, Marie Wilbur, and I took off.

It took some time to get accustomed to the winding mountain roads on the way to California, with sheer drop-offs and no guardrails. Every passing car was a heart stopper. But we learned to relax and enjoy the spectacular scenery. Lake Tahoe was a turquoise gem glistening in the sunlight, and the Sierra Nevadas, split by the Donner Pass, were awesome. We dropped down into the Sacramento Valley, and by sunset we could make out the Golden Gate Bridge, opened just the year before. There from across the Bay we saw the shining jewel of the Pacific, San Francisco.

We had less than forty-eight hours to savor some of the magic of that magnificent city. Marie Wilbur was completely familiar with San Francisco and its surroundings. She whisked us from one attraction to another, so we saw the Presidio, Golden Gate Park, the Embarcadero, and Chinatown, ending with dinner on Fisherman's Wharf. We even squeezed in a ride on a cable car. The Opera House was dark and the glorious San Francisco Symphony was off-season. The sights and sounds of that fabulous city would have meant much more if Bruhs could have shared them with me. After only a few brief hours in San Francisco, I had seen enough and loved it so much I vowed to return someday with Bruhs, and I kept a dream of making our home there. I have remained, even half a century later, captive to its charm. Today San Francisco is bursting with the vitality of thousands of gay people and warm with the memory of the gay political pioneer Harvey Milk.

Time seems never to stand still when you most wish it to. Before we knew it, my sister and I were saying goodbye to our mother and brother in Reno and boarding the train for the East.

8

The Big Move

After the longest rehearsal period in theatrical history, *Sing for Your Supper* finally opened in April 1939. The critics felt that a mountain of talent had labored to bring forth an artistic gnat. Only one number, "The Ballad of Uncle Sam," received any critical recognition. Later, as "Ballad for Americans," it went on to wide and long-lasting popularity, especially with American ethnic minorities. Its spirited exploration of the meaning of democracy, and the varied contributors to the melting pot we call America, had a strong appeal to those who felt ignored or disenfranchised. It stirred feelings akin to those of the "Battle Hymn of the Republic" and became a rallying cry for many who considered themselves low on the totem pole and yearned for the recognition that they, too, were participants in the American parade.

In spite of its poor press, *Sing for Your Supper* ran for several months. The ticket prices were low enough to attract many who could not afford other shows on Broadway, and the audiences enjoyed seeing flesh-and-blood actors at movie prices. Meanwhile, those flesh-and-blood actors were able to survive one of the toughest periods of their lives, thanks to the assistance of the Federal Theater Project.

To pass the evenings while Bruhs was in *Sing for Your Supper*, I worked at the piano with Mr. Haga, a pleasant young Japanese man who also lived at 23 Downing Street. He was studying voice and needed an accompanist. We practiced his songs; I made corrections and suggestions for his English pronunciation.

He sang only popular ballads. Among the songs we worked on were "Where or When" and "The Folks on the Hill." "Where or When" went well and he sang the English words with clarity and feeling. However, with "The Folks on the Hill," try as I might, the word *folks* seemed to give him great difficulty, and it always came out rhyming with *ducks*. Today, with the permissive vulgarity of many lyrics, perhaps no one would raise an eyebrow at Mr. Haga's interpretation.

Meanwhile my regular job at Paramount had settled into a routine that seldom brightened my day. I did ride in a cab with Bing Crosby and tried to enlist his interest in the songs Bruhs and I had written. He was polite but noncommittal.

On another occasion, Jack Benny and the cast of his radio show were scheduled to take the Broadway Limited from Penn Station to do a picture in Hollywood for Paramount as soon as they finished an appearance at a Broadway theater, and there was little time. With applause still ringing in their ears, I hustled Benny, Mary Livingstone, and Don Wilson into a cab and began the dash for the train. Everyone seemed unusually glum and we traveled in total silence. Suddenly Benny shattered the stillness: "For chrissake, will somebody open a window!" Those of us who remember Jack Benny's unique style of humor from his radio shows can just picture it! The public always viewed Jack Benny's donning of female attire as hilarious. His superb performance in drag as "Charley's Aunt" no doubt led comedian Phil Harris to remark, "Put a dress on Jack and you can take him anywhere!"

One of the outstanding events of 1939 in New York was the spectacular World's Fair, which we visited over and over. We poked our noses into every nook and cranny of the gigantic conglomeration that sprawled over Flushing Meadows. One of the features was Elsie the Borden cow; as our personal tribute to the legendary bovine queen, Bruhs and I turned out a song. Although we performed it for our friends on many occasions, the song was never brought to the attention of the Borden company. A sample of the lyrics may suggest its potential:

ELSIE THE BORDEN COW

Lyrics by Bruhs Mero; music by Gean Harwood

She's Elsie the Borden Cow
A great scientific wow, now
Gives up her milk to a milking machine
Gives so much milk, among cows she's a queen

They play on a zither, when she's in a dither
From too many in her boudoir.

She's Elsie the Borden Cow
Lives in great style but somehow
She can't forget things down on the farm
No bulls around to give Elsie alarm
And there's no fun in life,
When you're no bull-ly's wife
But just Elsie the Borden Cow.

Sometimes she wonders when people all stare
If they really know what goes on in her mind
Do they think she's happy and free from all care
Or musing on sweet joys behind.

Oh!—She's Elsie the Borden Cow
Rates with the glamour girls now
Has pictures up on all the billboards
Throngs crowd to see her in gay maddening hordes
Where she used to say "Moo," now she's learned to say
   "Coo"
For she's Elsie the Borden Cow.

About this time, Bruhs's brother's pedigreed wirehaired terrier
had somehow met a roving spitz. From the terrier's litter of mixed-
breed puppies, all adorable, we finally selected a male pup with big
soulful brown eyes. We named him Geebee (*G* for Gean and *B* for
Bruhs). With both of us away all day it was a catch-as-catch-can
proposition to housebreak him. Bruhs rigged up a wooden gate
between the kitchen and the living room to keep Geebee in the
kitchen, which had an easily mopped tile floor. But as Geebee grew,
his teeth got bigger, stronger, and eventually he could chew through
the gate. Not satisfied with this freedom, he then began to attack the
wooden slats of a venetian blind that hung on the door to the street.
He sensed that if he could clear that hurdle, he'd be free to follow us
wherever we went.

We could never catch him in the midst of his chewing, and it was
useless to discipline him after the fact. He could tell by the tone of
our voices that we were displeased, but aside from looking guilty, he
gave us the stare that said, "Who, me?" We had to settle for replacing

the gate as fast as he chewed through it. With our vacations looming, we felt a change of scenery would give us all a respite from the "game of the gates."

For this vacation both of us felt that Auburn had little to offer. At Paramount I heard of a woman who rented her house at Fair Harbor, on Fire Island. I took the place for two weeks. *Sing for Your Supper* had closed at last and Bruhs could come with us. With Geebee in tow, we set off for legendary Fire Island.

We had always thought of Fire Island's Cherry Grove and its gays as representative of Fire Island. To our surprise, we discovered Fair Harbor was not what we had expected. No gay people were visible anywhere in this conservative community. But their absence did not immediately disturb us much since we had planned to unwind, not socialize. With plenty of sun, surf, and sand, we rested and got a good tan. Geebee of course relished his total freedom—when it came time to leave, we had to carry him bodily onto the ferry.

Back home, Bruhs solved Geebee's durance vile behind the gates. A little Kerry blue terrier puppy had caught Bruhs's eye every day as he passed a pet shop on his way to the Theater Project. When Bruhs brought little Bluebell of Topandy home, there was rejoicing on Downing Street. All was serene and Geebee's gate-chewing days were over.

But neither of us had given a thought to the fact that Topandy was a female and Geebee was a male. When Topandy had her first heat, she took it in stride, but poor Geebee paced up and down and cried all night. In a two-room studio we were unable to separate them. Once more Geebee was behind a gate in the kitchen, until Topandy's season had ended. We saw that it was unfair to Geebee to regularly subject him to such misery. We made the difficult decision to place him with another of Bruhs's brothers, who lived in the country. He could provide a good home, loving care, and space to roam around to Geebee's heart's content.

Other matters were percolating in Bruhs's mind. He had a perplexing assessment to make—where was he going with his career? The Federal Theater Project had been phased out of WPA, and he could no longer rely on that stipend. How would he manage without it? He was deeply into dancing, and it meant far too much to him to abandon it now. He realized that he could teach; he had much to offer students. But for that he needed a studio with suitable space. He directed his energy to finding the right place.

Among our friends were two older women, Ada and Annabelle. They both had been married, and their children had grown up. They had lost their husbands and due to their age were not seeking romantic attachments. They frequently visited us on Downing Street for a quiet evening of music and conversation. One of them, Annabelle, was a gifted psychic. She took a person's hand in hers and, stroking it, almost immediately began to see "pictures," usually dealing with the future of that individual.

One evening Annabelle held my hand and said she saw a place with which I was going to be closely associated. She described natural brick walls and a high ceiling. The only place I could connect to it was Paramount's studio in Astoria. But she insisted it wasn't a motion picture studio and that both Bruhs and I would be involved with this place. She apologized for not giving more details, but she said the "pictures" went by so fast she could only glimpse them briefly, and did not have time to study them in detail. I finally realized, much later, the place that she had described so accurately would be one of the most important places in our lives—the studio on West 10th Street, which we moved to shortly thereafter.

One of the dancers from the Federal Theater Project soon told Bruhs that a studio might be available on West 10th Street between Fifth and Sixth Avenues. She said that it was occupied by her brother, the well-known sculptor Isamu Noguchi, but Noguchi was planning a trip to Japan. After speaking with him, we contacted the owner, Alice MacMonnies, the widow of the then still well-known sculptor Frederick MacMonnies. She agreed that Bruhs could have the studio for $75 a month. Noguchi planned to leave in November, so it would be available in December of 1939.

In our brief visit to Noguchi in the studio we had given the place only a cursory glance, but when we came back to survey it, we were appalled by the debris scattered about, and the gargantuan task of converting a studio that had always been used by sculptors to a place suitable for dancers. Broken plaster of paris was everywhere, caked on the rough-hewn floorboards, piled high in every corner. I looked at Bruhs, and he looked at me.

"Do you think you can make something of this god-awful mess?" I asked.

He didn't answer right away, but I could tell by his face that he would do it or bust a gut trying. His jaw tightened. "The sooner I get started, the better." I couldn't believe that he could take on this superhuman task virtually single-handedly. I was not taking into account the depth of his commitment to his dancing and its importance to his very existence.

Moving to the big studio on 10th Street meant negotiating the lease at Downing Street first, to figure a way to extricate ourselves— and the piano. Our landlord at first rebuffed every proposal of ours. Even though we had only two months to go on the lease, he wouldn't budge on letting us out earlier. In addition, he flatly refused to let us touch the steps again.

When the first of November came, we withheld the rent. Later that day, a notice of eviction was posted on our door by the city marshal. An eviction would have solved the problem of breaking the lease, but it did not take into consideration the removal of the piano. The owners really felt they had us, and in truth, they did.

Surveying the situation, the city marshal's office suggested that we go back to the bargaining table with our landlord. So we talked— and talked—and ultimately got permission to break down the steps one more time if we bore all expenses of breaking them and replacing them. The landlord allowed us to shorten the term of the lease when we agreed to sacrifice the one month's rent he held as security. This amounted to $35 for rent and about $40 for the masonry, a total of $75, the exact cost of the monthly rent we had assumed at the new location. We still considered ourselves lucky.

The studio on West 10th Street was a converted carriage house. A large double door at the street entrance opened to reveal a hall approximately thirty-five feet in length and twelve feet wide. This housed a small boiler at one end to supply heat and hot water for two apartments up above. Two hall doors opened on a space that would accommodate the piano. Built up three feet off the floor was a separate bedroom enclosed by plywood.

Beyond this was the studio proper—a room with enormous possibilities, as Bruhs had grasped on first viewing. The interior walls were all natural brick, as our psychic friend had foretold, and the floor was easily sixty feet in length with a forty-five-foot width. The ceiling vaulted to a height of forty feet, with skylights on the north side to get that precious even light so desired by artists. Mrs. MacMonnies later told us that her husband, Frederick, had had the ceiling raised to provide him suitable working space.

MacMonnies had completed his statue *Civic Virtue* there. For a time the controversial sculpture sat in City Hall Park, until a storm of protest forced its removal to Queens Borough Hall Park. The cause of the controversy was self-evident: a muscular man representing civic virtue, nude except for the proverbial fig leaf, and brandishing a sword and shield, had one foot planted on the prostrate figure of a nude woman, presumably representing civic corruption. The male, triumphing over the fallen female, seemed to epitomize male chauvinism and was utterly demeaning to all women. It was a shocking display of dubious taste, with questionable artistic merit. A far better example of MacMonnies's work can still be seen on the Broadway side of City Hall Park, a statue of the American Revolutionary War hero Nathan Hale, just before his execution by the British. It exhibits a depth of feeling and sensitivity.

At first it seemed impossible to make any headway against the shambles in the studio. But gradually under Bruhs's backbreaking labor, the place began to take shape. His first concern was the floor, because he needed it in prime condition for his work with teaching and performances. He cleared up the plaster accumulation and put down linoleum that made the floor look like highly polished wood. At the back he hung yards of dark terry cloth, from a bargain fabric center. To support the weight of the material he had to use steel cable, and this necessitated drilling into the brick walls for supporting fixtures. He installed inexpensive coach lanterns on the side walls of the studio, and hung tapestries on the walls behind the piano to give it warmth. An old-fashioned potbellied stove provided the heat for the studio, and it made up in quaintness for what it lacked in efficiency.

Although Bruhs was as frugal as possible, all our money was going out, and nothing was coming in except my salary from Paramount. We were beginning to worry in earnest about how we would meet the rent. Seventy-five dollars never seemed as large as it did then. But with Bruhs's hard work on the studio, after two months it looked as if we were at last on our way.

Blanche and Magda, two lesbians we had long known, asked us if they could rent the studio for two evenings. Money was so desperately needed we saw this opportunity as heaven-sent. They were expecting about fifty people, and they would need seating. They knew of a place going out of business glad to dispose of its equipment. So for the cost of cartage, we acquired the requisite tables and benches.

We checked with the women about hard drinks, and they assured us they would only sell mixers; patrons would bring their own liquor. When case after case of soda and ginger ale arrived marked "Club 52," we began to have misgivings. However, we tried to pocket our fears and enjoy the rent, paid in advance.

The night of the party arrived. Instead of the fifty people originally mentioned, there must have been well over one hundred! Blanche and Magda were ecstatic; their take would exceed their wildest dreams. It was a noisy crowd who grew more raucous as the evening wore on. Many became so loaded with alcohol they had to be carried out.

We had one toilet to accommodate this mob, and it was dreadfully overworked. Things went reasonably well until one witless soul tried to flush a sanitary napkin down the toilet. Disaster!

If we were near panic before, just picture Bruhs trying to stop the overflow by using a plunger, and me standing guard at the door, trying to hold back a horde of desperate women. Their desperation almost matched ours. Some of the more aggressive patrons shouted, "Let's rush him!" But I held my ground and they held their water; there was no way they were going to get to that john except over my dead body. But even though Bruhs labored over the plugged toilet for hours, it had to remain off-limits for the balance of the night.

We have known many lesbians among our closest friends. They have been thoughtful, caring, considerate human beings. We had never encountered a group like this. We were shocked at such crass and thoughtless people, bent only on having a roaring good time. Perhaps they were carried away by mob abandon. Perhaps under different circumstances their behavior might have been different. They certainly were not representative of the wonderful women in the gay community today, nor of our lesbian friends then.

After what seemed an eternity, the nightmare was finally winding down. When the last of the patrons had left, Blanche and Magda came to us and apologized for things getting out of hand. They could tell by the grim expression on our faces that there would be no more sessions of their Club 52 on our premises. They tried to make amends by giving us the furniture and not asking for a refund on their canceled second evening.

Meanwhile, we were left to reflect on how dangerously close we had come to jeopardizing our whole enterprise—the dream of a school and a showcase for Bruhs's talent, for which he had toiled unceasingly. We had our next month's rent, but at what price!

9

Dance Gallery and Nucleus Club

At last we were embarked together on the most creative and productive period of our lives. The wild evening of Blanche and Magda's Club 52 seemed to have little impact on our next-door neighbors, one of whom was Maurice Evans, the Shakespearean actor, who occupied 50 West 10th Street. We christened our studio the Dance Gallery. Early in 1940, Bruhs began enrollment for the dance classes he would teach and started planning an opening concert.

I had always loved the piano without any thought of playing it professionally. I had taken some classes in composition at Juilliard, but to move from musical dilettante to full-fledged "accompanist" was a big step. There was the double burden of working at Paramount from nine to five, then rehearsing with Bruhs until the early-morning hours. My job helped to stabilize our finances and meet the expenses in running the studio. Although Bruhs put together several dance classes and added to our income by renting space to rehearsal groups and other dancers, there was the ever-present threat of not being able to keep the Dance Gallery going. So much of us had gone into building the place, just its survival became our obsession.

Somehow we sensed that time was not on our side, and every-thing we did had an urgent, almost feverish quality about it. We gave ourselves impossible deadlines and pushed ourselves doggedly to meet them, with a proverbial monkey on our backs. I discovered quickly that in working on a creative effort with Bruhs, he totally divorced himself from personal feelings and concentrated completely on the business at hand. He was as insistent on the perfection of my performance as he would have been with a complete stranger. It took me some time to adjust to this new person in charge; his criticism and corrections often rankled. On many occasions, if there had been time or if I had received any encouragement to do so, I would have sulked. I was often hurt and discouraged by his attitude, which no amount of placating endearments after rehearsal could change.

It took me some time to settle into my new role of accompanist, and to realize that Bruhs was asking no more of me than he asked of himself, and that somehow, the end would justify the means. I eventually learned to accept that he simply would not tolerate anything shoddy. It had to fit or it didn't belong, period! By alternating cajolery with intimidation, he convinced me to attempt things I had not dreamt I could do. In retrospect, the potential he sensed in me needed this prodding to bring it to life. None of the piano music I composed for him would have evolved if I had been left to my own devices. Even though, more often than not, I chafed under his impersonal manner, the finished product made me proud of our labor together, and pleased with what I had accomplished through his continuously insistent demands.

At times I was lost in wonder at how Bruhs could move. There was never a gesture that didn't eloquently proclaim the idea behind it. There was always the evidence of unlimited strength, yet as the moods changed, mingling the dramatic with the lyrical, I was struck by the economy of his movement and his almost effortless style and grace. His precision, control, and cleanness of line were beautiful to behold. So often I wanted to grab and hug him from the sheer joy of sharing these moments of ecstatic expression. His body was such a beautifully tuned instrument that he kept me in a constant state of emotional involvement, so much so that I often missed a beat in the music. This, in turn, would evoke a stern reprimand from him. But we were sharing our lives in the most meaningful way, and what we achieved together was a tribute to his artistry and a testament to the successful subordination of my fears of inadequacy.

For our opening concert Bruhs asked me to personally intro-duce each number instead of using a printed program. At first, I shrank from what seemed an added burden. The thought of speaking to an audience was terrifying. I had only begun to feel at home on the piano and able to acknowledge that I could express myself in that medium. I liked his idea of acquainting the audience with the meaning of each number, but why did I have to do it? I thought it would take weeks to overcome my trepidations and face an audience with some ease. After I finally agreed to attempt it, there were awkward moments at first as I fumbled with my notes. Gradually, I found that abandoning the notes altogether made things go more smoothly. Before I knew it, I began to relish the explanatory remarks before each number. I warmed to my assignment, and the audience responded.

Every concert we gave had a host of details. It required all our effort, and we could not have handled it alone. Fortunately we had the support of several creative people who gave their talents to us without remuneration. Herbert worked wonders with the lights and suffered artistic agonies because of our extremely limited electrical equipment. Rosary had magical fingers with a needle and thread and provided costumes that had style and flair. Ellis produced fresh and inventive ideas for masks and scenic designs. Everyone worked on a ridiculously low budget.

Another factor that contributed to the success of the Dance Gallery and brought us all close was that the entire staff was gay. It would be hard to find the equal of this group, whose long hours, unstinting loyalty, and devoted dedication made this whole project a labor of love. And Bruhs and I seemed to draw ever-increasing inspiration from each other as well. Something in the atmosphere of our Dance Gallery, and the creative talent that surrounded us, enabled us to produce program after program of strikingly original works.

We hoped one day to draw upon our expanding repertoire for a Broadway debut. We steadily added names to our mailing list, and we were helped tremendously through our friendships with John Martin and Walter Terry, dance critics of the *New York Times* and the *Herald Tribune*. Week after week, our programs were listed in their Sunday editions. As a matter of policy, they never reviewed studio recitals, but the listings helped us draw an audience. This free publicity spread the word that the Dance Gallery was a unique showcase and advanced Bruhs Mero's reputation in the dance world as a solo performer and choreographer.

Shortly after we moved to the Village we met two young gay women, Dorothy and Rosary, the one becoming our costumer. We all grew very fond of one another, and we spent many hours together.

They introduced us to other young lesbians. Our circle of friends, who up to this time had consisted principally of gay men and a sprinkling of straight men and women, grew by leaps and bounds. We found that we were always comfortable with gay women, and they were among our closest friends.

It wasn't surprising, therefore, that the friends who congregated at the Studio on the Saturday nights when no concerts were scheduled were fairly evenly divided between gay men and gay women. Bruhs and I played host. After a time, however, the friends began to feel guilty about imposing on us so regularly. One of the regulars, our seamstress, Rosary, spoke up: "We've sponged off you guys long enough! Why don't we form a gay club? Right here, we have the nucleus for it." And so the Nucleus Club was born.

With the memory of the Club 52 disaster still fresh in our minds, we had many reservations about "clubs." We decided that if there was to be a Nucleus Club, it would have to be under strict control. We drafted bylaws that limited the members at each Club gathering to one guest, whose future invitations were subject to approval by the regular members. If the guest's behavior was objectionable in any way, that person was denied admission to future gatherings by majority vote of the members.

Membership cards were made up for all regular members. On Saturday nights, upon presentation of the card and payment of one dollar, the members were each given three tickets for three drinks that evening. This way no liquor was sold on the premises, and the possibility of a person's having too much to drink was eliminated. Bruhs set up tables and benches for the club, and I tended bar and handed out peanuts and pretzels.

The first meeting of the Nucleus Club was well attended. About thirty people seemed pleased to enjoy attending a safe, congenial place where they could dance together and be themselves. To our knowledge, it was the first and only club of its kind with an equal number of lesbians and gay men. From the beginning, there was no feeling of separateness. Dance partners were frequently inter-changed, men and women dancing together. Lesbians and gay men got to know one another and discovered how much they had in common.

But the relationships remained gay. And we sometimes had to help out. Bruhs was once talking with one of the members of the Club who confessed he was attracted to another man who seemed to be unattached. But he didn't know what approach to take. Bruhs offered a simple solution:

"Why don't you just go over to him and talk to him?"

To which the member replied, "It's Saturday night! Who talks?"

Around midnight, everyone gathered around the piano. Bruhs and I did many of our own songs—rhythm, patter, and ballad—and the regulars began requesting their favorites, which were "Elsie the Borden Cow," "Take It Easy," and a song that was special to all of us, "Come and Take My Hand."

We set a curfew of 1 A.M. for closing. As a precaution, a man always accompanied a woman on leaving, so that to anyone outside, it appeared to be a straight party breaking up.

In the three years that we operated the Nucleus Club, we never had an unpleasant incident. We were mindful of our neighbors and avoided anything that might draw unwanted attention. We kept the music at a reasonable volume. The Studio was so far back that it was never apparent from the street that a social gathering was in progress. When the weather got too warm, we would need to open the skylight windows for ventilation, so we suspended operations rather than risk outside interference. We needed every precaution for the security of the regulars and for the continuance of the Club, and we could not afford to jeopardize Bruhs's teaching and performing.

The Nucleus Club meant hard work for Bruhs and me, setting up the tables and benches, and cleaning up afterward. We never made money; even if we had hoped to, it was not possible, at the prices charged! In fact, we were lucky if the Club broke even. Nevertheless, it was a wonderful experience. Some of the original members are still around, and they have warm memories of the happy times we shared at the Nucleus Club.

War clouds had been thickening in Europe and Asia for some time. No one was surprised when, in 1940, the U.S. government began registering men for the draft. We all complied with this request, but with a heavy heart. We knew that this was the first step, the prelude to involvement in the bloody conflict that was sure to follow. Both Bruhs and I were ardent pacifists, but we had no religious affiliation whatsoever to back up a claim of conscientious objection. All we knew was that neither of us would ever be capable of killing anyone, and we decided to bide our time until we could make our views known creatively.

The exhausting effort on concerts, teaching, and operating the Club, and our concern over the impending military situation, forced us to get away for a vacation and a change from the Dance Gallery. Dorothy and Rosary had told us of a place where they had stayed in Provincetown—Captain Jack's Wharf. The idea of checking out P'town appealed to us.

We wanted to include our dog, Topandy, in our plans, but I learned that no passenger trains went directly to Provincetown. This meant we would have to send Topandy by Railway Express. We provided a special crate for her, put in food, and attached a good leather leash. The agent assured us that our pet would be fed, watered, and walked to relieve herself. We followed the express company's instructions explicitly, but when we picked her up in P'town, we discovered the abominable treatment to which she had been subjected. Her leash was missing and a worn piece of rope had been substituted. But she obviously had not been walked at all because she was filthy from having to lie in her own excrement.

As quickly as possible, Bruhs got her bathed, combed, and brushed. When she had been given something to eat, she was her old sweet self again and ready to forgive us. Even though it was our first night in P'town, we didn't have the heart to leave her alone. Instead, we had a dinner of sandwiches on Captain Jack's Wharf and watched the moon come up over Provincetown harbor, with our baby between us.

The next day we rented bicycles. This, too, presented a problem, as I had never been on a bike in my life. Bruhs had to use up precious vacation time to teach me. He ran alongside my bike to keep me in balance. I finally got enough of the hang of it to try the long trek to the beach. Bruhs's bike had a wire basket on the handlebars, and Topandy proudly rode in it to the beach and back.

The other vacationers on the Wharf were all gay men, and very congenial. We spent time together sight-seeing during the day and then at night joined the group for dancing in a place where men could dance together.

Rumors circulated about how unfriendly the local Portuguese population was toward gays. There were stories of physical assaults on gay men, and of trumped-up charges of "disorderly conduct" pressed by the local police. We tried to ignore these threats. Besides, we knew gay patronage formed a large part of the town's income from tourism, and we were therefore a necessary "evil." We liked the freedom the place seemed to offer. By traveling in groups we made use of the safety in numbers.

One thing about P'town that neither Bruhs nor I liked was that some of the gay men we met there referred to each other as "girl." We never thought of ourselves in such a way, at any time. Even though the appellation was tossed about only in a campy manner, we found it unnecessary and in fact offensive. We felt the careless use of such terms only served to reinforce the stereotypes so dear to every homophobe.

When our two weeks were almost over and it was time for the return trip, we were at a loss about Topandy. We were disgusted by the callous treatment she had received at the hands of Railway Express, yet the first point at which we could hope to get her into a railroad baggage car would be Yarmouth. By great good luck, the last day we were in P'town, we ran into Tina, a dancer whom Bruhs knew from Helen Tamiris's dance group in New York City. Tina and her husband, Bill, were leaving the following day, and they had a car! We explained our predicament over Topandy. Even though their car had very limited extra seating space, Tina offered to squeeze us in and get us to Yarmouth.

Bill was gruff and undemonstrative, and at first he was dis-pleased about having to accommodate us, even for the relatively short trip to Yarmouth. However, when we reached Yarmouth, we discovered that the next train out was hours away, and Bill suggested that he take us farther, where we could pick up a train on the main line from Boston. We were all very cramped, but we were grateful that Bill had volunteered to carry us farther. By the time we reached New Haven, Bill had thawed out completely and had become quite affable. As we were getting ready to get out for the train, he said, "What the hell, you've been uncomfortable for hours. If you can stand it a little longer, you might as well ride to New York with us."

After that we saw Tina and Bill often in the city and at their home in Paramus across the Hudson. Bill spent an entire evening taking photos of us in the Studio on 10th Street. Those photos are almost the only pictorial record we have of the many dances Bruhs did in the Dance Gallery.

10

Protest and War

The summer of 1940 was over too soon, and in the bustle of activity at the Dance Gallery, it almost seemed we had never been away. We wanted to keep the momentum of the recitals going, and Bruhs devised new dances with my musical accompaniment to present to our developing audience. Bruhs's dances always had a rich feeling of theater. For the musical backgound I experimented with modern composers. Bruhs enjoyed moving to the vibrant, evocative music of Poulenc, Satie, Debussy, Scriabin, and Shostakovich; these composers were a source of never-ending inspiration for him. Some of the recitals were so well received that we repeated them, which carried us to the end of 1940.

For New Year's Eve we held the first of our special holiday parties for the Nucleus Club and made it a dress affair. It was fun to usher in the New Year with friends, and it began what we hoped would be a tradition.

In January 1941, Felicia Sorel, who in her dance career had always been associated with Gluck-Sandor, decided to break out on her own as a solo dancer. She called Bruhs because of his friendship with Sandor and Sorel, dating back to 1933. She contracted for several dates with him to try out material at our studio. Bruhs was happy to offer the Dance Gallery as a showcase for Felicia's solo debut. In addition to helping Sorel, the advance press notices gave more valuable publicity to the Dance Gallery. Since Felicia Sorel was a well-known figure in the dance world, she attracted a sizable audience, and she was able to repeat her program three times.

Bruhs and I, always anxious to keep the Dance Gallery lit and lively, followed her appearances with a series of three programs of our own in February and repeated them in March. These presentations acquainted more and more people with the Dance Gallery as a place where something novel and interesting was always taking place. In 1941, we took time out from our rehearsing to see a striking dramatization of Richard Wright's explosive novel, starring a newcomer to Broadway—Canada Lee, a young black actor. Fresh from a pugilistic career, Canada Lee was catapulted to stardom by his electrifying performance in *Native Son*. Born Lee Canageta, he received his stage name when an announcer in the ring had stumbled over the pronunciation of his name and it came out as Canada Lee. Since Canada won the bout that night he considered it a good omen and chose to keep it professionally.

Bruhs and I were both deeply moved by Canada's performance, and even then, Bruhs felt it would be a privilege to work with this man. Next Canada assayed the role of Caliban in *The Tempest,* followed shortly thereafter by *The Duchess of Malfi,* performed in whiteface makeup. We were impressed by the quality of Canada's talent.

When the producers of *Out of the Frying Pan* approached us to use our space for rehearsals prior to their Broadway opening, we felt we were at last on a roll. There seemed nowhere to go but up. At the show's rehearsals in our Studio we met a talented young actress, Barbara Bel Geddes, on the threshold of her career.

In 1939, Dalton Trumbo published his powerful book *Johnny Got His Gun;* in it he told the agonizing story of a man so incapacitated by war injuries that he was incapable of motion or speech. It wasn't until 1940 that we read it, and we were so fascinated by it we could think of nothing else. Bruhs began to visualize how he could translate some of the vibrant, despairing words of Trumbo into dance and heighten its searing indictment of the mass violence we call war.

As Bruhs started putting his ideas on paper, I began to think of the music we would need. Bruhs finally developed a script that had a prologue, twelve scenes in two acts, and an epilogue. The setting of the dance would be largely left to the imagination, suggesting a room in a hospital, with a bed, and a table with a radio on it. The time: outbreak of World War II (September 1939) to the present. The program stated, "Psychoanalysts tell us that in every man's mind is a censor that allows only the things we want to know to enter our conscious minds, forcing the others into the subconscious. This presentation is an excursion into the mind of an imaginary individual, a product of the drama that exists in a modern world of greed and competition. The voice you hear is the censor in his mind, talking to him."

Bruhs included two other dancers and had an actor read portions of the script; Bruhs was the protagonist. The action of the drama unfolds by flashback, to the man as a country boy in a bucolic atmosphere. From this carefree, idyllic existence he slowly awakens to an awareness of life. He finds love, but all too soon he is buffeted by the overwhelming turbulence of a world that has seemingly lost all sense of balance or perspective.

To underscore the basic concept of man's inhumanity to man, in one scene we are taken to the deep South and witness a lynching. In another, we suffer the plight of Jews—exiled, wandering, fleeing the violence of anti-Semitism.

In a more personal flashback we share the man's sorrowful farewell to his loved one. The woman has offered him love, but his needs are too great for her to fulfill. Too many of his unanswered questions still burn in his brain, as, disconsolate and isolated, he is conscripted into the army. Here he feels completely lost; there is no focus for the inner rebellion that consumes him.

As Bruhs dances, a disembodied soldier speaks, and the full, shattering impact of the war is poured forth in a bitter poem, written by Bruhs, that is a desperate and passionate plea for peace:

I AWAKE

I have died so many times, it seems—
Can I not raise my voice against foul dreams?

I awake from the dead to speak
(Awake and speak!...awake and speak!).
I seek you out, but no one pays me heed.
I bleed from wounds that never dry—
I cry out in horror of this folly.
(I died in pain as millions have before—
I sought no gain but fought with many more.)

I take no bread from the weak,
The peak of the quisling's deeds
(Take from the weak...take from the weak).
I needs must hasten my lament.

I meant to rid the world of hate and fear.
(Kill! kill!...hide!—run and hide!)
(I died in a world on fire,
Trusting there was a plan
That from the ashes there would arise
A new world of the common man.)

Forsake the dread of the meek
(Dread of the meek...forsake...forsake).
They shriek with untold anguish.
I languish for want of peace,
Surcease from pain and sorrow.

I return to my grave,
Home of cheerless nights
And unhallowed days—
Dreaming...
Dreaming endless dreams
That man will learn
To change his ways.

The audience is given no release from tension in the story's relentless drive toward a tragic ending. The soldier, unable to stand such strife and suffering, loses all touch with reality and tries to escape. He twists and turns on a high ladder, then in an agony of despair comes down to earth to seek his lost self.

We presented this dance drama, *Awake and Speak*, at four performances. The audiences gave rapt attention to the action. Those who did not share our antiwar views, such as Paul Nathan, the associate play editor at Paramount, were nevertheless unanimous in their praise of the production. Our only regret was that we had reached too few with our message.

We had wanted to make the strongest possible statement about the futility and obscenity of war. With war already on our doorstep, *Awake and Speak* was controversial. This striking—in parts electrifying—production made our point as clear as possible. Given the climate of the times, it was fortunate that we presented it before Pearl Harbor. Later it would have been labeled "unpatriotic" or even "subversive." *Peace* was already becoming a dirty word, comparable to *cowardice* and *capitulation*. Such unpopular opinions were soon silenced.

There is a parallel between expressing antiwar sentiments and public disclosure of being gay. As long as conformity was outwardly observed, American society was, if not completely satisfied, at least mollified; that way, no one got hurt. One had to swallow the queasy feeling this hypocrisy generated. It was all part of the game of "cover up" and "don't make waves."

Awake and Speak was a tough act to follow. What to do for an encore? Performers must continue to grow, raising their sights and struggling toward some future goal. *Awake and Speak* had been a satisfying blending of intense conviction and esthetic involvement, but we felt we had to put aside our evangelical efforts and find some escapist resolution. We could not, in good conscience, contribute to the superpatriotism of the moment, but we could entertain, and into that we channeled our creative energy.

Besides the work I did with Bruhs in the Dance Gallery, I had expanded my musical activity to include appearances with a choral group organized by employees at Paramount Pictures. Their spring concert at the Hotel Biltmore on May 21, 1941, featured two of my piano compositions, "Prelude in E-Minor" and "Spanish Caprice," which I performed as soloist. One of the tenors in the Choral Society sang "Come and Take My Hand" and another song Bruhs and I had written, "Solitude."

The evening at the Biltmore not only meant my solo debut, but it came between performances of *Awake and Speak*. I had to scramble and suffered stage fright. But the concert, attended by all the executives at Paramount Pictures, was a success. After the performance many came up to me to express their pleasure and good wishes. Barney Balaban, the president of Paramount, came over, shook my hand warmly, and said, "I enjoyed your work tonight very much. In fact, I've never heard finer at Carnegie Hall."

In the audience that evening was Edith DeLara, an accompanist and coach at the Metropolitan Opera. She wrote me a note saying how much she liked my "Spanish Caprice." She had worked with the composer Joaquín Nin in Paris and felt that my composition had something of the rhythmic quality and picturesque atmosphere of his works. She asked for a manuscript copy to perform. I never had the opportunity to hear her play the "Caprice," but of course I was enormously pleased.

After the Biltmore concert, the Paramount Choral Society did a program on New York City public radio station WNEW. I played a portion of "Come and Take My Hand" as the opening and closing theme, and the entire song was done in the program. These appearances gave me valuable experience and confidence as a performer.

The summer of 1941 we headed back to Fire Island on vacation. This time we invited Frank Westbrook to go with us. Frank had taken intensive dance training with Bruhs and had performed in *Awake and Speak* and assisted me at the Solovox, a precursor to the electronic keyboard. With its own electronic amplification system, it was attached to the piano and had a four-octave range, but could not produce chords and was limited to one "voice," hence the name. Eight tabs simulated various string or wind instruments; the cello was the one I favored. At several points in *Awake and Speak* Frank played the melody on the Solovox, which left me with both my hands free at the piano for a richer, fuller musical background.

This time at Fair Harbor on Fire Island the sun set each evening in a fiery burst of color, promising a day of clear skies and incomparable sunshine to come; but each morning we awoke to the dreary sound of rain on the roof. Of the thirty days of June, we had ten out of doors. There were no other gay people in the area, and no social life for us whatsoever. Indoors, we read everything in sight, played cards until demented, and were bored out of our minds. We vowed never again to try the island in June, and we had had it with Fair Harbor.

Back at the Studio, as soon as the temperature dropped a little, we resumed the meetings of the Nucleus Club. We began rehearsing programs for the fall. One of the novelties we introduced in the fall of 1941 was a suite of dances from the Transvaal. I arranged these Boer songs of the South African veld, and Bruhs gave them some charming dance settings. The songs were descriptive and lent themselves admirably to movement. We decided they would be most effective if sung. Our problem was to find a vocalist. Bruhs finally looked straight at me. "You try it, Gean," he said. "I'm sure you can do it. We don't have a singer and you are the only one I can turn to."

I had been expanding my musical activities at the Dance Gallery. I had become an accompanist practically overnight. I had been pressed into service as an announcer at the recitals and had learned the Solovox to augment the musical accompaniment. Now I had to consider singing, too! It seemed a little too much, and half in jest I said, "If I show you the proper aperture, maybe you could insert the broom handle, and at the same time I can also sweep the floor!"

Bruhs saw that I was upset and dropped the matter for the time. But later, going through an old scrapbook of mine, he came across a clipping on my reputation as a boy soprano. It was useless to protest, or even to point out my voice had changed. He persuaded me to try one of the songs, and more to my surprise than his, it went well.

I have always admired song stylists who play their own accompaniment. It takes something akin to a split personality to pull it off, and I did not credit myself with the ability to concentrate well enough to be successful. At one of the performances I invited my boss from Paramount to hear my composition, and my performance at the piano and the Solovox. He greeted me at the end of the evening with a hearty handshake, but to my amazement said, "Gean, you have a lovely singing voice. I enjoyed the songs so much!"

At this point, my mother's mixed-up philosophy crossed my mind and expressed my feelings: "You can't sometimes most always tell what you least expect the most!"

But all these promising developments ended with the close of 1941. Pearl Harbor meant the country was at war at last. At our annual New Year's Eve party the Nucleus Club members tried to be light and gay, but they held their breath in anticipation of how our lives would be shaped and changed by events to come.

11

Wartime

Early in 1942 a difficulty emerged about our living at the Studio. Mrs. MacMonnies notified us that even though she had rented it to us as a working studio with living quarters, she was in violation of the city building code. The building was in fact classified as a "two-family and business dwelling." As there were two occupied apartments on the second floor, this meant we could have the Dance Gallery but would no longer be able to live on the premises. As compensation for this disruption, Mrs. MacMonnies reduced the rent.

Further west on 10th Street we managed to find an apartment that had a big living room and two bedrooms. As luck would have it, both Rosary and Herbert, who worked so diligently on costumes and lights for us at the Studio, were each looking for a room. They both had split up with their partners and welcomed the opportunity to share quarters. Rosary took one of the bedrooms, and Herbert the other. Bruhs and I shared a double studio couch in the living room, so we were one big happy family, and expenses were kept to a minimum for everyone. It was not as convenient as living at the studio, but with everyone's future so indefinite anyway, we made the best of it.

The Nucleus Club flourished, as a safe and pleasant meeting place for our gay friends and associates. Because of our determination to keep the Club within bounds, there was even a waiting list for prospective members.

The beautiful collaboration in dance and music that Bruhs and I enjoyed with each other seemed to come to full creative flower, and we were thinking of broader horizons, expanding our activity beyond the confines of studio performances. But the military draft raised a sword of Damocles over our heads, and put our dreams on hold. We knew that we would eventually be called, and it was useless to plan too far ahead.

The call-up of young men was beginning to cut deeply into our circle of friends. Bruhs taught a class for men that featured exercise with limited dance movement. When duties at Paramount did not interfere, I usually joined the class, which met after work twice a week at the Studio. After each session we would go to dinner together at the little inexpensive China Bowl Restaurant on 8th Street. After seeing *Awake and Speak,* everyone knew how passionately Bruhs and I were opposed to war and military service. We still talked of peace to everyone. But the imminence of the draft made the men in the class all very much on edge. They knew the military did not want gay people in the service, but with many of them there was an overriding conviction that they should serve anyway. When the conversation turned to the subject of military service, as it invariably did, the views that Bruhs and I held grew increasingly unpopular. At one point one of the young gay men snapped, "Lay off the peace talk! We're at war, and it's our duty to go if we're called!"

We realized sadly that we were championing a lost cause. We would have to stifle our true feelings to preserve some semblance of congeniality with our associates.

The fact that many held a different opinion about military service did not sway us in our conviction, and we were not alone, by any means; countless others felt as we did. But they, too, were forced to wrestle with the question of serving. We never made an actual count, but I recall that as many chose to stay out as to go in. It was a choice they and they alone could make.

Finally the men's classes ground to a complete halt. The young men who had been concerned about the soft and graceful balletic terms—*glissade, jeté, assemblé* and *relevé*—one by one left to march to a different drummer. In a few weeks Bruhs and I ourselves, both on the same day, got the familiar greeting from our draft board.

I remember the day we reported for induction. The skies were overcast and a light drizzle was falling, matching our mood perfectly. We each packed a razor, shaving cream, and a toothbrush. At the door we stopped and threw our arms around each other. We clung to each other as though the fierceness of that embrace would somehow prevent our separation. We had shed parting tears before, but this rupture of our lives together had a frightening finality about it. We both shivered as we made our way to the subway that would take us to the induction center. I'm sure that many young men were fearful that day, and we were not alone in our apprehension.

Bruhs and I were separated as soon as we checked in, and we went with completely different groups from doctor to doctor for the physical. Eventually I reached a man I assumed was an army psychiatrist. His manner was purposefully disarming and designed to put me at ease. I anticipated his first question:

"Do you have a girlfriend?"

"No."

"Do you have male friends?"

When I answered "Yes," he went on quickly, asking, "Have you had sexual relations with any of these men?"

When I replied in the affirmative, he asked only one more question: "How recently?"

My reply was brief and to the point: "Last night."

He did not look at me again, but at the top of my form in bright red crayon he scrawled "Admitted Homosexual." His parting shot was: "On your way home, don't pick up any girls, Harwood."

I waited until Bruhs had finished. For him, too, everything had been routine up to the psychiatric interview, and Bruhs's doctor had also shown his bias, once he saw the pattern of the answers he was getting. We both had been totally truthful, but I could see that Bruhs was shaken. Somehow he felt that his masculinity had been challenged and diminished by the psychiatric questioning, and the effects of this trauma were to stay with him for a long time. As for me, I tried my best to shrug it off as an unpleasant experience. Actually, the relief I felt far outweighed any damage that might have been done to my psyche.

What bothered me most was how I would answer questions at my office when they found out I had not been taken into the service. A deferment had to have a reason. What excuse could I use without the damaging admission that I was gay! I would have had to invent some physical deficiency serious enough to give me a deferment. But, fortunately, no one ever asked. Maybe they knew more about me than I thought they did!

When we returned from the induction center toward evening, we were met at the door by Rosary. She gathered us both in her arms and held us without a word. As soon as she found her voice, she said quietly, "This morning when I went into the bathroom and saw the empty shelf where your razors and toothbrushes usually sit, I sat down and bawled. I just felt so empty. The desolation you both must have been feeling this morning when you started out settled over me like a cloud. Now, I just want to hold you close and share this precious togetherness with you."

Later that evening I called Frank Westbrook. He had to answer an induction notice in the very immediate future, and his first words were, "How did it go today? What did they ask you, and what did you say?"

I tried to be as offhand as possible to reassure him about the situation he would eventually face. "The physical tests take a long time," I said, "a little wearing, but bearable. The most important thing is, when you finally get to the psychiatrist—you'll know which one he is quickly enough by the type of question he asks. It's all pretty routine until the last moment." Here I paused briefly and added, "Then you're ushered into a private room and with a red-hot iron they brand 4-F on your forehead."

I expected him to laugh uproariously at my preposterous account, but instead there was dead silence: I had sent him into shock. I quickly tried to rectify matters. "Frank, Frank, are you there? You know I'm only kidding!"

After a moment he rallied and laughed weakly at my grisly joke. But I don't think he ever forgave me. I should have been sensitive to how uptight everyone was, and how hard it would be to appreciate any attempt at humor about the situation.

A few days later we were rehearsing late at the Studio when our doorbell rang. Much to our surprise, there stood Isamu Noguchi. We had assumed that he had left the country before the outbreak of the war with Japan. He mumbled something about being in the neighborhood and wanting to look at the Studio. He had apparently been drinking heavily and his speech was slurred. We ushered him through the long entrance hall and into the Studio.

When we had rented the Studio, Noguchi had left it in shambles. Herbert, who handled our lights so capably, was also a talented sculptor, and he had pieced together plaster-of-paris figures of a man and of a woman that Noguchi had thrown on his piles of refuse. We used these figures as a decorative touch at either side of the stage, but we were not displaying them as original works of Noguchi.

As we walked Noguchi through the Studio, he commented on

the remarkable cleanup job we had done. He seemed scarcely to recognize the place he had once occupied. Finally his attention was caught by the two plaster figures at either side of the dance floor, and his whole manner changed. His face livid with rage, from beside the potbellied stove he seized an ax that we used to chop kindling and proceeded to demolish the figures, screaming at the top of his voice, "How dare you use these without my permission! How dare you exploit my work in this fashion!"

We were speechless. After a moment Bruhs, fighting to control his temper, his face tense and white, said tersely, "Mr. Noguchi, you left these discarded pieces of statuary in a god-awful mess of rubbish that I had to clean up before I could make any use of this place. I worked like a dog to make it presentable, and you have no right to accuse *me* of exploiting *you*. I'm an artist, too, and you have no right to litter the clean floor I need for my livelihood! Now, I have to ask you to leave!"

Without another word, Noguchi flung down the ax and stalked out of the Studio. That was our last visit from Noguchi.

Under the heading *Dance Moods,* we put together a winning combination of dances, performed several times during early 1942. Bruhs had visualized a group of dances relating to sports. To start with, he chose fencing as the motif, and I wrote "Tango del Florete" to accompany it. Later Bruhs added a second section portraying tennis, which I set to a fox-trot rhythm. Both were well received.

Our Dance Gallery series was interrupted by a request to perform at a giant victory rally, planned by a great number of civic organizations, at William Howard Taft High School. This helped to publicize us and to contribute to our growing popularity.

Felicia Sorel attended our concerts regularly; she had fond memories of her performances at our Dance Gallery. She huddled with Bruhs to devise a joint program to feature solos by each of them, along with numbers danced together. As usual, I accompanied Bruhs's solos. Felicia used two supporting musicians: Wallace House, guitarist and folksinger, for some of her solos, and for the others, Tiger Haynes, whom she had discovered singing in a bar on 47th Street, to provide a deeply moving, hypnotic blues background. Tiger went on to forge a brilliant musical-theater career, appearing in such Broadway hits as *The Wiz, My One and Only,* and the paean to graceful aging *Taking My Turn.*

We launched our joint endeavor with Felicia on June 14 under the banner *Sunday Nights at Nine,* for three performances. With no air-conditioning it would not have been comfortable for performers or audiences during the summer, so we closed on June 28.

In the *Brooklyn Eagle* of June 30, 1942, Arthur Pollock captured the essence of *Sunday Nights at Nine:*

> *Sunday Nights at Nine* is what goes on these Sunday nights at 9 in the Dance Gallery, 52 West 10th Street, and what goes on is the dancing of Felicia Sorel and Bruhs Mero. You go in through doors large as an entrance to a stable, pass through a pleasant foyer, take your seat in a Studio with polished floor and a skylight far above. The lights go out and in a moment the darkness is cut by a sliver of light from a little spot, and there before you in the beam one of them is dancing. It's pretty lovely.
>
> They dance many things. First, to a fluid and lyrical accompaniment by Gean Harwood, Mero does a dream dance that begins half-way up a ladder, takes him under a street lamp, then on to a bench before a mirror and back onto the ladder again. The lights go out, the ladder disappears behind a tall screen, the tender spotlight is on again and Sorel, seated on the bench far away, rises slowly and, while a dark young man named Tiger Haynes beats his guitar and sings, dances the St. Louis Blues. Now Mero is back to dance to songs of the Transvaal. Together they do a thing called "Nickel in the Slot" that takes you back to when the juke box was young and boys and girls thought they had discovered something new because they called it "necking." That is a swell number, brief and pointed.
>
> After that there are many things. Sorel dances to Langston Hughes' poems, sung and played by Tiger Haynes. On his eloquent lute Wallace House plays an old Greek song of women who threw their babies over a cliff, and as he sings, Sorel dances, gravely dramatic. She follows this sombre piece with a light-hearted Mexican dance with drumming heels. Then they are a team for an easy, lazy, languid, beautiful thing called "She Ain't Nowhere." The closing number on the program is a Haitian voodoo dance called "Ouanga." To the beat of a Haitian drum, a young wife employs black magic

to get rid of her husband so that she can keep a date in the adjoining jungle with the man she fancies more.

This is finely tempered dancing, a blending of nice poise and suave agility, a picture book of flitting variegated figures.

By now the Village had taken on a different hue. Uniforms began to dot the crowds, and at gay bars like Main Street, men lined up six deep on Saturday nights without a question from passersby. Washington Square Park, long a meeting place for gays seeking a date for the evening, became a popular rendezvous for servicemen on the town looking for companionship or amusement. As free as the bars had become, restrictive measures began to crop up in other places. One eating place, the Jumble Shop, that was popular with gay men and lesbians displayed a card in its window: "We are not obliged to serve women wearing slacks." This was directed at lesbians; imagine how many straight women would be affected by such a ban today!

Herbert had entered military service, and Rosary had begun a new relationship and moved to Long Island. Without their rents, Bruhs and I felt a financial pinch and had no choice but to pack up our belongings at the 10th Street apartment and, on the q.t., take up residence at the Studio again.

As soon as the summer heat abated, we resumed the Nucleus Club and welcomed back many members in their new uniforms. One of them brought with him a man in a Marine uniform whom I recognized as someone I had known in my hometown of Auburn years ago, Joe McDonald. He had steadily dated a girlfriend of my sister's for a long period. I had never realized that he was gay and that the dating was merely a cover-up. He saw my look of astonishment when I greeted him, and he chuckled, "Small world, huh, Gean? Guess you never expected to see me at the Nucleus Club!"

I threw my arms around him and gave him a big hug. "Welcome aboard, Joe. We have a lot to talk about." Later that evening we got together for a chat and we remarked how many gay men in Auburn had never come out, never sought out other gay company, and felt more comfortable pretending to be straight. He also commented that my sister's dates had been mostly with gay men, and he named several that I knew were gay. Yet though she was literally surrounded by gay men, she never caught on. It is just possible that unconsciously she preferred it that way. She had the pleasure of interesting male company for the evening without the threat of any physical overtures. When we finished discussing my sister, I tried to draw him out about his military service.

"Joe, why the Marines? They are the toughest branch of the military!"

His answer was to the point. "I know they're tough, and it has been rugged for me. I guess I had to prove something to myself, and I picked the Marines as the best way to do it!"

Joe visited the Club whenever his leaves permitted. He had adopted the wartime philosophy that everyone seemed to share: "Enjoy yourself today! Who knows what tomorrow will bring!"

12

Career

As 1943 started, there was universal preoccupation with the war. People seemed to face each day with resolute optimism, and Bruhs and I were no different. We went about our daily tasks with as much enthusiasm as we could muster.

On a frigid morning in January, Bruhs was preparing to teach his first class of the day, consisting entirely of young women. To his dismay he discovered that the fire in the potbellied stove, the sole source of heat for the Studio, had gone out. With newspaper and kindling he set about starting a fire to make the Studio warm enough for the class. But there seemed to be no draft to keep the fire going. The room started to fill with smoke, so he opened the skylight to let the smoke out. This caught the attention of neighbors, who turned in a fire alarm.

Within a short time Bruhs heard the sirens of fire engines in the street and dashed to the front door. One of the firemen shouted, "Do you have a fire?"

"No!" Bruhs quickly replied. "I'm trying to start one!"

The fireman signaled his crew, "Here it is, fellas," and in they came with axes held high and hoses dragging behind them. The man in charge surveyed the situation and dispatched a man to the roof to check out the chimney. Meanwhile, the students had arrived and stood in shivering clusters around the stove, which was smoking but giving off no heat.

The fireman asked Bruhs for a pail of water. There was no pail, but Bruhs got a large basin filled with water. He was afraid the fireman would douse the stove in one fell swoop. But instead the fireman carefully dipped his hand in the water and delicately sprinkled the smoldering mess inside the stove, neatly avoiding wetting the floor. He kidded with the young women:

"I'd like to join your class, but I don't have my dancing shoes with me!"

Classes that day had to be suspended. But after the chimney was cleared out and the stove was working again, the Studio's activities could be resumed.

The idea of a Broadway recital was uppermost in our minds. We felt that our experience with the Dance Gallery performances had prepared us for the big step. Professional skill is crucial for a recital, but one has to wrestle with other factors: a suitable theater or concert hall that is affordable, plus the services of a concert management to handle advertising and ticket sales. All of these required one ingredient—money! Neither Bruhs nor I had the reserves to cover the cost of such an event. Bruhs discussed the situation with Bill, one of his older brothers. When Bill was assured that this was the way Bruhs wished to proceed, and that a Broadway showing was necessary to advance his career, Bill agreed to act as sponsor.

Shopping around, we settled on the New York Times Hall, which has had a colorful history. The newspaper had acquired the Little Theatre on West 44th Street as part of its holdings and was endeavoring to compete with Town Hall for concert bookings. They changed its name to New York Times Hall to attract concert business. Several years later, it reverted to its former name, Little Theatre. In the 1980s it was renamed the Helen Hayes Theatre, home for several years to Harvey Fierstein's memorable *Torch Song Trilogy*.

When Herbert went into the Army, we had lost a valuable member of our staff. But we were able to enlist another young man, Berry, to handle the lights. Using Herbert's cue sheets, he quickly adapted to our limited electrical facilities. He worked with us on several recitals at the Studio—dress rehearsals for the main event.

The date of our concert, April 24, 1943, finally arrived. We were cheered by the news that Herbert, having reached age thirty-eight, had been discharged from active duty. He would be able to join Berry in overseeing the light cues for our concert that evening. The electrician's union would not permit either of them to even touch a light switch, but with quick changes in lighting critical to the performance, it was crucial that they be there to relay instructions with split-second timing.

We were permitted one walk-through of the program in the afternoon. Playing the piano, I knew it would need tuning. I left orders for this to be done, but it never was tuned. For the "Flight from Reality" number, which Bruhs performed on a ladder, a complicated support structure was needed. This special construction did not arrive until after the run-through, so there was no chance to see how well it worked. These were just more contributors to the nail-biting jitters of opening night.

While Bruhs was getting into makeup, I did a last-minute rehearsal of the Transvaal songs with our tenor. Before we knew it, the signal for "curtain up" was sounded.

The opening number was "Fanfare," which Bruhs performed in a long, black, sequin-lined velvet cape, done to one of my compositions. He did spectacular leaps and turns with the cape; the overall effect was electric; the audience response was enthusiastic. The next piece was "Tango del Florete," my composition. Bruhs used a fencing foil to accentuate the mercurial movements of the dance. From the stark and somber lynch story told in the third dance, "Strange Lullaby," the mood changed swiftly to the bright and lilting "Dances for the Young," done to the songs of the Transvaal.

For the fifth piece, the mood swung again, this time to a tense, decadent picture of the effete Spanish aristocrat who contributed to the betrayal of a great nation. This was performed to my "Spanish Caprice," which I had played hundreds of times. But at this critical moment I suffered a momentary lapse at the climactic finish—I actually added eight extra measures to the music, which forced Bruhs to improvise a completely different ending. When I realized what I had done, I was mortified. How could I have done such a thing on this night, of all nights! I knew he would never forgive me and felt I deserved anything he might do.

The intermission immediately followed my debacle and I went to his dressing room prepared to take my punishment. To my utter surprise he said absolutely nothing about the havoc I had created in destroying the climax. On the contrary, he was sweet and reassuring and said he felt the concert was going well.

I don't know which unnerved me more—the blunder I had made, or the sunny calm with which Bruhs ignored it. He may have known how much I had suffered already and felt a reprimand from him would only exacerbate my condition. With the second half still to be done, he couldn't run the risk of my coming completely unglued.

Thank God, the fifteen-minute intermission gave me an opportunity to calm down. By the time the curtain went up on the second half, I had managed to pull myself together.

The last half started with a bouncy portrait of high jinks in a "Country Lad," then moved swiftly to three unrelated tragic episodes taken from *Awake and Speak*. In one part, done without music, I read the lines from the poem "I Awake." As in past performances of this work, the audience seemed deeply moved. For comic relief, "Afternoon of a Reluctant Faun" followed. The closing number, "Flight from Reality," featured the spectacular dance on the ladder. Fortunately, I carried off my part of the second half with no more flubs, and the supporting props for the ladder worked securely. If anything, using the ladder with the extra construction gave an even greater effect of Bruhs's being suspended in midair.

The audience demanded lots of curtain calls, and many streamed backstage to greet us. We could feel that we had launched a new career and could build on it for the future. One thing we discovered, however, was that starting a performance at 8:45 P.M. on a Saturday evening did not give reviewers time to make the Sunday editions. In spite of this, we did garner some good notices, and we were encouraged to feel that we were on our way.

The prop construction used in the performace at Times Hall was brought down to the Studio, but arrived when Bruhs was teaching a Saturday-morning children's class. He excused himself, but in the confusion, as the delivery truck started away, Bruhs suddenly realized that an item was missing and dashed after the vehicle, shouting to get the driver's attention. Just as Bruhs neared the truck, stopped by a light, the light changed and it drove quickly away.

When Bruhs panted back to the class, his sister Pnina, who had brought her daughter to the Studio for dance class, and who sometimes helped us with mailings and ticket taking, listened as he breathlessly recounted what had happened. Her immediate response was, "Why didn't you whistle?"

Worn-out by weeks of rehearsal for the recital, tension with children's classes generally, and the irritation of never having been able to whistle, Bruhs blew his stack. Pnina was aghast at his outburst, and deeply hurt. I would remember this incident months later when it would become significant as an aspect of Bruhs's physical crisis.

Apart from my work with Bruhs at the Studio, which had become the most important part of our life, another matter having a direct bearing on my job at Paramount was beginning to surface. Several of the employees approached me about using the Studio for meetings. These meetings were being kept secret because their purpose was to organize the office workers at Paramount. The low wages for office personnel throughout the industry had convinced many who worked there that nothing short of a union would ever persuade management to improve conditions. At first, by offering the would-be organizers free use of the Studio, I felt I was doing enough toward promoting a union. Gradually I became even more convinced that this action was necessary and began to participate more actively in its planning and strategy. These meetings went on for many months before we felt we were ready to go public.

When the time came to hold an open meeting, I was selected to chair it, another totally new experience for me. I knew that I was sticking my neck out by this public stand because there would be company observers planted throughout the hall. To my knowledge I was the only gay member of the organizing committee, and I secretly delighted in the fact that I was considered the only one with enough guts to chair the open meeting. (The thought has since occurred to me that perhaps no one else relished playing the role of sacrificial lamb.) In any case, the meeting stimulated considerable interest in forming a union. Fortunately for us, President Roosevelt had in the 1930s encouraged the formation of a new industrial union federation, the Congress of Industrial Organizations (CIO). We eventually affiliated with their United Office and Professional Workers of America. Ironically, when we had approached the AFL, which included all the craft unions in the movie industry, they were not interested in organizing office workers. The militant and enterprising CIO, however, jumped at the chance to welcome us into their organization.

The time and energy I spent in trying to secure a union contract for my coworkers was not lost on the Paramount management. They never forgave me for rejecting their paternalistic attitude and "betraying" them by joining the union cause. They bided their time, but when the time was right, they dealt me a coup de grâce.

Summer may not be the best time of year to start a Broadway musical, but when such an opportunity knocked for Bruhs, it seemed such a propitious moment. Felicia Sorel approached him to assist in choreographing her first Broadway show, *My Dear Public*.

From the moment Bruhs took on the assignment he realized that it would be rough going. Felicia was so insecure that her tentative attempts at forming routines for the dancers confused them to the point of almost total disorganization. On several occasions Bruhs took over and managed to inject some form and discipline into the proceedings. By laboring with individual dancers on the mechanics of doing lifts, he tried to prepare them for executing some of Felicia's ideas, but it was a backbreaking ordeal. Such extreme exertion in hot weather began to take its toll on Bruhs's health. He had been in good physical shape when he started these rehearsals, but the demands made on him were beyond the bounds of physical endurance.

Another problem that Bruhs had not anticipated began to surface. He had joined the company through Chorus Equity with the understanding that he would be acknowledged as assistant choreographer, and due to his long friendship with Felicia he thought this was clearly established. When he finally realized that the work he was performing would not be recognized, he felt not only frustration and betrayal, but the abysmal sense of having been used. Felicia tried, rather lamely, to excuse the situation by explaining that she was allowed only one assistant. Henry Letang, who was an expert in tap dancing, had been brought on the show to work strictly in his field of expertise, and Felicia claimed she was powerless to give credit to any additional choreographers.

Bruhs realized the extent to which Felicia was depending on him, but he was so physically and emotionally drained that he was determined to call it quits and leave the show. With this in mind, he paid a visit to our family doctor, a good friend, to discuss it with him. The doctor gave him a thorough examination and agreed that Bruhs was endangering his health. To back up his diagnosis the doctor also gave Bruhs a document that would release him from the show.

When Bruhs presented his doctor's statement to Felicia, she was adamant in her refusal to accept his departure for any reason, and they exchanged bitter words. Actually, Felicia was panic-stricken at the thought of losing Bruhs's vital support, and in a last desperate effort to hold on to him, she threatened to have him blacklisted so any future work in an Equity production would be foreclosed to him. Nonetheless, her threats fell on deaf ears, and as of August 15, Bruhs severed all connection with *My Dear Public* and Felicia Sorel.

The days that followed were a letdown after the exhausting daily chores of rehearsal. Bruhs still smarted from the hostile and unreasonable attitude that Felicia had exhibited. His resentment continued its relentless impact on him, and his days and nights were filled with a burdensome replay of all the unpleasantness that had gone before. He gradually seemed to lose his sense of direction and began to question where his career was headed. The morass of unresolved outrage—and guilt—at the way he had been compelled to deal with the situation combined to make him deeply depressed. I was painfully aware of his torment, but my words of support and comfort could not reach into the depths of his depression. We even sold my much-loved Chickering piano, because it wasn't being used.

On a hot evening near the end of August, we walked our dog, Topandy, to Washington Square Park and sat trying to get a breath of fresh air. There was not the slightest ripple of a breeze; we finally gave up and headed back to the Studio where a floor fan could give us a little relief from the sultry night air.

It must have been well after midnight before we settled into bed, and as I leaned over to kiss Bruhs good night, I realized that for days our physical needs had been sadly neglected. When we embraced, some of the bitterness that had possessed him so completely seemed to dissolve, and the love we shared at that moment was, as always, richly fulfilling.

I was awakened around 3 A.M. by a strange thumping sound. I looked over to where Bruhs should have been in the bed and was shocked to see him sitting up banging his head against the wall! He was experiencing a crushing pain in his chest and the only way to distract himself was to hit his head.

I had never been faced with this sort of emergency before and was at a loss. Aspirin was the only pain reliever we had in the house, and I did not know whether it was hot or cold applications that would help. The pain seemed so intense I strongly doubted that aspirin would have any effect on it, but my only thought was to try to make him more comfortable. I suggested we go to a hospital emergency room, but Bruhs vetoed that. He said he would somehow try to hold out until he could see his own doctor in the morning.

It was one of the longest nights of my life, because in addition to my concern about Bruhs's condition, I was wracked with guilt for encouraging our earlier lovemaking. I was filled with a sinking sense of apprehension. After what seemed an eternity of waiting, morning came; the pain had abated somewhat. I got Bruhs dressed, bundled him into a cab, and we took off for the doctor's office.

13

Medical Crisis

The doctor, our friend, heard the urgency in my voice when I called, and he agreed to see us even before his regular office hours. He was gay, a rare find for us. Because he chose not to come out to his family, I will refer to him as Harry.

There had never been a question too embarrassing to ask, and we were always comfortable in that rapport between a gay doctor and a gay patient. I felt no hesitancy in telling Harry that Bruhs and I had made love several hours before the attack. Harry's assurance that there was no connection between those events helped ease the guilt that had settled over me.

Harry gave Bruhs a minute, lengthy examination. He reported that upper-respiratory-tract infection was the basic cause of the problem, plus a physical depletion ensuing from the exhausting rehearsals for *My Dear Public*.

Harry wrote out a prescription that he felt would give Bruhs relief from any recurring chest pain. After cautioning him to call if there was any change, Harry sent us on our way. We filled the prescription, and after assurances from Bruhs that he could manage by himself, I put him in a cab and sent him on home alone, while I went on to my daily office duties at Paramount.

Shortly after Bruhs arrived at the Studio, however, there was a phone call from the doctor. Harry lived by the Hippocratic oath. I have never encountered such selfless devotion to duty from anyone else in the profession. After we had left his office, he had had a change of mind about his diagnosis of Bruhs's condition and had dashed out to tell us but missed us. He now said he would like to reexamine Bruhs, but this time in a hospital. He explained that, as head of the Department of Internal Medicine at Bellevue, he could treat Bruhs there without charge. However, when Bruhs heard him mention Bellevue he cringed, because in his mind the name Bellevue was associated with the Psychopathic Ward as it was called in 1943, and he wanted no part of that. The only other hospital with which Harry was connected was a private one, Medical Arts Center, at 57th and Sixth Avenue. If Bruhs was to keep Harry as his attending physician, he had no other options to consider.

Bruhs tried to call me to tell me that the doctor wanted him to go to the hospital as quickly as possible, but I was out of the building. He then called his sister Pnina; as a housewife she was available to go with him.

Bruhs was admitted to Medical Arts at about 3 P.M. on August 26, 1943 (a date indelibly planted in my mind), and shortly thereafter Harry began intensive testing. At about 4:30 P.M. he called me to tell me that tests revealed that Bruhs had suffered a coronary thrombosis. It was further complicated by a virus infection of the nervous system. Harry also told me that due to a shortage of beds, Bruhs had been assigned space in a ward with five other patients. He said that he would leave word at the nurses' station for me to be permitted to see Bruhs at any time.

I hurriedly closed up my desk. With a hasty word to my boss about what had happened, and highly agitated, I took off for the hospital. When I arrived at Medical Arts, I discovered that Bruhs had been placed in an oxygen tent. When I approached the bed and took his hand, it felt as if it were on fire. Harry had told me that Bruhs was running a temperature, but I was not prepared for the terror-stricken look in Bruhs's eyes, nor for his hallucinating. His grip on my hand was like forged steel, and he fairly bristled with tension. His voice came in hoarse gasps:

"They are closing in—the walls are closing in! I have to stay here—but *you* don't. Get out—*get out*—while there's still time! In a minute it will be too late! Go, please *go!*"

I was at a total loss as to what to do. His agitation seemed to be mounting steadily, and I didn't want to add to it. I realized he must be suffering a claustrophobic attack triggered by confinement in the oxygen tent. Finally, with great reluctance, I left.

The chain of events that followed has been put together from accounts of Harry and nurses on the floor. Bruhs broke out of the oxygen tent and lunged toward the windows that opened on the street, two stories below. One of the ambulatory patients grabbed his arm to hold him back, calling frantically for the nurses. Bruhs struggled and managed to free himself, but an orderly got to him just as he was mounting the windowsill and fumbling with the latch.

With Bruhs back in bed, a reassessment was clearly called for. The precarious state of his health had made it seem unwise to move him. But after this episode, it seemed urgent to change his environment as quickly as possible. Unfortunately, a private room was not immediately available. In the meantime, there was no choice but to put restraints on Bruhs and wait.

As the night dragged on, Bruhs's temperature soared. Sulfa drugs had proven ineffective. All available penicillin was commandeered for military use, and there was no satisfactory substitute. The fever and the restraining bonds combined to increase Bruhs's hallucinatory fantasies. Through a murky haze, Bruhs saw nurses and orderlies with mops and pails busily trying to stem a river of blood that coursed over the floor. All their actions seemed speeded up, as in a silent moving picture, but no matter how frantically they worked, the bloody tide kept rising higher. Bruhs closed his eyes to shut out the frightening scene and, worn-out by the events of the day, finally surrendered to the sedative he had received and lapsed into a deep sleep.

Some time after 11 P.M. that evening Harry was able to transfer Bruhs to a private penthouse room. That dedicated doctor spent the rest of the night at his patient's bedside.

When I had left the hospital, I had lost all track of time. I knew a little dog was waiting at the Studio to be fed and walked. I managed to get downtown to the house on 10th Street, and as I opened the door, Topandy gave a joyful bark and jumped up into my arms. She showered me with licks, an outpouring of affection that was a blessing at that moment. Later I walked her to Washington Square Park and just sat there dumbly, not wanting to eat, trying not to think, most of all not wanting to go home to the empty Studio.

As it grew later and later, I knew I must get up and go home. Once inside the house, I fixed myself a sandwich, made a cup of tea, and sat down at the table. Finally I got undressed and lay down on the bed. Topandy usually slept at the foot of the bed, but I needed her comforting presence and I picked her up and made her lie down beside me. All the events of the day came crowding in again and overwhelmed me. Never in my life had I felt so completely powerless. I started to weep uncontrollably. I held Topandy close to me, and through my tears I kept repeating, "Topy, baby, what are we going to do?"

I have always believed in the power of prayer, and I had no other source to which I could turn. In a desperate appeal I asked for divine intercession in my hour of need, to swing the balance in Bruhs's favor. I pleaded for the divine presence to enfold him and hold him in its embrace and restore him. I entreated Providence to calm me and allay my fears. After a time my tears stopped, and I began to feel an inner peace and quiet settling over me.

It seemed as though I had not slept at all, but I must have drifted off. Suddenly, the insistent ringing of the phone awakened me, and I sat bolt upright. I looked at the clock. It was about 7 A.M. I picked up the receiver and it was Harry's voice, very grave. "Gean, I think you should come up to the hospital right away. I don't know which way this thing will go, but I want you to see Bruhs anyway. We'll talk when you get here."

Bruhs's family had been contacted about the gravity of the situation, and I found three of his brothers already at the hospital. They had talked with the doctor and had discussed the medical expenses. Bill, who had so generously underwritten the cost of the concert, assumed responsibility for the hospital charges when he learned that Bruhs had no health insurance and a bank balance of only $200. Another brother, Gilbert, offered to pay a share of the expense. They encouraged the doctor to consult with specialists about Bruhs's condition and what could be done for him.

After Harry called me, he suddenly thought of a drug, aminophylline, that he had not previously tried. He administered it when Bruhs was at his lowest ebb. It acted as a temporary stabilizer and bought a little time for other efforts. Harry brought in Dr. Applebaum, the heart specialist from Bellevue, who gave the grim report that Bruhs's heart was three-quarters gone.

His case grew ever more baffling. Bruhs clung to life by the slimmest thread, slipping in and out of consciousness. Each time he lapsed into coma, there was the possibility that he would not come back. Harry felt my presence was a comfort to Bruhs and made arrangements for me to spend night after night at the hospital. I sat in a chair by Bruhs's bed and held his hand. It was heartening that when he was awake, he always knew me and spoke my name, which he did with no other person.

Bruhs's older sister, Anne, and her husband, Brenner, although both had jobs, managed to devote hours to Bruhs at the hospital. They ran interference between their brother Bill, the doctor, and the hospital administrator. Bill was often irked by the size and frequency of the hospital bills, which continually escalated. Since he was bearing most of the expense, he felt he could legitimately gripe.

Pnina, too, came during the day and spent long periods with Bruhs. He was rarely awake, and when he was, he made strange requests. He asked her to trim his fingernails and also to cut his eyebrows. Because he usually went back to sleep almost immediately, she never did either. He ate mostly raspberry Jell-O, and he asked for it frequently. Only much later did we learn that these requests were part of an ongoing hallucinatory fantasy in which he was turning into a werewolf. He felt his nails were becoming clawlike and his eyebrows were growing over his eyes like an animal's. He thought that he was being force-fed red Jell-O as a substitute for the blood he craved in his nocturnal foraging. A place on his thigh became irritated from the bedsheets, and he thought this was a wound from a silver bullet fired at him during his midnight marauding. Each time orderlies gave him the urinal, his face darkened in a resentful scowl. He later told me it felt like the orderly had put something across him to prevent him from urinating.

Bruhs grew weaker each day. He lost all control of his muscles, so that he had to be turned like a baby. His weight dropped steadily; Harry was grateful that Bruhs's initially well-nourished body provided reserves to draw on. We took developments one day at a time. Each time Bruhs roused himself and spoke, no matter how irrationally, we took it as a sign that he was going to make it after all.

In an ongoing search for answers in this perplexing case, Harry called in a reputable neurologist from Montefiore Hospital, a Dr. Sevitsky. For more information, Dr. Sevitsky asked members of the family to be present during his examination. At one point, he asked each person in turn if he or she had ever observed Bruhs behaving irrationally before the illness. Only Pnina had a ready response, as she remembered the incident at the Studio.

"I said a very simple thing to Bruhs once, 'Why didn't you whistle?' when he'd been unable to get a truck to stop. With no warning or reason, he flew into a real rage!"

The doctor gave no indication that her comment was significant.

His final words repeated the gloomy forecast given by the other doctors. He stated that if Bruhs survived, he would spend the rest of his life in a wheelchair.

I had to put aside my preoccupation with Bruhs and the hospital to face another problem. The lease on the Studio was to expire September 30, and we were well into the month of September already. I had to make a decision, probably the most difficult choice I had ever been asked to make. I knew what the Dance Gallery meant to Bruhs—the blood, sweat, and tears that had gone into creating it, and the dreams that were inextricably bound up in it. In his present condition it was impossible to discuss it with him. After days of agonizing about it, I had a long talk with Harry. He was very positive and told me firmly, "Gean, we have to look at the practical side, separate from any sentimental considerations. We both know that Bruhs will never dance again, and it's pointless to keep that place in the hope that he will. He has to have a comfortable place to recuperate in when he leaves the hospital, and the Studio is definitely not the place. You have to give it up."

I realized Harry made sense, but it did not tell me how to break the news to Bruhs. And I faced the staggering task of dismantling the Studio by myself—nothing in my life so far had prepared me for that. Nonetheless, I acted quickly, once my decision had been reached. I notified the landlord and arranged with my office for a week's vacation to take the Studio apart.

A providential boost was Herbert's offer to work with me evenings on the electrical equipment. He also took the backdrop down from its heavy cable. Each night when I finished, I offered a prayer of thanks, and each morning I somehow miraculously found the strength to make it through another day. There was no time to dispose of furniture or studio paraphernalia, so I decided to get everything into cartons and put it in storage, where it would have to stay indefinitely. Fortunately, since we had sold the Chickering grand piano before Bruhs's illness, that was one large item that did not have to be stored.

On the final day of work at the Studio, a host of last-minute details remained. Suddenly the phone rang, and when I got down off the ladder to answer it, it was Bruhs's brother-in-law Brenner. He had taken over the visits to Bruhs for the week so that I could give undivided attention to the studio chores. He was calling to tell me that Bruhs was awake and wanted to see me, and that I should come right away. I tried to demur, filthy as I was, but he wouldn't listen. Resignedly, I hung up the phone and, as quickly as I could, cleaned myself up and hurried to the hospital. When I got to Bruhs's room, as I had anticipated, he had lapsed back into the comatose state with which I was so familiar. I bit my lip, stifled the sharp things I wanted to say to the well-meaning Brenner, and headed back to the Studio to work far into the night to finish the job.

Although by September 30, I managed to dismantle the Studio, where were Topandy and I to live? As luck would have it, a chance meeting with René Ferraris on the street that same day offered a partial solution. Reminiscing about the studio he had shared with Bruhs and me back in 1935, I brought him up to date about what had happened to Bruhs and my closing of the Dance Gallery. His reaction was immediate.

"I have a room on Washington Place and you can stay there," he said. "It isn't very spacious, but we could make do for a while."

I smiled and said, "That's great. When could we move in?"

René looked puzzled. "What do you mean, *we?*"

"Oh, I meant Topandy and me."

René's face fell. "Oh, I love Topandy, but the house doesn't allow pets."

This was a problem I had not anticipated. But again a benign Providence provided a refuge for Topandy with another of Bruhs's brothers, Nat. He called and offered to take care of Topandy until we could be settled permanently. I hated the thought of being separated, but I could hope that it would be only a short time until we were all reunited.

More than ever I felt that God was in His heaven and did look after His own. Bruhs was alive: where there's life, there's hope. I was ready to face the future with confidence reborn.

14

Recovery

On a crisp day late in October, as the air raid siren began its dismal noontime wail, Bruhs suddenly opened his eyes. It had been almost eight weeks since he had been admitted to the hospital; his life had hung in the balance for days on end. For the first time in these many weeks he seemed aware of his surroundings. The sunlight streamed through the window catching his face in its glow. Like a child's, his eyes were large and questioning.

"What was that sound? Where am I?...Why am I here? What's happened to me?"

It had been so long since he had said anything rational, I pressed his hand almost in disbelief. I was so overcome I could hardly speak and struggled to answer.

"That's the air raid siren, which sounds every day at noon while the war is on. You're in the hospital because you have been very sick, but now you are getting better."

He squeezed my hand with surprising strength, and his brimming eyes told me clearly his emotions. I knew how weak he was and I didn't want to put any strain on him. I released his hand and called the nurse to give her the good news.

Impressed by the remarkable improvement in his condition, the nurse went up to him, and asked, "Bruhs, what would you like for lunch? Name it and you've got it!"

Bruhs smiled wanly and said, "Oh, anything would be nice, as long as it isn't Jell-O!"

I lost no time in contacting his family. They were soon gathered in the room.

Suddenly Bruhs turned to his older sister, Anne, and asked, "Why doesn't Mama come to see me?"

Our hearts sank. Bruhs's mother had died eight years earlier. We had all been wrong in assuming that his irrationality, which had clouded everything he'd said for the last eight weeks, had disappeared. It still seemed to control his thinking. It gave us a sickening jolt to see he was not yet fully recovered, if he ever would be.

None of us knew at this point that the high fever, which had persisted for days, plus the complications with his nervous system, had played havoc with Bruhs's memory. What had happened to his thought processes only slowly dawned on us. A large chunk of his life experiences had been completely obliterated. Bruhs had reverted to age fifteen, when he had been in the hospital for a mastoid operation. His mother and father were both still living then, so his question about his mother's visiting made sense. The days I'd spent in agonizing over how to break the news to him about giving up the Studio had been totally unnecessary. Almost all memory of his life from age fifteen to thirty-two, which contained his treasured experiences of dancing, had apparently vanished. It would take all the patience and skill we could summon to bring him into the present and step-by-step rebuild his memory and confidence.

Harry was anxious to move Bruhs out of the hospital environment. As soon as he thought it advisable, he had his patient discharged. We had to deal with the thorny question of where Bruhs would get the best care so that he could commence his long recuperation and find his way back to a productive life.

Bruhs's sister Anne and her husband, Brenner, shared their Central Park West apartment with their daughter, Jean. Jean insisted on giving up her room so Bruhs could stay with her mother and father.

The day Bruhs left the hospital he weighed about ninety pounds. It was simple to make a chair of our arms and carry him from his brother's car to their elevator, and up and into the third-floor apartment. Anne had engaged a practical nurse to take care of Bruhs during the day. I would occupy the room with Bruhs and serve as his "night nurse."

Harry visited the apartment every day to check on Bruhs. Mrs. Bayer, our practical nurse, was conscientious and responsible. Her accurate and consistent records showed that the extra systoles in Bruhs's heartbeat indicated the necessity for restricted physical activity. At first Bruhs used the bathroom, but guided by the daily record of his heartbeats, Harry decided that bathroom privileges must be revoked, and a bedpan and urinal substituted. Oddly, much of Bruhs's use of them took place at night, so I got plenty of practice with them.

To help Bruhs build up his weight and regain his strength, Harry started his nutritional supplements with hepovex. This worked wonders for Bruhs's weight and color, and gradually he showed improvement in many other ways. In trying to walk, however, he had to shuffle his feet, as his legs just would not obey commands from his brain.

When Bruhs was strong enough, we decided to reunite our little family by bringing Topandy to live with us. When Nat walked in with her, it took two of us to hold her back when she saw Bruhs. We were afraid to let go of her for fear she would overwhelm Bruhs with her sheer exuberance. Little by little, we calmed her down. When she finally got to Bruhs's bed, she showed her determination never to be separated again. She refused to leave his side and could barely be coaxed into eating her meals. Even when picked up bodily and taken for a walk, she was a bundle of impatience until she could return to Bruhs.

Days lengthened into weeks and the season changed from autumn to winter. With Bruhs on the mend, the practical nurse became unnecessary, and Anne began to feel her daughter should return to her own room. Anne was not happy about Jean's temporary living quarters. Bruhs's improvement indicated that shifting to another location would not unduly affect his health and well-being.

Bruhs's other sister, Pnina, who was four years older than he, lived with her husband, Leslie, and their eleven-year-old daughter, Joan, in Washington Heights. Pnina offered to have Bruhs stay with them. It was a good stopgap arrangement but meant that we would be separated again while I returned to René's Village apartment for an indefinite period. But Topandy would be able to remain with Bruhs, a joy for both of them. Pnina's husband was probably the least enthusiastic member of the family about having a "boarder" under his roof, but his attitude softened when Bruhs's brother Bill volunteered financial assistance toward Bruhs's maintenance.

There was a side agreement to this offer, however, of which neither Bruhs nor I was aware. Bill made a proviso that I was not to be permitted to visit Bruhs; if I did, the financial aid would stop. Yet the first weekend that Bruhs was in Pnina's home, she nevertheless invited me to dinner. Although she was not aware of Bruhs's relationship with me, she knew the psychological benefit Bruhs seemed to derive from seeing me, and she was determined to follow her heart, whatever the cost. During dinner that night, Bill arrived unannounced, and Pnina's kind gesture resulted in their being immediately deprived of Bill's help. Added to that, she had to constantly mollify her disgruntled husband, who never tired of proclaiming that he was the "breadwinner" of the family.

Pnina, ever eager to show support for her brother Bruhs, never gave a sign that she had problems with her husband over Bruhs's tenancy. For that matter, Leslie himself was always the essence of cordiality to Bruhs and to me, giving no hint of his other feelings. But as time went on, the atmosphere there became charged with tension, to which Bruhs was extremely sensitive. He felt uncomfortable and unhappy, coupled with his general sense of confusion and insecurity due to the ravages of the illness. He began desperately to cast about for some solution.

To add to the behind-the-scenes drama, I had a call from our doctor, who said he would like to talk with me in his office. When I arrived, Harry was pacing up and down and I could see he was agitated. His first words were, "When I presented my bill to Bruhs's brother, he was outraged. He said it was exorbitant and badly inflated. He refused to pay it until I reconsidered it and scaled it down. You know Bruhs's case was difficult. In fact, it was so unusual I'm preparing a paper on it for the medical journals. I felt that my fee was equitable and, in view of the circumstances, I deserve to be paid. Bruhs is a dear friend as well as my patient and I'm overjoyed that I could do what I did for him. Let's face it—God cures the patient, and the doctor collects the fee, but in this case, as His agent, I certainly feel entitled to be paid for my services."

I took Harry's hand in mind and just held it. I was really stunned by his account of Bill's attitude. None knew better than I the depth of Harry's commitment to the handling of Bruhs's case. The devotion he was showing Bruhs was above and beyond all reasonable professional demands, and I considered it absolutely priceless. It would be hard to put a monetary figure on such magnanimity. I knew what I was about to say was absurdly inadequate, but I had to say something.

"As far as Bill is concerned, I suppose he feels overwhelmed by the expenses for the hospital and all, but I am sure he appreciates what you have done for Bruhs and will come through eventually.

Harry, you know our financial circumstances, but the $200 we have in our account is yours, and I know Bruhs would want you to have it as a tiny token of our gratitude."

Harry's response was quick. "No, Gean, I want nothing from you, either of you. Bruhs would not have made it without your love and your devotion. That goes beyond any material considerations. You supplied the missing ingredient of love. No, Bill will pay me the fee. I'll see to that!

"But there is something else I'd like you to know about Bill. I think he would like to see you and Bruhs separated. He simply doesn't realize what you mean to each other, or the vital part you played in Bruhs's recovery. What you and Bruhs have together goes beyond Bill's narrow outlook. Don't let him destroy it!"

I relayed Harry's suspicions of Bill's intentions to Bruhs. Bruhs was able to carry on a lengthy discussion with me about a plan to resolve our difficult living arrangements. Bruhs was in fact well enough to write a letter to his brother Gilbert indicating how depressing the atmosphere had become at Pnina's and how much it was impeding his recovery. He asked for suggestions as to how to remedy the situation.

Gilbert's reply was speedy and reassuring. He said he had discussed the problem with Bill and together they would finance a move to other quarters that Bruhs could share with me! This surprised us both and showed that Bill had either had a change of heart or had never had the sinister motives attributed to him. In any event, neither Bill or Gilbert ever hinted that he considered me an undesirable companion.

Given their decision, I began to scour the Times Square vicinity for a small residential hotel that we could afford, one that would allow us to keep Topandy with us. I finally found the Hotel Nash, on West 47th Street. The only thing left was to have Bruhs see it and give his approval.

February 15, 1944, was Bruhs's thirty-third birthday and I was determined to go all out in celebrating it. I was able to get tickets for *Carmen Jones,* which was playing to packed houses at the Broadway Theatre. It proved a magical choice for this very special evening.

I picked Bruhs up at Pnina's in Washington Heights, for dinner and then the theatre. This was our first night out since the illness had struck in August, and we both reveled in the sheer joy of sharing it together. *Carmen Jones* was performed by an all-black cast headed by Muriel Smith and Luther Saxon. The Bizet score was used in a special arrangement, the Carmen story retold by Oscar Hammerstein II in a modern war-plant background. The staging was superb, with striking choreography and brilliant lighting. In the hands of such expert performers the score had never sounded better.

After the theater, we walked slowly one block north to the Bryant Hotel where I had reserved a room for us. It was almost a second honeymoon. We both knew what limitations we had to observe; just being together totally by ourselves was enough.

The following day, after Bruhs had given the Hotel Nash his stamp of approval, I gathered up his belongings, and with Topandy in tow, we took up residence in the hotel. There were no facilities for cooking, so we always had to eat out. In the same block we found a Chinese restaurant that ignored Board of Health regulations to allow us to bring Topandy in, if we kept her under the table. Occasionally I brought up sandwiches to our room and we ate lunch there.

The Nash was conveniently located for me; I could walk to work at the Paramount Building at 44th Street and Broadway. We began to feel very much at home. The desk clerk was friendly and the elevator operator thoughtful and considerate. Several times the elevator was out of service, but as Bruhs was still unable to climb stairs, the operator carried him up three flights on his back! All of the hotel staff adored Topandy and went out of their way to show they cared about our comfort.

We had been living at the Nash for a few months when an incident occurred that left us shaken. West 47th Street off Times Square was a busy, noisy street; this was wartime and there was always the hustle, bustle, and hullabaloo of people moving through the amusement area even long after midnight. We usually listened in our room to our radio until 10:30 P.M. and then got ready for bed. But it was difficult to get accustomed to the street racket. Bruhs was a light sleeper, but luckily for me, once I managed to drift off, I could sleep through a typhoon or a volcanic eruption.

On this particular evening we had been in bed for about two hours when I felt Bruhs tugging on my arm. His voice was shrill with alarm.

"Gean, did you hear that noise? Something gave a terrible thump just now!"

I was slow to recover my senses, and I tried to be reassuring as I said, "Oh, it was probably Topandy rustling the papers on the foot of the bed."

Bruhs was not satisfied by my reply and snapped on the light at the head of our bed. We couldn't even see each other! Something like fog or smoke had completely filled the air and made it impossible to distinguish any of the familiar objects in the room.

I bounded out of bed. There at the foot of the bed on the rug was a great heap of plaster that had fallen from the ceiling. It easily measured three feet across; as the dust settled in the room, we could see the gaping hole in the plaster ceiling. The falling plaster had just missed Topandy.

When the hotel manager saw what had happened, he was appalled. The mess was quickly cleaned up and the ceiling repaired. He gave us a rebate of a week's rent.

To while away the hours when Bruhs was alone during the day, he frequently walked Topandy slowly to Rockefeller Plaza to sit and enjoy the fountains and the flowers. One day, quite by chance, Dhimah Goldsmith, a woman whom we had known in the Village when she ran a health food restaurant with her husband, sat down beside him. Dhimah reported that they had given up the restaurant and were living on West 79th Street near Riverside Drive. She invited Bruhs and me to dinner.

In the meantime, Bruhs filled me in on Dhimah's colorful background. As a young woman she had been a dancer and had fallen in love with a black writer, Richard Wright, and married him. They traveled extensively and they had a son named Peter. In those days, interracial marriages were far from acceptable in a country whose climate was still one of bigotry. Landlords and hotels would routinely create problems for this beautiful family. Finally, Dhimah left, no doubt overwhelmed by the frustrations of living with Richard Wright. Does one ever really know why some couples do not stay together? I only surmise that racial hatred played a part in their separation. Dhimah and little Peter began a new life. When she married Arthur Goldsmith, he was very happy to have a new son and a new wife.

A week later, on our way to Dhimah's for dinner, as we stepped off the Riverside Drive bus, we saw a brownstone being renovated that advertised apartments for rent. There was no one at that hour to give us information, but Dhimah volunteered to get details and call us. We learned from her the apartments would be available in mid-July at a rent we could afford.

We lost no time in signing a lease on a rear basement apartment at 64 Riverside Drive. This would at last give us the stability of having our own home again. It became the place where we were to spend a considerable part of our lives.

15

New Careers

For the first two weeks in July 1944, Bruhs's sister Anne and her husband were leaving the city for a vacation, and she invited us to occupy their apartment. We saved on hotel rent for that period, to apply to our new apartment. Our friend Milton helped us transfer the few belongings we had at the Hotel Nash to Anne's place and then to Riverside Drive, where we were allowed to take possession two weeks in advance of our lease. We spent the two intervening weeks shopping for furniture to supplement our limited household equipment. Bruhs had discovered a shop in Rockefeller Center that was closing out its furniture selection. There was a tremendous discount on chairs and occasional tables finished in driftwood gray. We selected several pieces as our motif and started refinishing our old pieces to make everything compatible. This was to be a residence, not a studio, and we wanted to make it livable and homelike.

When I closed the Studio on 10th Street, I had put everything except clothing in storage. Many items that had been appropriate for studio use just didn't fit in an apartment, and I left many things with the storage company. But the dozen or more wooden shutters that we had used to screen off portions of the entrance hall on 10th Street were useful at 64 Riverside Drive as partitions to separate the kitchen from the rest of the apartment. The layout was a rambling affair resembling a farmhouse, with two large rooms connected by an archway. They looked out on a private courtyard.

Among the cartons that I retrieved from storage were some full of pictures and programs from Bruhs's dancing career. We pored over these together. But at no time could Bruhs feel a relationship with the pictures. He felt as though he were learning about some other person's past, that person still a stranger. As time went on, he

98

began to realize that the part of his life that had had the greatest meaning to him had been wiped out, and he was absorbed by an aching sense of deprivation.

In 1944, on one of her occasional visits to New York, I took my mother to see *Oklahoma*. This was a milestone in the musical theater, not only for the magnificent score of Rogers and Hammerstein but for the revolutionary treatment of dance by Agnes de Mille. Gone were the traditional chorus routines designed to merely entertain. Instead, de Mille had introduced modified ballet that told a story and advanced the plot in a meaningful way. But Bruhs did not accompany us. This would have been of enormous interest to him when he was dancing, but now he felt the loss of his dancing so strongly that it was too painful to witness others doing what he could no longer do.

Because of his confusion and unhappiness, Bruhs asked our family doctor about seeking help through psychotherapy.

Harry was very firm. "Bruhs, I don't recommend seeing a psychiatrist. If you think you're mixed up now, you will be infinitely more so with psychotherapy. You have suffered a tremendous setback in the pursuit of a career, but it isn't the end of the world. You will find yourself and how to channel your energy in some other direction. Trust me, Bruhs. Stay away from the 'mind doctors.' They will not help you!"

He repeated the physical restrictions he felt Bruhs should observe for the balance of his life—no walking up stairs or riding in an airplane or ocean swimming. Bruhs left Harry's office more depressed than when he went in and was secretly determined to test some of these restrictions at the first opportunity. Bruhs said to himself, I can't go on to the end of my days living like an invalid. I'm still a young man, and I have to adjust to making a new life. If I die in the attempt, so be it!

To get another opinion on his prospects, Bruhs made an appointment to see Dr. Sevitsky, the neurologist from Montefiore Hospital who had examined him at his lowest ebb. Dr. Sevitsky was surprised that Bruhs had not only made it to his office under his own power, but had in fact disproven his prognosis about Bruhs's being confined to a wheelchair for the rest of his life. The doctor was no more optimistic than Harry, however, about the future of a man with Bruhs's case history. As Bruhs left, the doctor wished him well and graciously waived his consultation fee. Bruhs considered this visit fruitless, but it did confirm his feelings that doctors, even the most sensitive, rarely, if ever, took into account the human potential for recovery. The talk with Dr. Sevitsky only strengthened Bruhs's resolve to do some cautious experimenting on his own, and not submit to the severe inactivity the doctors had prescribed.

Bill and Gilbert had been generosity itself in paying for Bruhs at the Nash Hotel. Now that we had relocated on Riverside Drive, Bill went even further and put Bruhs on his office payroll, providing ongoing financial support. When Bruhs felt physically able, he began to spend time in Bill's office to take phone calls and help with bookkeeping. It was a valuable boost to his morale: it made him feel useful to be paid for contributing a needed service.

Another event made Bruhs aware of how many friends he had and how much his welfare concerned them. Milton Goldman, with his abiding love, organized a welcome-home party for Bruhs. He assembled a group of Bruhs's friends, many of whom had attended the Nucleus Club. Milton hosted the affair; at its conclusion, a war bond was presented to Bruhs. It was an expression of caring and a friend's deep concern.

Living on Riverside Drive was advantageous in many ways. A great place to relax, Riverside Park, was at our door, a wonderful playground for Topandy. The 79th Street Boat Basin was so removed from city traffic and noise that it had all the charm of a suburban resort, and we spent many hours in its tranquil surroundings. Even after nightfall there was no danger, and we felt perfectly safe at any hour. Sometimes we walked up the Drive to 90th Street to observe the comings and goings at the Soldiers and Sailors Monument; it rivaled Washington Square Park as a meeting place for gay men, but we remained only friendly spectators.

Over the years, many interesting neighbors lived at 64 Riverside Drive, but we were especially fond of one young newly married couple. Helen and Murray Tonken moved into the front of our basement floor in 1944. Helen was a dancer who had teamed with her husband for a time before she found steady work in the chorus of *Follow the Girls*. Murray waited tables to supplement their funds while auditioning for shows. He finally landed a part in the Mae West play *Catherine Was Great*, which gave them a steady income. Then Helen, expecting a child, stopped dancing.

Their daughter, Yon, was born in 1945. As soon as Helen was able to, she started auditioning again for a spot in a Broadway musical. Bruhs often took charge of the little one so Helen could answer a chorus call. For Bruhs it was a vicarious association with "show business," and looking after little Yon, he became very attached to her and she to him.

In the evening, male dancers with whom Helen had worked would drop by her apartment, and Helen often invited us to come in, too. No one ever identified himself as gay, but it was understood and taken for granted. Yon grew up in this atmosphere and exhibited a sophistication that belied her age. At three, she often requested one of the men to "do some more of that *campy* stuff."

Yon was frequently backstage with Helen and at age four had picked up a theatrical vocabulary. Bruhs often put her on his shoulders and danced with her as if they were a ballroom team. One day, when Bruhs's sister-in-law Martha unexpectedly stopped by, they were finishing a "number." Martha blurted out, "Yon, you might fall and get hurt! I wouldn't do that if I were you!" The child listened in visible disbelief, and then replied disdainfully, "I think that's utterly ridiculous!" Martha was so taken aback she didn't open her mouth again for the rest of her visit.

One night rather late Bruhs and I were preparing for bed when there was a knock on our door. With the chain in place we opened it cautiously and were surprised to see our neighbor Helen standing there with Yon in her arms. Murray was working late and had not yet come home. Helen's doorbell had rung insistently, several times. Not expecting anyone, she was startled. She hadn't pushed the buzzer to release the lobby door, but she needed someone to talk to.

Yon was hanging on every word with alarm creeping into her eyes. Helen tried to be casual: "It was probably someone who had forgotten his key and just rang to get in the house."

Yon turned her angelic face toward her mother and in a thin little voice exclaimed, "You know when that doorbell rang just now...it sure scared the hell outta me!"

Helen rolled her eyes heavenward and quickly added, "That's our show for tonight, folks. Say good night, Yon."

Another friend, Ada Penick, lived on the Drive at 90th Street. We were frequently invited to supper parties at her apartment. She had many friends of her own and met many more through us. The groups were mixed—part gay, part straight. The respect for talent among the guests made the question of sexual preference totally irrelevant. After dinner we usually gathered around the piano. Since there were singers and pianists in the group, there was plenty of entertainment. Bruhs and I did some of our songs which, oddly enough, had remained in his memory.

Two straight women, the sisters Shirley and May Frank, friends of Bruhs's sister Anne, had attended the concert we gave at Times Hall. They promised to keep in touch and, shortly after we moved to the Drive, invited us for dinner at their apartment on West 86th Street. We wondered if Shirley and May speculated about our relationship, but they never gave any sign that they regarded us as "different."

May was a superb cook, and her dinners were works of art. Frequently we joined them, usually on Friday evenings. Lil, another friend of theirs, occasionally had dinner with us all. On leaving, Lil always singled out the only store-bought food among the many dishes that May had made from scratch and, beaming at May, would say, "Such delicious bread!"

Due to chaotic wartime transportation, my work at Paramount grew increasingly difficult. The motion picture industry had always received red-carpet treatment, but with accommodations in short supply, I had serious problems providing the expected services. Space was allotted to the highest bidder, and a staggering premium was exacted for services that had previously been offered free. I had to work every connection I could think of. Even the surrender of Germany and then Japan in 1945 seemed to have little impact on travel problems. In fact, ever more returning military personnel jammed the already overburdened railroads. In handling movie stars and executives I had become accustomed to their unreasonable demands, but the state of transportation by the end of the war was totally unacceptable to people accustomed to getting the best at the snap of a finger. "Don't you know there's a war on?" was a cliché I could not use. Although I tried not to bring my problems home to Bruhs, I still spent sleepless nights worrying about each new situation. I was extremely short-tempered and difficult to live with.

Food was rationed. It was distressing that the affluent could always purchase what they wanted by lavishing gratuities on merchants or by patronizing the flourishing black market. Yet although we may have been denied some of the luxuries, rationing had allowed us to obtain the essentials and we never experienced hunger. The depth of our commitment to each other sustained us through the lean and difficult times so many had to endure because of wartime shortages.

By 1946 I had been without a piano for over two years and missed it dreadfully. An old-fashioned Steinway square piano was for sale by a private owner for $40. I couldn't wait to get my hands on it. But when the movers brought the instrument into our apartment, I was not home. It had not occurred to me in advance to prepare Bruhs for its size. Detached from its legs, the body of the piano looked like a great, black coffin. Once attached to the legs it looked more like a piano, but its seven-foot length took up one whole end of the room and filled Bruhs with dismay every time he looked at it.

We tried to remove the badly scratched finish, but the ebony stain was too deep to respond to a sander. We ultimately did it over in a velvet gray that harmonized with the other furnishings. Our piano technician marveled at the fine condition of its parts; with only modest repair, it became the centerpiece of the apartment. It was largely responsible for helping me to unwind each day after wrestling with my job, and to express myself musically again. Its fine mellow tone gave me the satisfaction that only communion with music can bring.

Marion, a young woman we had known at the Nucleus Club, who lived in Brooklyn, had kept in touch with us throughout Bruhs's hospital stay. She called us one day and asked if she might stay with us on the Drive until she could find a place in Manhattan. We welcomed this opportunity to supplement our income, although Bill continued to aid Bruhs. He said that helping Bruhs had brought him good luck. He had secured several lucrative government contracts during the war, and his trucking business had enjoyed prosperity beyond his fondest hopes.

While Marion was with us on the Drive, our social life seemed to blossom. She knew many people in the theater and loved to widen her circle of friends. At one of these gatherings at our apartment, Thelma Carpenter, a popular singer, gave us her poignant rendition of "Happiness Is Just a Thing Called Joe," accompanied by Erroll Garner, the great jazz pianist. During a break in the program Garner looked out at the guests and, flashing his beautiful smile, said, "Sitting at this piano, I feel just like Mozart."

In 1941 Bruhs and I had seen *Native Son*, starring a newcomer to Broadway—Canada Lee. It was a sizzling performance that propelled him from a promising career in boxing to a stellar position in the theater. Bruhs had been so impressed by the quality of Canada's talent that in the fall of 1946 Bruhs sought an opportunity to work with him in the newly formed Canada Lee Productions.

In a long conversation with Canada, Bruhs outlined the many ways in which he might be helpful. As a trial, Bruhs came daily to Lee's office and soon had an unsalaried position with Canada Lee Productions. This rewarding association lasted until Canada's untimely death in 1951.

Also in 1946, the *Daily News* carried a story of a musical to be titled *The Reluctant Virgin,* based on the Puccini opera *Turandot,* as the first offering of Canada Lee's fledgling production company. Bruhs Mero was to do the choreography, and Albert Hague the score. Fortunately for Bruhs this effort never materialized, for he no longer had the vaguest idea of how to choreograph. However, it did get Bruhs's name back in circulation as an active theatrical participant. Within a few weeks, the Canada Lee School of Acting came into existence, and Bruhs became a member of the faculty to handle the Body Movement Department. This did have a modest stipend attached to it. But the school was not markedly successful and closed after two semesters.

Marion, who had joined us on the Drive as a "temporary roommate," stayed on with us until 1947. Early that year she acquired a new friend, Ethel Gladys, who as "Eegee" became one of our closest friends. Marion and she decided to share a place together. To celebrate, they invited us to a performance of *Finian's Rainbow.* It was a memorable evening and generated an extraordinary warmth of feeling; I hummed the score for days. A week later Marion and Eegee decided to drive to Florida and invited Bruhs to come. It was a simple matter for him to take time off from Canada Lee, and Bruhs needed the change. So we persuaded him to accept their invitation. On the way back Bruhs stopped off in Richmond, Virginia, to spend a few days with his brothers Gilbert and Lee, whom he had not seen since his illness.

Meanwhile, we had heard so much about Tennessee Williams's new play *Streetcar Named Desire* that I had to see it. Marlon Brando oozed animal magnetism from every pore, and his brooding intensity, combined with his guttural speech, was utterly compelling. Jessica Tandy brought to the role of Blanche Dubois a wistful vulnerability that was a perfect achievement. A critic's description of *Streetcar* as "shattering" captured the impact of this great theatrical experience.

In 1948 the federal government won its suit against the motion picture companies and they had to break up their monopolistic hold on the production, distribution, and exhibition of their films. Rumors were rife about all the changes that would result. In part through my efforts, the United Office and Professional Workers of America (UOPWA) had been certified as the bargaining agent for the Paramount office employees and won much-needed raises for us. When 1949 dawned, everyone was still talking about impending changes, but not until July did the ax fall—squarely on my neck!

Much has been said and written about the unconscionable power of unions. The irony of the situation was that even though I had been a prime mover in bringing the union to Paramount, the union was powerless to save my job. The job had been "abolished" and no one had the strength to demand its restoration. The union tried: they set up a picket line in front of the Paramount Building, handed out leaflets describing my twenty-year tenure, the outstanding service I had rendered to the company, and so on. In addition to the union's efforts, some employees took up a collection that equaled my weekly salary ($65) and plunked it down on President Balaban's desk. They thought they could buy another week's time for me in which negotiations might put me into a different position. It was all to no avail. Management didn't want to keep me on: I had committed the unpardonable sin of foisting another union on them. Although it had taken a while, they finally had the perfect excuse—the government's lawsuit—to justify my dismissal. Because of this breakup they had carte blanche to downsize personnel. They had achieved one objective—good riddance to me as a troublemaker. The only satisfaction I could muster was that I had not been fired because I was gay. Gean Harwood was a free agent at last. After picking up the twenty weeks' severance pay (one week for each year) and saying goodbye to all my friends and fellow workers, I hit the unemployment line.

I learned that to qualify, one was expected to be ready, willing, and able to work. I explored my contacts in the airlines and railroads, looking for work with which I was familiar. It was fruitless—the airlines were only interested in young people for apprentices, and I had passed my fortieth year! The railroad employees were unionized, and it was impossible to pry loose an opening. I had one offer of a job from United Office and Professional Workers of America. They wanted me as an organizer, but I couldn't visualize that as a career.

A young woman I knew in Paramount's personnel department, who felt I had been treated unfairly, let me know of a job opening with Consolidated Film Industries. This company shipped film; she felt that with my knowledge of rail and shipping lines, I could qualify. At this point I was clutching at straws and lost no time in arranging an appointment to see a Mr. Reilly, the general manager of Consolidated. A brusque man, he seemed bent on making the interview as brief as possible. He offered me five minutes to sketch my background, then broke into that with an impatient gesture that implied I was wasting his time.

"Yeah, Harwood, you handled big shots at Paramount, but this job is different. Here you have to handle tough customers, real tough, and you have to be tougher than they are. You seem too soft to handle this job. I have to tell it like it is."

I could not wait to get out of his presence and hurried back to Paramount to report my brush-off to my friend in personnel. She met me with a crestfallen look.

"I'm sorry I sent you over there, Gean. Reilly called me about five minutes ago and I couldn't believe what he said. I wrote it down word for word. Do you want to hear it?"

I nodded, and she gave it to me:

"That guy Harwood that you sent over was just a waste of time. He couldn't possibly handle this job. I have interviewed women who were stronger than he is. Next time, if there is a next time, don't send a 'fruit' to handle a man's job."

My twenty years with Paramount, and what had finally happened there, had soured me on private corporations. I began to think of a civil service job in local government. There would be no more periodic "hitting up the boss" for a raise. At least promotions would be earned and based on what I knew rather than whom I knew. At the first announcement of the New York City clerical entrance exam, I applied and started boning up for the test.

When the day of the exam finally arrived, I felt amply prepared and I earned a good grade. I knew I would be sure of an appointment. It meant starting over—but I have never regretted my decision to leave private industry and take the unglamorous role of civil servant.

16

Postwar Recovery and Depression

If 1949 was a hectic year for me, it was also a disturbing one for Bruhs. He was concerned about the psychological effect on me of losing my job, and he wondered how we would manage financially. As an employee of his brother he had no real security, and he knew that when I had exhausted my severance pay, I would have only the meager sum of $21 per week provided temporarily by unemployment insurance. My civil service appointment would eventually materialize, but many months remained for the bureaucratic machinery to grind out a list, and we had to stay afloat somehow for that interval.

As a wartime measure, the government had instituted rent control on buildings that had been constructed prior to 1947. The building we occupied fell in this category. Our starting rent had been $45 per month, and we had only an increase of $10 overall before rent control became effective. Thus our rent was frozen at $55, which included gas and electricity. Our only additional expense was for a telephone, which had been hard to obtain during the war; our doctor secured the necessary priority due to Bruhs's health.

Taken as a whole, 1949 was not all bad. It was the year that a long and beautiful friendship began quite casually. One Friday afternoon Bruhs had finished his daily volunteer stint with Canada Lee and was relaxing in Rockefeller Plaza. He struck up a conversation with a young man who gave his name as Lenny and said he lived in Brooklyn. Until his enrollment at New York University he had rarely if ever come into Manhattan. His manner was so open and flavored with such guileless naïveté that Bruhs was delighted by him. Bruhs invited him to visit us on the Drive, and early the following week he paid us a call.

Lenny had started summer vacation from college, and he would become almost a daily visitor at 64 Riverside Drive. He seemed totally intrigued by us and asked endless questions about our lifestyle. Without any sexual involvement, by degrees we became aware of his awakening sexual identity. We both functioned as a combination of companion, confidant, father confessor, and role model for him. Watching him develop, we were delighted by his pixieish sense of humor and his insatiable curiosity about everything and everyone associated with the gay milieu. I introduced him to modern music, and he had a burgeoning appetite for, and an uncanny comprehension of, the other cultural riches we three explored together. Lenny became so much a part of our life, and we shared so much with him, that it was hard to believe that his luminous presence had not always been with us.

Besides the bright spirit that Lenny brought to our household, we had a large circle of friends, with lots of parties at our place and theirs. We did not patronize the gay bars, which were becoming numerous and popular. We attended the theater or a concert when we could afford it. We never seemed to lack for entertainment and amusement.

I often regaled Lenny with accounts of personalities I had encountered at Paramount. He particularly enjoyed hearing about one of my last official duties there. Gloria Swanson had been signed to do *Sunset Boulevard,* and the studio was extremely anxious to get her to the Coast so that shooting could start as soon as possible. Miss Swanson's requirements were for a drawing room on the Twentieth Century Limited to Chicago and the same accommodations on the connecting Santa Fe Chief to Los Angeles. Time was of the essence, but try as I might, I could not come up with a drawing room. I had offers of compartments, bedrooms—everything except what I needed. Each day that her departure was delayed, Miss Swanson grew more impatient. In desperation, she would have settled for something less than a drawing room, but there were physical complications (never explained) that compelled her to have a separate lavatory. At times, she seemed practically on the verge of tears because the part in *Sunset Boulevard* was a comeback for her and she felt her career was on the line. The studio kept up its cries of distress, and the home office added to the tension by its petulance over my "failure" to produce the required accommodation. At the eleventh hour, with practically all hope abandoned, a drawing room reservation became available on the Broadway Limited, the Pennsylvania Railroad's competition to the Twentieth Century Limited. Gloria Swanson was finally able to embark for Hollywood to play Norma Desmond, the greatest role of her career.

In 1950, Canada Lee was selected to play the lead in a film being made from Alan Paton's book *Cry, the Beloved Country*, on the divisive force of apartheid. Many scenes were to be shot on location in South Africa and the final footage at studios in England. Canada portrayed the Reverend Stephen Kumalo, whose struggle to save his son from the injustice of the prevailing system of oppression dominates the story. The Paton book had been done in 1949 on Broadway as a musical, *Lost in the Stars,* for which Maxwell Anderson had written a script with a score by Kurt Weill. Canada's friend Todd Duncan had triumphed on the stage in the same role that Canada would portray on the screen, and it was a challenge Canada relished.

Under the terms of Canada's contract, his salary was to be paid to Canada Lee Productions. He could begin reimbursing Bruhs for the years he had devotedly worked for Canada. This helped our strained finances and contributed to Bruhs's peace of mind.

In 1950 things looked brighter for Bruhs and this was reflected in his attitude at home. Lenny continued to visit us frequently and often had supper with us. He was always interested in the preparation of food, and my modest attempts at culinary surprises were greeted with great enthusiasm. Lenny always arrived bearing gifts, some so extravagant and expensive that we were embarrassed to accept them. He never tired of proclaiming that Bruhs and I had become a second family for him, and one where he could be himself.

Although the activity surrounding Canada Lee's film had made a marked improvement in Bruhs's morale, I was steadily slipping into depression. I chafed at the interminable waiting to be employed again. The mandatory weekly visits to the unemployment office were irritating, and the pittance received was demeaning. I began to think of myself as a failure and to question myself endlessly. In addition, there were unpleasant symptoms in my urinary tract.

A Dr. Hotchkiss, a specialist in urology, had saved the kidney of our friend May Frank, at whose suggestion I contacted the doctor for an office examination. He asked me many questions, including one about my military service. I didn't want to disclose that I was homosexual and had to do some fast thinking. On the spur of the moment I came up with the explanation that I had been classified 4-F because of "inadequate personality," a term I had heard used but whose exact meaning I did not know. I hoped the doctor would be unsure of it, too. I knew Dr. Hotchkiss continued to see May, and I did not wish to openly declare myself, for fear this would reach May and Shirley. I was still traveling the corridor of fear, and its constraints weighed heavily on my spirit.

When Dr. Hotchkiss heard that I was unemployed, he agreed to ask a fee only for the initial examination. As Bellevue Hospital's chief of urology, he arranged to admit me there without charge, to undergo a procedure that he had devised himself. With a trans-urethral instrument called an indoscope, he planned to remove prostatic tissue and reduce the enlargement of the gland. He felt this operation would give me relief from my constant discomfort.

It was several days before Dr. Hotchkiss could perform the procedure for which I had been admitted. In the meantime, our own doctor, Harry, who was chief of internal medicine at Bellevue, looked in on me frequently. Bruhs, the soul of invention, managed to visit me every day, no small accomplishment considering that visiting hours were limited to two days per week. But by carrying a small black bag that looked like a doctor's, Bruhs was accepted as part of the staff by guards and virtually had the run of the place.

Dr. Hotchkiss repeated the procedure, known technically as fulguration of the verumontanum, a second and third time. At first, the operations seemed to yield some benefits, but as time went on, the unpleasant and painful problem returned and had a profound effect on my sexual drive. The discomfort I felt was often so intense that the thought of sex became actually repugnant. I began to be assailed by doubts about the cause of the pain. Maybe it was not physical at all but some deep-seated psychological problem that had surfaced, some leftover remnant of sex-related guilt. Maybe it was a signal of midlife crisis. Whatever it was, it was difficult to explain my feelings to anyone. I tried to talk with Bruhs about it, but talking only made matters worse. For some unaccountable reason I seemed unable to bridge the gap in our communications. Bruhs, with a comforting exhibition of patience, let me know that he was standing by and would wait it out while we exhausted every effort to find a solution.

For some time, Bruhs had had a developing conviction that

psychotherapy would be of benefit to him. This feeling built up in him despite Harry's low estimation of psychotherapy. I, too, began to feel that perhaps psychotherapy might provide some answers for my problem. The intense bond that held us together meant that our relationship did not suffer as badly as it might have from our enforced celibacy, but we both realized that some action was urgently called for to preserve our lifetime commitment. We knew that several friends had had psychotherapy, and we asked them about possible referrals. One of them shook his head and sighed as he gave his gloomy forecast: "Take it from one who knows—if you both go into therapy, I give your relationship six months!"

The main stumbling block to starting therapy was our lack of money. As everyone knows, therapy is expensive and beyond the reach of modest incomes. Again Providence seemed to smile, as if to give approval. I received my long-awaited city job and began work in February 1951. At the outset I drew only $28 per week. It was only $7 per week more than I had received from unemployment insurance, but this was a permanent job! And I knew there would be an early opportunity to move up the ladder and improve my income.

When I arrived home one afternoon from work, I found we had a visitor, someone I had not seen for a long time. Belle, who had been Bruhs's steady girlfriend when I first met him, had kept in touch with Bruhs over the years by exchanging birthday cards. She had learned of his earlier illness from his sister Pnina and had visited the hospital, but he had still been comatose. Later, when Bruhs was at his sister Anne's, Belle came to see him again. They brought each other up-to-date on their lives. Now at our apartment she still seemed to feel no resentment toward me and greeted me cordially when I came in.

Belle had married a doctor and had two children, yet somehow she had never become reconciled to the break in her relationship with Bruhs. This day she had a particular purpose in mind. She was enrolled in "orgone therapy" and asked Bruhs to visit her therapist. We invited her to have supper with us, but after getting Bruhs to promise that he would see her therapist, she left. It was the last time either of us ever saw her. Bruhs did visit the orgone therapist, but his visit did not help resolve Belle's problem. I learned a short time later from Pnina that Belle had taken her own life.

Pnina made me promise not to tell Bruhs. Belle's brother, Mike, had always bitterly resented Bruhs's "rejection" of his sister, and

Bruhs's family were fearful that Mike might create an ugly scene if Bruhs attended the funeral. Pnina promised faithfully to bring the family together to break the news to Bruhs. Days stretched into weeks and months; in spite of constant reminders from me the family never did tell Bruhs. When Belle's birthday came again, he prepared to send her a card as usual. I had to tell him not to send the card and why. He was crushed by the news and very angry with me for a time. Eventually he realized the difficult position in which his family had placed me. I learned a valuable lesson—never harbor secrets from the person you love. Candor may be painful, but it is wrong to make decisions for others when the heart is deeply affected.

At the completion of *Cry, the Beloved Country,* Canada Lee Productions was dissolved and Bruhs no longer had an income from that source. At just the right moment for him, and as I started working for the city, Pnina found an opening for Bruhs in the Letters of Credit Department of the goverment of Israel Supply Mission, where she was employed as an executive secretary. This meant that Bruhs and I both had steady jobs and could direct our attention to locating a therapist. This was more easily said than done because of the fee involved.

There are many schools of therapy to choose from. In the early fifties, some followed Karen Horney, and some the methods of Carl Jung, but Freud was the predominant figure in the field. In Freudian treatment the patient was left with no guidance or suggestions from the therapist. There was no discussion in advance about a desired goal or the aims of the therapy. The patient was cast upon a turbulent ocean in a leaky craft without rudder or sail and felt the total desperation of sink or swim.

It was our misfortune that Bruhs and I both landed in a Freudian trap the first time around. I was never privy to what Bruhs encountered in his therapy, but his anger and confusion after the sessions spoke volumes about how stormy they must have been.

I did not fare much better in my initial exposure to therapy. My therapist instructed me to lie on the couch, then adjusted the window blinds so that harsh sunlight fell directly in my eyes. He asked no questions of me nor did he do anything to encourage me to talk. I spent the entire "hour" (a euphemistic term for a session lasting fifty minutes) in dead silence. At the end of the session I paid him the fee and he gave me an appointment for the following week.

The next visit was on a cloudy day so I had no problem with sun in my eyes, but the therapist had another card up his sleeve. This time he smoked a big cigar throughout the session and every now and then would deliberately blow some smoke in my face. For the full fifty minutes I endured this "treatment," again in stony silence, and concluded that the man must be a sadist masquerading as a therapist. As I was leaving, he said to me, "I'll see you next week," to which I replied, "No, you won't see me next week! These two sessions have accomplished nothing except to expose me to unbelievable discomfort. I can't afford to go on with you in this manner. We're obviously not suited to work together."

His reply surprised me but did nothing to change my estimation of him or his "methods." "I knew the sun in your eyes was uncomfortable," he said. "I also knew the cigar smoke was unpleasant. Those were deliberate devices to get you to assert yourself—to speak up, to protest. It's your prerogative to seek another therapist, but you will continue to have the same difficulty in communicating your displeasure unless you learn to open up and let it out." His explanation shed some light on his behavior, but I felt it was not the approach I was looking for. I experienced vast relief at leaving for good.

After these abortive attempts at therapy, both Bruhs and I decided to wait awhile before giving it another try. We felt it was unfair to pass judgment on a scientific system without further trial. With a bit of luck, we would find the right person to administer the therapy for what we wanted most—relief from my pain, and to see that some of the scrambled pieces of Bruhs's life puzzle were put back in place.

17

Jobs and Dreams

Bruhs and I settled quickly into our new jobs. They were both routine clerical jobs taking a minimum of concentration; at the end of the day they could easily be forgotten. Bruhs's supervisor was a humorless martinet whom we privately dubbed Herr von Schtunk. He made unreasonable demands, but since Bruhs was a perfectionist in any assignment, he never offered an opportunity for criticism at his job.

On the other hand, Herbert Pine, my supervisor in the city Bureau of Records, was a methodical and even-tempered man. He delighted in retelling stories of his exploits as a building inspector before he was elevated to senior statistician at the Bureau. A wiry man, he had remarkable energy for his age. His morning walk from our office down a long corridor to the lavatory was accompanied by audible flatulence, and he frequently rooty-toot-tooted his way down the hall as if by jet propulsion. This down-to-earth man quickly endeared himself to me. He was thirty years my senior and adopted an almost fatherly attitude toward me. His only criticism was to chide me for finishing my tasks too quickly. On many things we saw eye to eye, but I differed sharply with him about politics. He was a staunch admirer of the most conservative men in government and loathed any politician or policy with the slightest taint of liberalism. He had served during La Guardia's entire tenure and literally hated his guts. Franklin Roosevelt was another of his "most disliked." When Eisenhower became president, Mr. Pine was ecstatic.

I will always remember Mr. Pine fondly for his referring to Bruhs as my "partner." Both Bruhs and I have never been comfortable with the term *lover*. It has always had a subtly illicit connotation, and we were happy to adopt *partner* as more apt and used it exclusively after that.

That same year Lenny met a young man who was to change the course of his life. There were complications because the young man was a widower struggling to raise a son. At first it seemed that their relationship would be difficult to work out, but when love is genuine, it triumphs. For a time we saw less of Lenny while he explored an emotional experience that differed completely from the platonic relationship he had with us. Eventually we were introduced to his new friend, and the four of us became close. We were enormously pleased by the transformation this meaningful event had wrought in Lenny's outlook. He was no longer an emotional drifter now that he had an anchor in his life. With his feet set firmly on a new path, his love would be channeled away from transitory affairs to a durable relationship, which he truly needed and deserved.

One day late in the year I noticed in the *Chief,* the civil service newspaper, an announcement for a test for the music librarian post at the city's WNYC radio station; it sounded much more attractive to me than statistical tabulating at the Bureau of Records. I had listened to the classical music programs on WNYC and WQXR for years, and with my musical background I could handle the job well.

It was an esoteric position, and to prepare for its civil service exam there were no study books or previous exams. I went into the test with absolutely no preparation but my musical background and a determination to pass. I had to draw on memory in plotting sample programs. Only one person did better, by a fraction of a percentage point.

I was summoned for an interview; my qualifications were fine. The first question from the interviewer yanked me out of my complacency by zeroing in on my critical vulnerability: "Did you serve in the military?"

When I explained that I had been classified 4-F, the interviewer made a dry, matter-of-fact statement: "A position in a radio station is considered sensitive and a careful screening is done to rule out security risks. If you have any reason for not wishing your army records to be examined, you can ask to have your name removed from the eligible list. Think it over and let me know what you decide."

This was a stumbling block I had not anticipated, and I found it difficult to respond. Before my eyes flashed the bold red letters "Admitted Homosexual" on my records. I rallied and asked for time to consider.

I sought the advice of a man at the Bureau of Records with whom I had become friendly. He had held responsible positions in other administrations and was very knowledgeable. He was also gay. At that time, there was no executive order that protected a gay person's job. My friend agreed with me that if knowledge of my sexual preference were known, it could jeopardize my present position as well as automatically deny me the WNYC post. I really had no choice. Crushed by the turn of events, I was forced to swallow my pride and ask that my name be removed from the list. This was one more example of the discrimination to which gay people were subjected, and a grim reminder of the "corridor" from which there seemed no escape.

However, a loosely structured organization principally of gay men, known as the Mattachine Society, had begun to surface about this time in New York City. Its main purpose was to organize common pursuits and identify common aims of gay people. Neither Bruhs nor I was impressed by reports we had of Mattachine meetings, which seemed too often merely to provide a meeting place in which to make out. The greatest emphasis was placed on social activity, with more serious discussion sandwiched in only when there was enough time. We did not question the sincerity of participants, but it did not appeal to us particularly, either. We failed to take into account that gay people were very diverse with many different interests. If there was to be any movement to bring them together, it would probably have to originate in a kaffeeklatsch atmosphere. Unfortunately in those days gay people did not take themselves seriously, and it was a big step for them to visualize anything even vaguely approaching the concept of community. We had not yet even begun to use the term *gay* to identify each other, and it would take many years of fertilization by the Mattachine Society and others to yield any gay liberation.

Marion and Eegee had moved to a little two-story house on Water Street, which they shared with two other lesbians. One evening at one of their many parties, where we entertained the company with our songs, we were watching the boats come and go on the East River. Twinkling lights glistened on the dark water, and as we glimpsed the busy river traffic through the windows, we seemed visitors in some foreign port and not in New York City at all. Our reverie was broken by a young man who introduced himself as Dr. Howard Brown. He was on the administrative staff at the Health

Insurance Plan (HIP), so we kidded with him ironically about how much Bruhs's care there would have been improved if we had found a family physician who was gay. He agreed, but said he knew of none on the entire HIP roster. Years later, as a high official in New York City government, this remarkable man became a symbol of courage by publicly admitting being gay. His forthright stand made him a man to be remembered, and the Fund for Human Dignity is a fitting memorial for his inspiring example.

One evening at Ada's home on the Drive, Elton and his wife, Ethel, two regular guests at all of Ada's affairs, asked a medium they knew to conduct a séance. With the guests assembled in the living room, the psychic asked to be doubly blindfolded and, with a minimum of preparation, went into a trance. She called on her spirit guide to help her communicate with those close to the assembled group. At first there were general messages, rather somber and vaguely expressed, not directed to any specific person.

Suddenly, with almost no warning, the medium's voice brightened. It took on a totally different timbre. "Is there someone named Bruce? There is a dark-haired young woman here who is anxious to give you a message."

Bruhs was so unnerved he could barely speak. "I'm 'Bruhs.' I'm here."

The medium went on, "There is so little time but she wants to tell you that everything is all right. She is at peace. Things are clearer now, and you must not worry about her. Everything is all right." The medium's voice trailed off, as though coming from a great distance, and the last words were barely audible.

When we were leaving Ada's that evening, Elton and Ethel each held one of Bruhs's hands and squeezed them. He was still in shocked disbelief. He wanted to accept the message as valid and comforting, but found it difficult. He walked in total silence. At home he turned to me and said, "Do you think it was really Belle speaking to me tonight?"

"Yes," I replied, "I believe the message came from Belle. She knows how distressed you've been over her. She wanted to reassure you, and you're not to suffer anymore."

This seemed to satisfy him. We never discussed the séance again.

One day, I was walking at lunch in the Wall Street area when I noticed a small magazine partially hidden behind other periodicals on a newsstand. I could not believe the title and the logo under it: *ONE: The Homosexual Magazine.* I made sure no one was watching me as I put down my twenty-five cents and took a copy.

When I got back to the office, I went to a bathroom stall where no one could observe me and opened the cover. I read a first-page paragraph:

> *ONE* is a non-profit corporation formed to publish a magazine dealing primarily with homosexuality from the scientific, historical and critical point of view...to sponsor educational programs, lectures, and concerts for the aid and benefit of social variants and to promote among the general public an interest, knowledge, and understanding of the problems of variation...to sponsor research and promote the integration into society of such persons whose behavior and inclinations vary from the current moral and social standards.

That statement boggled my mind! It really seemed the millennium had arrived! Here was a sober, well-intentioned periodical that embraced many of the ideas that Bruhs and I had held for years. It was a masterstroke of consciousness-raising that reached to the core of what being gay was all about. I was delighted and couldn't wait to get the following month's issue. Each month included a fiction piece, a thought-provoking discussion, reports on changing attitudes toward homosexuality, a book review, and other items of interest.

When I had to go to the hospital for an appendectomy in December, I mulled over some ideas for a story. I hadn't written anything since high school, but *ONE* had inspired me and I felt the time was ripe to write something that they would publish.

My recuperation at home clinched my resolve. I was still too closeted to use my own name, so I selected a nom de plume, Curt Merrick.

HALF A WORLD

by Curt Merrick

Dick Lovett held his eyes on the control tower visascope. What he would see in a few minutes could change everything in his world. The minutes ticked slowly, steadily on, but his mind raced back—back into the past. All of his own past since he had been aware of himself passed in shadowy review. He was young and he had inherited a new and better position in society than others of his kind before him had enjoyed. Now his runaway thoughts were traveling farther back into those difficult days about which he had only read or been told.

It had all started with the transposition of the letters in the word, homosexual, so that the "sex" connotation was eliminated, and a new designation provided for that group which had borne this onus for so long. From that point on things began to slowly change for the better. With a new name, the ranks of HEXOSOMUALS, as they were now called, swelled to an unprecedented number. Many heretofore unsuspected individuals, to whom a "movement" involving organization of homosexuals was anathema, came forward and joined with their brothers and sisters in the march toward a new concept in society.

Of course, the heartbreaking labor of the pioneer workers in organization was not to be minimized. Now that so much had been accomplished, it was hard to believe that it had taken all those years of persecution to make the homosexuals desperate enough to really begin to organize in earnest. Some of the early organizers were pilloried and all but boiled in oil getting things underway.

The heterosexual majority, termed, with a high degree of inaccuracy, as "normals," had received a new name, too, in the shuffle, and were now referred to as MORNALS. The more open the HEXOSOMUALS' organizing activity had become, the more frenzied and violent the MORNALS made their opposition. All the biggest batteries of the Law and the powerful influence of the Church were brought to bear in trying to strangle the nascent movement...

Dick halted his parade of thoughts as he reached for a capsuled stimulant. He must keep himself alert while he remained at his lonely vigil in front of the visascope. But his thoughts would not remain captive for long. They were off again on their journey into the past.

There was considerable difficulty from another segment of society—the VERPERTS. Many of those emotionally distorted people, whose compulsions directed their attentions only to youngsters or other perverted acts, had to be dealt with and controlled. The MORNALS had to be convinced that these unfortunate persons were no more a part of the HEXOSOMUALS per se than they were of the MORNALS, and that their activity was justly abhorrent to society, both the Old and the New.

Thus, in retrospect, the integration of HEXOSOMUALS into a friendly and productive coexistence with MORNALS seemed easy, but in reality it had been anything but that. Yet, the resulting sense of security for the HEXOSOMUALS in society was enormously increased, worth all the superhuman efforts to achieve it....

These were some of the thoughts that crowded into Dick Lovett's mind as he scanned the screen in front of him. So much—everything, in fact—depended on the outcome of the strategy he and his staff had evolved. This was the big test.

He had read and reread the history of the last half of the 1900s leading into the new century. It seemed like some tragic nightmare that the homosexuals, as they were then archaically termed, were jailed and persecuted, kept from participation in government and civil affairs on the flimsy pretext of being considered "security risks."

As the light caught the bars on Dick's shoulder, bespeaking his powers of command, he smiled. Yes, the HEXOSOMUALS had come a long way since those dark days of the 1950s. Now he must stop this woolgathering and give his undivided attention to matters at hand.

For years the conflict with the SURSIANS had seemed ready to break wide open. But each side had held back, mindful of the awful consequences involved. This teetering on the edge of doom couldn't go on forever. Every new mental hospital kept being filled the same day it opened its doors. MORNALS and HEXOSOMUALS alike were at the breaking point.

Then it was that he himself, as commander of the Air Squadrons, had evolved the strategy now about to unfold before his eyes. His own squadron, composed entirely of HEXOSOMUALS, the most popular group in the Air Command, had volunteered to spark this mission. They were to act as a decoy and lure the reluctant SURSIANS through an atomic curtain, the existence of which, it was hoped, would be completely unknown to the enemy. If the plan succeeded, the victims' airships would be disintegrated.

It seemed feasible and would certainly be decisive. If any sanity was to be preserved, quick decision was imperative. A status quo, with both sides armed to the teeth sitting in quiet desperation waiting for the other to make a move, couldn't be maintained indefinitely.

The first indication of action was beginning to show up on the screen. Dick's mouth became tense, his lips a thin line, as he watched. The lead plane piloted by Gaylan Carr, ace flyer of this special HEXOSOMUAL Corps, was of more than tactical concern to Dick. Gay was not only his Aide—he was his reason for living. Every dream, every hope of their lives together, flew in that plane.

It was dawn—and this was it! The first gray streaks of light filled the sky. Now all his gallant men should be coming into view—and if the plan worked, the SURSIANS in pursuit.

Dick felt hot and cold by turns as he adjusted the controls of the screen. Why didn't they come? Time was running out.

Suddenly they were there! Gay's ship and the other and—Dick caught his breath—the SURSIANS! Something had gone wrong—impossibly, horribly wrong. His own men were being crumpled and twisted by atomic fire but the SURSIANS, seemingly untouched, came on with a piercing supersonic scream. Gay was lost—everything was lost. The whole world was crashing about his head and all because his plans had miscarried. He, Dick Lovett, had brought about the end of the world!

A ring of fire closed around Dick's throat. He could no longer breathe, and his eyes were swallowed up in the deadly blue atomic fog. He tried to speak one name, Gay, but no sound would come....

The fog was lifting but the shrieking drone of aircraft still sang in Dick's brain. His mind strained to return to reality and his hands reached out for reassurance. His fingers touched the dear face of Gay, whose lips he suddenly heard speaking:

"Dick! Dick! What is it?" they said. "What is the matter?"

Dick shook his head. Things were getting clearer now.

"Are you all right, Baby?" Dick's voice was very unsteady.

"I'm all right, but how about you?" Some of the concern was beginning to leave Gay's face. "You were making such awful noises!"

"What day is it—I mean what year?" Dick was still tense.

"Sunday, August 29th, 1954—it's about 6 A.M.—we went to bed at 4. Remember?"

"Then there are no...HEXOSOMUALS!" Dick's returning awareness couldn't conceal the disappointment he felt, coloring his voice.

Gay looked puzzled. "HEXOSOMUALS? What's that?"

"A dream," Dick answered. "A dream for the future—a wonderful dream, up to a certain point. It all seemed so plausible, somehow, being accepted by society and no longer under a cloud." By now Dick was sitting up in bed. "Oh, if only..."

He didn't finish the sentence, for Gay's arm had gently but firmly made him lie down. "It's sleeping time now," Gay proclaimed. "Let's try to get some before we really do have to get up. You can tell me your dream later"—his voice trailed off sleepily. Only a few minutes had passed and Dick realized that Gay was asleep.

But Dick could not sleep. Somehow he knew that he could never again be content with half a world. Today, "a dream" but tomorrow—maybe tomorrow!

ONE magazine liked my story well enough to publish it in 1951, and the editor urged me to contribute others. I wrote "Appointment in Arcadia," about a personal psychological experience, which the magazine held for some time but eventually returned as too long to use. I never reworked it, and so my literary career was sidetracked indefinitely. I was pleased to learn later that *ONE* was started by the Mattachine Society—an admirable step toward gay awareness.

18

CT Therapy and Early Memories

The year 1953 became significant to Bruhs and me because of the discoveries we both made in our separate therapy sessions. At a private party we had attended, Bruhs made a valuable connection. One of the guests was Arthur Mann, a young psychologist actively engaged in social work with the Thomas Mott Osborne Foundation and Catholic Charities.

As Bruhs talked with the young man, he felt a rapport that prompted him to ask if Arthur was available for private therapy, which he was. Bruhs wanted to start at the earliest opportunity.

This encouraged me to ask Arthur about my seeing him also, but he felt there might be problems if he saw us concurrently. Inasmuch as Bruhs had spoken first, I felt he had priority and was pleased that he would at last be starting therapy with someone empathetic. But I envied his advantage, at least slightly. I couldn't resist telling Arthur that when I was four years old, my mother had taken me to hear Thomas Mott Osborne himself play the piano at a musicale held in the Auburn city school auditorium. Osborne was a well-known figure in Auburn because of his activity in the prison reform movement, which he had started at Auburn State Prison.

That evening program of music in Auburn had been progressing nicely, but then an evening meal I had topped off with fresh cherries and a glass of milk proved too much for a four-year-old's stomach. Almost without warning, I upchucked noisily. My mother struggled desperately to contain the mess and hustled me out of the auditorium and into a restroom to clean me up. When I was halfway presentable, she brought me back to our seats, but by this time Mr. Osborne had completed his program and was acknowledging the applause. When my mother looked around for me, I was nowhere to be found. Suddenly a neighbor who had come to the concert with us grabbed my mother's arm and pointed to the front of the hall. There I was, with coat in hand, totally undaunted by the disturbance I had caused. I had walked straight up to Mr. Osborne and in a small but firm little voice said, "Mr. Osborne, would you help me on with my coat?"

He towered above me, but he bent over and beamed at me as he replied, "Why, of course, young man, I'd be delighted to help you." Which he did.

My mother retrieved her brash offspring as quickly as possible and, with mumbled apologies to Mr. Osborne, ushered me out of the building. I have often wondered what happened to the self-assertion that a little four-year-old utilized so naturally; it seemed to have evaporated as I grew older and left no trace.

Arthur was amused by my story, but of course he had never met the man. There were rumors that Osborne's sexual preference differed from the "norm" and oblique references to his propensity for dressing in women's clothes. Fortunately, the gossip was never widely enough distributed to discredit the contribution Osborne made to prison reform.

Bruhs settled into his therapy and in Arthur's skilled hands seemed to be improving his self-image to a remarkable degree. Arthur was fascinated by the illness that had changed Bruhs's life, and he suggested that Bruhs visit a narcotherapist.

The doctor who administered this type of therapy had a long and detailed discussion with Bruhs about the illness and decided that, in his case, it was unwise to attempt to reactivate the trauma. The doctor felt that if the condition that caused the collapse were to be brought back to a conscious state, it might well trigger another, possibly fatal, episode, and for that reason he completely ruled out the use of narcotherapy. Bruhs had felt that if new light could be shed on what had caused his collapse, it was worth taking a chance, but he also recognized the inherent danger that the doctor outlined. Bruhs had no choice but to abide by the professional judgment, and he tried to deal with the disappointment he felt at another fruitless attempt to unravel the mystery of his collapse.

When I observed how well Bruhs was responding to the work with Arthur, it made me all the more eager to get started with therapy myself. My continuing dull pain in the genitals had caused me to lose interest in intercourse with Bruhs, and I was aware of the effect this was having on him. I saw the pain in his eyes that could only come from my distancing myself. I realized how unfair my coldness was, and yet I seemed powerless to change. I knew that no relationship could survive under these circumstances, and unless this perilous drift was reversed, a complete breakup would be the result.

In fact, at this point in my life I had begun to feel that life was slipping away from me. I had passed my fortieth year, and before I put myself on the shelf sexually, I thought maybe what I needed was something new to stimulate my sexual urge. I had never lived the type of gay life in which promiscuous, even anonymous, sex is commonplace. I had never frequented bars where one makes such contacts, and going to a Turkish bath scared me. Suddenly and quite unexpectedly an opportunity to explore this side of gay life presented itself when I began working for the city of New York.

To get to my job I had to ride the subway from 79th Street and Broadway to the City Hall area, way downtown. In the 1950s the subway system operated some very old equipment. The cars all had separate, dimly lit vestibules to accommodate standees. During rush hours riders were packed in like sardines. The first day I boarded the train, pressed against other men, I suddenly realized all the passengers in the vestibule were male. The train trip took about thirty-five minutes with occasional express stops about thirty blocks apart. This gave those who wished the uninterrupted opportunity to grope the man nearest him. At first I could not believe what was happening to me, but the determined, clandestine approach, never apparent on any countenance, fascinated and tantalized me.

I began to relish the morning experience, and the ride home in the late afternoon provided an extension of the morning activity. The same crowded conditions existed. Sometimes I found pants already unzipped as an open invitation for fondling.

Eventually I became more aggressive and began to follow the person with whom I had been intimate when he left the train. If the young man wished something more, he would stall until I caught up with him, then after an exchange of greetings go to his place to continue.

One such encounter had a bizarre finish. When we arrived at the young man's home, I discovered he had a huge Saint Bernard, whose presence in the bedroom made me uneasy. The dog watched intently what was taking place and, when it was finished, gave two joyful barks and, putting his great paws on my shoulders, licked my face. This almost seemed the Good Housekeeping Seal of Approval.

As I settled into this new outlet for sex, I finally became bold enough to exchange phone numbers. One attractive young man responded willingly to my advances and promised me that we would get together. He did call and we arranged for a meeting. But on the appointed day and time, he did not appear. Later, in an abjectly apologetic call, he explained that he had in fact kept our appointment, but at my door he had been collared by his wife, who had followed him and taken him home—one woman's way of handling marital infidelity!

Only one time was I turned off by the prospect of having sex in one of these encounters. My previous experiences had always been with men who were circumcised. This young man had a fine physique but longer than average foreskin. Unfortunately he also was careless about his personal hygiene. I blurted out, "With this, you really should serve crackers!" He pulled away from me sharply and fairly spat in my face, "Listen, you bitch, I don't need your smart-ass remarks. There's a waiting list dying to have it. If you don't want it, get the hell out!" I made a hasty exit, realizing that my remark had been cruel, but I hoped that my gibe might get him to give his equipment better attention for future encounters. In spite of its hypnotic influence on my libido, I had managed to retain at least a sense of humor.

My intense sexual activity lasted well over a year. During that time I led a double life, pretending to our friends to have a stable relationship with Bruhs. But at every opportunity I abandoned myself to this sexual indulgence.

I realized that I had become jaded with a cynical outlook and a deep sense of self-loathing. I seemed satisfied with these shallow contacts; I had allowed people to use me, and I had gone along with it, following some blind, undefined urge. My extended walk on the wilder side of gay life had really accomplished nothing for my life and its future except to make me feel degraded. I had somehow begun to realize that I had miscalculated my needs. Making such sexual contacts provided only a temporary exhilaration and did nothing to diminish the bodily or psychic ache that I lived with daily.

I knew I must take stock of where I was going. I was too ashamed to confess to Bruhs. I did not even want to think of what damage I had been doing to our relationship. But I knew that if it was to be salvaged, I had to summon enough willpower to stop the subway cruising and forgo the temptation of the vestibules, which had been my downfall. I had to once more take charge of my life.

I had exhausted every medical possibility in an effort to end my sexual pain and looked to therapy as a last resort. Maybe some deep-seated emotional problem, some long-buried guilt, was causing the pain and if brought to consciousness could set me free. Spurred on by the urgency of the situation, I had an earnest talk with our friend Milton, who finally found a therapist for me, one whom I could see immediately and could afford.

On a frosty fall morning, I walked the few blocks from where we lived on Riverside Drive to 86th Street. Dr. Glen Boles had arranged with Milton to see me at 7 A.M. at a special rate. As I walked briskly along the nearly deserted street, I pondered what my reception would be like. As directed, I went to the penthouse and was greeted by a man in his thirties whose warm smile soon put me completely at ease. He ushered me into what I took to be his bedroom and asked me to lie on the couch.

I didn't know what method of therapy Dr. Boles used, but I felt it was best to be completely frank about my misgivings regarding Freudian therapy. Dr. Boles's immediate response was reassuring: "I know exactly what troubled you. I had the full Freudian treatment in my preparation to become a therapist, and I found it often discouraged rapport between the doctor and the patient. I'm a disciple of Harry Stack Sullivan. I find it much more effective for therapy. It's easier on the patient, and on the therapist, as well."

He paused and then continued, "I want you to go back in time, as far back as you can remember."

"Are you going to regress me to a former life, like Bridey Murphy?" With my firm belief in reincarnation, I had hoped to have such an experience.

Dr. Boles smiled. "No, not that far back. Let's talk about your earliest childhood memory."

I thought a moment, then something did come to mind, but it was sexually oriented and I felt embarrassed. To avoid a direct approach to the incident, I launched into a circuitous account of my birth in Webster, a suburb of Rochester, New York, where my father ran a rented farm, and a subsequent move by my family to a tenant farm in Savannah, New York, when I was two years old. On the Savannah farm, my father employed a young farmhand by the name of Edison Wesson, who was about sixteen. This young man took a great fancy to me and I adored his attention. He would walk around with me on his shoulders, and in the early morning he would seat me on a great stone block that served as a hitching post at the front of the farmhouse. From this vantage point I would wave to the farmers in their wagons bringing their milk cans to the market. I frequently spent time with Eddie in his room. One day near suppertime he held me close and taking the nipple of my bottle out of my mouth, he substituted his warm, tumescent penis. It was only a fleeting moment, and no doubt the guilt-stricken boy was terrified at the consequences if he were discovered. My father and mother must never have been aware of what had happened in Eddie's room. They would have dealt harshly with Eddie if they had ever known. Years later I still remembered the encounter with Eddie; his show of affection was bathed in a kind of golden glow. I asked my mother what had become of him. She replied, "Oh, when Eddie left us, he went to the Midwest. He was drowned in a flood. He was such a nice boy and he was very fond of you, dear." He remains a warm and loving memory, one that makes me perspire freely.

Would Eddie's behavior be categorized today as child abuse? I am sure it happened more than once, and yet I never felt in any way threatened by what Eddie did. He was obviously a lonely adolescent who probably, due to his isolated situation on the farm, satisfied himself by masturbating. His approach to me was always gentle and loving, and I did not equate it with "naughty" behavior. A homophobic psychiatrist would pontificate, "Aha! The perfect early conditioning for development of a homosexual pattern." Perhaps technically this is true, but children have an uncanny sense about honest expressions of affection, and I think those feelings can be trusted rather than denigrated with the typical observation, "He was just a child! What did he know?"

When I was around three, my father forsook the life of a farmer and brought the family to Auburn, New York, a radically different environment. In Savannah my father had worked an isolated farm, and I had no opportunity to be with other children. But on Foote Street in Auburn I played with children my own age and slightly older. I was eventually introduced to "playing doctor." I remember how much I relished the curiosity and revelations common to all the children, and the wonders of the differences in anatomy that never failed to intrigue the boys and the girls.

A somewhat older boy seemed to supervise the exploratory excursions, but even though he was older, the differences between male and female genitalia had not truly registered with him. He was present one day when the boys and girls were playing leapfrog. One of the young boys made an audacious leap over a hydrant, but when a little girl, not to be outdone, tried to clear the obstacle, she couldn't quite make it and clutched her groin in pain. She struggled to keep back the tears as she cried, "I think I hurt myself!" The older boy came over to her and lifted her dress to examine the damage. He gave a low whistle as he exclaimed, "Boy, I'll say you hurt yourself! You knocked your cock off!"

But my happy days there soon ended when my father rented an entire house on Lansing Street in another section of the city. He became a streetcar conductor, which provided us a better income. But this also offered temptations to my father. He was a man approaching forty who felt he must find the sexual fulfillment that my mother was apparently denying him.

By the time I was six, my mother and father's relationship had reached a total impasse. My mother locked my father out of her bedroom, and their times together were spent in acrimonious disagreements that often erupted in violence. I often fled the house and the strident voices of my parents and the barrage of dishes breaking.

During one of my parents' violent arguments I sought refuge in a woodshed some distance from the house. On Lansing Street I had difficulty making friends, as all of the boys my age seemed belligerent and quarrelsome. In the entire neighborhood I had discovered only one child with whom I had something in common, Claude, and he often joined me in the woodshed, which was our little hideaway. We amused ourselves by putting the curly wood shavings that littered the place in our hair, pretending they were curls. Claude was the only friend I had, and a feeling of closeness had grown between him and me. We also had mutual curiosity about our bodies. We felt the privacy of the place was assured and we tentatively began our exploration. This was a moment of rare communication for me and I wanted to enjoy to the utmost the warmth and exhilaration I was experiencing with Claude.

Suddenly the woodshed door was flung open with a loud cracking noise, and the figure of my mother, like some avenging goddess, was framed in the doorway. Her face was livid and her lips set in a thin, grim line. She grabbed Claude by his shirt and literally pushed him through the door as she hissed, "Go home and never come here again!"

Then she seized me by my collar and dragged me through the tall grass in the backyard, cutting a swath behind us. All the while she chanted, over and over, "This cannot be! This cannot be!" like some hysterical litany.

Once in the house, she took me up the back stairs to the second floor bathroom and made me lie down across the toilet seat. Then without another word, she grasped my father's razor strop and hurriedly, as though fearing she might weaken in her resolve to punish, gave me a dozen blows across my buttocks. I was too bewildered to protest; I was too humiliated to even cry. This was the first and only bodily punishment that was ever given me. I kept asking myself, what had I done to deserve this? I got no answer to that question and I was terrified to see my own mother, who had always been tender and loving, completely out of control.

When the ordeal was over, I stood up, went to my room, and threw myself on the bed. All the pent-up frustration and hurt of a six-year-old surfaced, and I sobbed uncontrollably. This incident was never referred to again by my mother or me, but the trauma was etched in my mind.

Dredging up the most painful memory of my childhood had left me agitated. I could have gone on, but Dr. Boles quietly reminded me that our time was up. His voice had a comforting warmth, and I welcomed his supportive manner as he said, "This has been a splendid first session. I've learned a lot about you, and your mother. Your behavior reflected a curiosity natural to all children. What happened between you and Claude should not have been threatening to anyone. Your mother's difficulty in handling any matter relating to sex blew it completely out of proportion and she reacted in panic. This was totally her problem. We'll work to erase any guilt feelings that you have from this experience."

Dr. Boles felt that we would make greater progress if I saw him at least twice a week. This meant my budget would be stretched to the breaking point. Bruhs showed me that we could manage by his paying more of our expenses, and encouraged me to expand my visits.

In the second session with Dr. Boles, I tried to follow a sequential train of recollections about my childhood. I realized that as I grew, I became increasingly shy. My mother continually placed on my frail shoulders the burden of her unhappy life with my father. These were problems too great for a six-year-old to understand. Sensing her pain, I spent most of my time feeling oppressed and helpless.

After the disastrous encounter with my mother, Claude avoided me completely. Since my mother had always discouraged my participating in any sports as too rough for my delicate frame, I was automatically denied any opportunity to form new relationships with other boys. Instead, I had to choose to play with little girls; with them there was no roughhouse and no competition. Because I was quiet and gentle, I became known as "Sissy" Harwood. On only one occasion, taunted beyond endurance, did I lash out at a tormentor and give him a bloody nose, though he landed several punches on my face. My mother's only comment on seeing my swollen and discolored face was, "Don't sink to the level of those bullies by fighting them. You are a little gentleman, and you are better than they are. Roughnecks never learn. They go through life using everything they dislike as a punching bag."

But contrary to my mother's theory, the bully who had forced me into a confrontation carefully avoided me from that day on. I never invited further encounters with anyone and never again had to defend myself.

My main goal in life was to always please my mother, and my report cards from school reflected my effort. The only blemishes on my record were my dismal showings in "manual training" and gym class. These were a horrendous ordeal for me. I could compensate for my failures in those classes only by trying to excel in every scholastic subject.

When my parents' divorce decree was granted, my father moved back to Rochester. But before he left, he arranged to see me one last time in Auburn. My mother's bitterness over the hurt she felt she had suffered at his hands had prejudiced me completely, and I thought my father was evil incarnate. My mother had hinted darkly that he would try to kidnap me, and the thought of being alone with him made me uncomfortable. When I finally did see him, he took me to an ice cream parlor and behaved not at all like the ogre I had anticipated. He lifted me up in his arms and gave me a big hug. There were tears in his eyes as he put me down and bent over me. He said softly, "You are my little boy, too. Never forget that! Your mother has custody of you, but you can always come to visit Cora [his new wife] and me. You are welcome anytime you want to come, and you can stay as long as you like!"

I was caught off guard by his affectionate words, and in spite of not remembering him as demonstrative earlier, mixed feelings about him began to surface. But my mother's poisonous picture won out. I felt that if I showed any affection for my father, I would somehow betray my mother's trust in me, so I was duty bound to ignore the depth of feeling he exhibited. When our meeting ended, I realized with relief that I had made no commitment to ever see him again, and I had shown little gratitude for his affectionate overture.

At this point, Dr. Boles interjected, "What you tell me of your father gives a perspective quite different from your mother's. He seems a loving man and to have loved you. He probably suffered from a problem in many relationships when one partner's sexual needs are greater than the other's. That partner seeks satisfaction outside the marriage, and if the conflict is not resolved, divorce is inevitable. Your father's sexual appetite was very close to the norm for a man of forty. Your mother's picture of him as a 'libertine' was a distortion, the outgrowth of her own emotional limitations. If she was not actually frigid, she certainly was fearful of her own short-comings. This woman—Cora—that your father married was not a prostitute or a loose woman, was she?"

"No," I answered, and added, "They had a marriage that lasted twenty-five years, until my father's death."

The provisions of the divorce granted child support for me from him but nothing for my older sister and brother, who both had to leave school and go to work to keep the family solvent. My mother was having great difficulty with the rent on the house we had occupied with my father. She discovered a place a few doors away that would reduce her overhead, and we made the move to the new location on Lansing Street.

This proved to be a boon for me! Next door lived Stuart, a boy of thirteen, who took me under his wing and spent hours with me. I did not understand why he took this willing interest in someone so much younger, but I was so starved for companionship that I accepted his attention as heaven-sent.

A small barn at the back of our lot housed a variety of cast-off machinery, lumber, barrels, and boxes. We worked together in organizing things and made a counter for what we termed our "general store." Stuart was always considerate of me and never permitted me to lift anything heavy. In every way he treated me like a younger brother, solicitous of my welfare, but always with a feeling that we were equal.

I was, therefore, totally unprepared when one afternoon in our "store" Stuart asked me to join him in back of the counter because he had something to show me. He unbuttoned his fly and displayed himself. I was fascinated by what I saw and was thrilled emotionally when he gave me permission to touch him. The episode was not sexual; Stuart seemed simply to want to share a prized possession with someone to whom he felt close. This was a closeness of which I had never dreamed, and at my request it was often repeated. When we were separated by my family's move, I was sad to lose this special friendship. Years later I learned that he had lost his life on active duty overseas with the army in World War I.

Our financial struggles finally abated when my mother remarried, and we all went to live with my stepfather in his large two-story house. His father and mother also lived there, and at first we were treated like interlopers. My mother strove valiantly to please her new husband and his parents. This was not without an ulterior motive, for by skillful maneuvering she was managing to keep a roof over our heads. Eventually the "old folks" were won over and to all outward appearances we became almost a "family." My stepfather, Charlie Wendover, was a quiet man, gentle and rather naive, and I don't think for a moment he was aware that he was being manipulated by my mother. Theirs was a marriage that can best be described as one of convenience, with little genuine feeling to breathe any life into it.

When we left our Lansing Street home and moved to the Wendover place on Adams Street, it opened up a whole new range of acquaintances and playmates. The Adams Street children liked me, and I seemed to fit in better than at any other time I can remember. We were enterprising, organizing such activities as backyard theatrical entertainments complete with costumes and makeshift scenery—we collected safety pins as admission.

Ralph, one of the boys who performed in our "productions," told me of an opportunity he had to appear with Paul Swan in a local concert hall. I had never heard of Mr. Swan, but he had come up from New York and was spending the summer at Owasco Lake, near Auburn. He was known for his interpretive dancing, and also for the fine oil paintings he had produced as an artist. Since Ralph's mother was planning to take him away for the summer, and Ralph would be unable to rehearse with Mr. Swan, he suggested that I take his place.

This proved quite an experience for an eight-year-old. I relished the idea but suffered the usual trepidations of a novice. For Paul Swan's program, I had to act the part of a slave. I bore a tray of burning incense and placed it before a statue that suddenly comes to life and frightens me away. For my role I was scantily attired, and Paul Swan was nearly nude. At the dress rehearsal I was nonplussed and uncomfortable. Mr. Swan was casual about undressing, and as he faced me totally nude, I blushed and looked away. He was quick to see my discomfiture, and in an off-hand manner he merely laughed and said, "Did you ever see anything like that?"

The night of the performance he gave tickets to my family and, in the dressing room at the close of the evening, invited me to visit him at the lake. He offered to do an oil portrait of me to compensate me for the time and assistance I had given him. But I was filled with apprehension at the thought of spending time alone with him at some remote cabin at the lake. I dressed hurriedly, and I thanked him for the opportunity to appear with him. It had been my first brush with "show business," and it made a deeper impression on me than I realized.

Later that year, on my birthday, my mother took me to see Walter Hampden play *Hamlet*. This was a rare appearance of a theatrical star in Auburn and was my introduction to the thrill of the theater. It enthralled me. It was the beginning of a romance with the magic of theater that was to deepen with the years and of which I dreamed of someday being a part.

19

Moving and Growing

At my next therapy session, I asked Dr. Boles if he thought I was giving him too much detail on my childhood.

"No," he replied. "Every detail has some significance, otherwise you wouldn't remember it. I need to hear it all, because these accumulated factors all shape our personality, and even the smallest event is relevant to you as a person. You're giving me insight for this exploration together. Your early-life accounts move the therapy along. You're fortunate you can remember as much of your past as you do."

Dr. Boles made me aware that my feelings were the paramount issue in every episode I discussed. I began to trust those feelings, and to value his respect for them. But like all patients, I chafed at how rapidly time in the session went by. I felt I had only begun warming to the subject when the time was up. Often I seemed to come to the session with something that, at first, appeared trivial. Before long, however, I was launched into an account that obviously had relevance, only to be stopped in my tracks by the clock on the wall.

But having launched this project, I plunged ahead and told Dr. Boles how in the house on Adams Street I indulged in a hobby— collecting movie star photographs. I clipped every photo I saw in magazines and newspapers and in no time at all had shoe boxes full to overflowing with pictures. I also became interested in the local theater ads and asked my mother to let me hang a part of a sheet on the dining room wall to which I attached the current ads for each of the four local movie houses. As the shows changed, I kept the ads current.

Sometimes this meant clipping from the evening paper before my mother or stepfather had read it. This drew a stern rebuke from my mother. She walked a fine line in the household between her loyalty to me and her need to placate her husband, given her mother-in-law's long unfriendliness and her father-in-law's overt hostility, so I could sympathize with her dilemma. I promised to mend my ways and curb my zeal, but it was a constant source of frustration to me that the members of the family, who were regular moviegoers, never consulted my bulletin board before going out.

Because my advertising efforts were largely ignored by my family, I hit on the idea of renting space for a framed bulletin board in a prominent main-street store where I would display ads for current shows and coming attractions. The fact that I was a local schoolboy would attract the other kids' attention and stimulate interest in the theaters' offerings. To sell my advertising scheme to one of the local theater managers, I set up an appointment to see a Mr. Schwartzwalder.

When I walked into his office, he was obviously taken aback by my young age, but he had the courtesy to let me make my pitch. When I had outlined my plan, Mr. Schwartzwalder asked with a straight face, "How old are you, son?" I answered truthfully, "Eight years old."

After a moment, he asked "Where do you get your ads for the coming attractions?" I felt he was really interested now. "I get them from the Sunday Syracuse paper, as they get the pictures a week before you do."

He settled back in his chair. "Your idea is okay, but bright colors attract and I don't think your black-and-white ads would stand out. Besides, to rent space in a store window would make it expensive for me. Thanks for stopping in to see me, and I want you to have this pass, good anytime for my theater."

That evening at home I told the family what I had done and my mother said, "Son, that was very courageous of you. I'm proud of you, and even though Mr. Schwartzwalder didn't buy your idea, you have a pass for all the movies you want to see."

A friend of my sister's added a sneering remark that bothered me, although I was too young to sense its full implications: "What did you expect from a New York Jew? They think they know it all." The manager had treated me with respect, and I felt he was being maligned. But the significance of anti-Semitism did not dawn on me until much later in life.

* * *

My participation in the friendly atmosphere of Adams Street lasted barely a year. My stepfather, having worked most of his life in a foundry, decided to indulge in a dream, farming. Although it meant forfeiting his pension and shifting his parents to his sister's care, with his life savings he purchased a seven-acre farm in Spring Lake, New York, a small village about twelve miles north of Auburn. My mother went along with her new husband's plans. After all, she was no stranger to life on a farm. She had had plenty of experience with my father in Webster and Savannah. What she failed to realize was that Charlie Wendover was totally unequipped to be a farmer and was making a serious mistake in giving up his pension.

I had developed a close relationship with a boy next door, Jimmy Flynn, who was a year younger than I. When I overheard my parents say that the Adams Street house had been sold and we were leaving Auburn, I ran to my friend Jimmy to break the sad news. He was not much help, for when I told him about our leaving, he began to cry. "You can't go, Gean. You're my best friend. I don't want you to go. You can stay here with me. We have lots of room. You can't go! You can't!"

He threw his arms around me and we clung together in a desperate embrace, too distraught for words. Finally as I walked from his house, I turned to wave to him in the window. Things happened so fast, with no preparation for the upheaval, that I never saw Jimmy again.

To make sure that I would be registered for the fall term in the Spring Lake school, I was shipped off to my maternal grandmother's home, across the road from the place my stepfather had bought. The few weeks before school were pure enjoyment. I had a special name for my grandmother, Baba, and I adored her. She was full-bodied, warm, and outgoing, with none of my mother's exaggerated sense of decorum. She had purchased a windup Victrola and, as an opera buff, had acquired a sizable collection of records. I discovered a whole new world of music listening to arias from *La Traviata, Madame Butterfly, Aida,* and *Carmen,* among many others. On some evenings I delighted Baba with my impromptu versions of Paul Swan dances.

I had heard about country schools where many grades were taught in one room by one teacher, but my first day at Spring Lake was so different from Auburn that I felt like a stranger in a foreign land. Getting used to this setting was difficult enough, but I was totally unprepared for the crushing hostility of my classmates. They immediately marked me as "that city kid." I was made a complete outsider, totally shunned except for the time the older and bigger boys spent bullying me mercilessly. I couldn't make friends with the girls either; everyone ostracized me. By the end of that first school day I was reduced to sitting numbly at my desk with my head on my arms. The teacher, who seemed a kind and considerate person, mindful of her duties, was unfortunately too occupied with operating seven grades to devote any time to mediating disputes. She must have been aware of my distress, for she dismissed me early, as the only option available. Once outside the four walls of that school I felt like a prisoner released from jail.

I walked the mile and a half from school to my grandmother's house. When she met me at the door, her face fell. "What on earth happened to you today?" she said. "You look awful!"

I put down my lunch pail, and the words came tumbling out. "Oh, Baba, I was so happy in Auburn—why did I have to come to this school? You can't imagine how terrible it was today! The kids treated me like a dog and did everything but spit on me! I can't go back there tomorrow and take that! I can't...I can't." I burst into tears.

She gathered me to her bosom and let me cry for a while before she spoke. "Sweetheart, you are smart and bright, and those kids were afraid you would put them to shame. That's why they were putting you down. They're not bad kids. You'll hit it off with them if you give each other a chance. Just show them you can take it, and things will work out. You'll see!"

For the moment, I took comfort from Baba's embrace. The next day, however, when I had to face that solid front of hostility, my grandmother's words quickly faded. No matter how hard I tried to tough it out, each day the school became more impossible to bear.

The situation seemed so hopeless I despaired of finding any solution, until one day by chance I entered the boys' outhouse and found it occupied by Grant, the younger of two brothers. As he started to button his pants, he looked over with the flicker of a smile. It was the first hint of friendliness anyone had shown. He reached out and touched me where I was peeing, and as I reciprocated his overture, I realized that I had an opening wedge, and I was determined to utilize it to the fullest. From that day on, Grant and I became pals. He engineered meetings with the worst of the bullies, his older brother, Wilfred, who after a careful inspection of my private parts invited me to spend a Saturday at their farm.

That was a day I will never forget. It was the first time that I had ever experienced complete freedom to explore other boys' anatomies. We began by taking off all our clothes and just romping around naked in the hayloft, grasping each other anywhere it pleased us. We played games where one of us would be blindfolded and try to guess whose organ he was holding in his hand. I suppose it was my initiation to masturbation, but it was exhilarating to participate with others instead of by oneself. At one point Grant suggested that I take Wilfred in my mouth, and then Grant promised that he would do the same for me. It was all so breathtaking I was almost beside myself to try it. But something kept me from doing it. So we contented ourselves with rubbing and feeling until it was time for me to leave. Wilfred's penis was perfectly shaped and I have never forgotten its image, nor have I forgotten the times when I sat at the same desk with him in school with my hand in his pants playing with that beautiful organ. That day of uninhibited pleasure at the farm changed my life. I can only speculate about how much more it might have changed if I had followed Grant's suggestion.

In the next session with Dr. Boles, I continued to talk about my life in Spring Lake. With Grant's efforts the boys became friendly, and eventually the girls thawed, too. While their acceptance was not complete, I was at least treated as a member of the human race. The improvement in relations with my schoolmates helped to console me for the loss of Auburn friends and gave me a brighter outlook on life in Spring Lake. I discovered, to my surprise, that the country teacher was several steps ahead of the Auburn grade school, and I had to devote considerable time to catch up.

The population of Spring Lake was about two hundred. There were two general stores and a Methodist church, presided over by an enterprising young pastor. He was anxious to raise money for the church and decided that the best method would be to produce a play using local talent. He conferred with my mother, and she recommended a play that had been used by her church in Auburn. This melodrama, heavy with pathos, was entitled *An Old-Fashioned Mother.* My mother agreed to act as combination stage manager and costume mistress, and the minister, the Reverend Mr. Weaver, took over directing. The casting was simple, as the country characters practically played themselves. There was only one part open for me to play, that of a young, gawky country girl named Sukey Araminty Pindle. I so much wanted to be in the play that I waved aside my misgivings about playing a female. My mother fitted me out with a dress and a bonnet to which pigtail braids were attached, and I made a reasonably believable girl. At eleven years of age my voice had not yet changed, and this helped the illusion.

We gave several performances locally, and then the resourceful Reverend Mr. Weaver decided we should play surrounding towns. We were well received everywhere. As an added attraction, I sang popular songs between the acts, accompanied by my sister. Although the rest of the family had moved to Spring Lake, my sister, Marie, had chosen to remain in Auburn, where she had started a civil service job. She visited us frequently and joined the company of *An Old-Fashioned Mother* for the out-of-town dates. After a dozen performances the company was disbanded, but the Reverend Mr. Weaver had netted sufficient funds to wire the church for electricity and to purchase a new organ.

One day my father and his wife, Cora, paid a surprise visit to our house in Spring Lake. They did not own a car, so they had come by train from Rochester to Port Byron, then hired a horse and carriage for the trip to Spring Lake. When my mother saw them drive up to the house, she exploded, "The nerve of that man bringing that hussy here! She's not setting a foot in my house."

My mother kept herself hidden behind the window curtains and insisted she had nothing to say to either of them. She asked me to go out to speak with them to see what they wanted.

I realized my father wanted to see me very badly to travel that distance, and as I approached the pair seated in the rig, I apologized for not asking them in. My father did not seem surprised by my mother's behavior. He was most disturbed that several letters he had written to me had never been answered. In fact, I had never received any letters and could not tell him what had happened to them. There was an awkward silence, then my grandmother came out of her house across the road and invited them and me to have lunch with her. Whatever her feelings were about my father and his new wife, she concealed them and did her best to make amends for my mother. Baba had lived in Rochester and was familiar with the city, which gave them all an opportunity for polite conversation. I felt totally uncomfortable throughout the meeting. When lunch was finished, my father repeated his invitation to visit him in Rochester. I mumbled something about starting school. My father picked up on that and smiled.

"You know we have good schools in Rochester," he said. "As a matter of fact, if you're interested in music, we could enroll you at the music school."

But tempting as it was, I didn't take the bait, because that would be a betrayal of my mother and would belittle her sacrifices for me. As they said goodbye and drove off, my father's eyes had a sad look. That was the last time I ever saw him.

The house adjoining my grandmother's was occupied by a Mrs. Mary Waterman, whose brother, Newton Swift, was on the faculty of the Boston Conservatory of Music. Mr. Swift usually spent his summers with his sister in Spring Lake, and each time he came, he was laden with wonderful phonograph records. I often went to see Mrs. Waterman, and she introduced me to Beethoven, Brahms, Tchaikovsky, and Rachmaninoff, and the world's great artists playing Chopin, Liszt, Mendelssohn, Schumann, and Schubert.

Mrs. Waterman saw how moved I was listening to music, and she began to sound me out about learning to play the piano. She owned one of the few in Spring Lake and offered her services as a teacher. She said that I was free to use her piano for practice, and if I worked faithfully at it, that was all she could ask for. I talked it over with my mother, and although she was reluctant to place us under obligation, she recognized the opportunity it represented and gave her consent.

I began to work with Mrs. Waterman, and it added a new dimension to my rather narrow and restricted life. She was patient with me as a rank beginner, and she always gave me encouragement even when the lessons did not go well. She sensed that my burning desire to learn would help me to rise above difficulties. I was beginning to show some progress when Mrs. Waterman became ill and was hospitalized. She had to undergo surgery, from which she never recovered. Thus my musical education's promising start came to an abrupt halt.

In any case, the Wendover-Harwood family's survival in Spring Lake had reached a critical stage. My mother did her best to keep us afloat by economizing in every conceivable way, but it was a losing battle. My stepfather had made one bad farming investment after another. He purchased virtually useless farm machinery unloaded at auction by local farmers. His livestock buys were also impractical—a cow that gave poor milk, and a horse that can best be described as a nag. His only smart purchase was a pig, and if it had not been for that animal and my mother's resourcefulness in serving pork in a multitude of ways, we could have starved to death our last winter in Spring Lake. My stepfather never plowed a single furrow, never planted any crop, and after he had exhausted his life savings, was finally reduced to hiring out by the day as a farmhand.

I had finished the final year of grade school at Spring Lake and had begun to think about starting high school. This would mean a seven-mile trip back and forth to the nearest school in Port Byron, and so a ride would be needed. The teacher with whom I had started grade school in Spring Lake had been offered a better-paying position in the Port Byron school. She would be starting in the fall and had room in her car to take me. Only the formality of registering remained.

My stepfather, whose morale was at its lowest ebb after five fruitless years of trying to be a "farmer," finally threw in the towel and made the trip to Auburn to see his former boss and plead for a return to his foundry job. He succeeded, but the company adamantly refused to reinstate his pension rights. It meant starting from scratch. But at least he would be earning a living wage.

My grandmother gave further impetus to the back-to-Auburn move by offering to share the cost of a house that would accommodate her as well. She had tired of the pastoral stagnation of Spring Lake and longed for the more lively atmosphere of Auburn, where it was possible to see movies regularly and even enjoy an occasional stock-company performance. Together they all settled on a two-story house on Fulton Street and sold the Spring Lake properties.

I was fairly well into my first term at Port Byron High School when, with the family back in Auburn, I found myself commuting by trolley to complete my semester. Each day a certain friendly older man seemed to gravitate to my seat. He introduced himself as Horace Fowler and was very ingratiating in his conversation. He told me that he had a son about my age, and that as a traveling salesman, his duties often took him to other cities. He invited me to accompany him on one of these jaunts, and unsophisticated as I was, I wondered why this older man would want the company of a fourteen-year-old. It began to dawn on me that his cozying up to me had an ulterior motive. I did not understand the situation, but I did feel threatened. From that day on I took great pains to avoid him. I had only a few weeks left of commuting to Port Byron, and in 1923, at midyear, I became a freshman at Auburn Academic High School.

Dr. Boles could hear the change in my voice as I began to speak of returning to Auburn. The balance of the first year of high school I spent in adjusting to new surroundings and establishing friendships. With my grandmother living under the same roof, it also meant resuming a close relationship with my beloved Baba. Saturday matinees at the movies became a weekly pleasure for both of us. *The Perils of Pauline,* in which Pearl White routinely risked her life, week after week, made us serial addicts. When a rival series appeared, with Ruth Roland as its star, we had new death-defying escapades to deal with, and it was a toss-up which one of us was more hooked by the continued-next-week thrillers. After the movie, there was always another weekly ritual—a visit to the ice cream parlor where Baba could indulge her sweet tooth in a pineapple sundae and I would have a banana split. I have felt to this day that there is no one in the world like a grandmother to make life truly worth living.

At the start of my sophomore year I got a fine teacher for English literature, and when I submitted a poem to her, she liked it and read it to the class:

PANORAMA

Day -	Night -
Hot, dry, exacting,	Like a great velvet curtain, rippling
Comes.	Falls.
Sun, with merciless rays	Stars in glorious profusion
Burns the land.	Peep through its folds.
Kings count their gold.	The beggar sleeps at the king's gate.
Beggars ask for bread.	The universe is still;
Men toil.	All is peace.
Little children weep.	

On the strength of that poem, the teacher recommended me for associate editorship of the school paper. It meant a prolific contribution not only of poems but of short stories and essays, as well. The fiction I produced was not exactly deathless prose, but I acquired a reputation and a following, particularly when I introduced to-be-continued stories that caught the reader and boosted circulation.

I told him about my private poetry, pieces too personal to submit for publication. He asked me to bring them to the next session and, after he read them, advanced this theory: "Gean, this group of poems dealing with a female figure can only be related to your mother—she was the only woman in your life. There is considerable passion. It appears to be a sublimated but incestuous feeling in which you merge the mother figure with the moon imagery. Here is one you call 'Moon-Fire':

O Moon, proffer on this night
A cup of hemlock to me—
And then arrayed in purple
Give me all thy light!

O Moon, I shall drink
The poison draught and die;
I cannot be thy lover
And thy son as well.

O Moon, thou'rt a fair mother—
But a fairer mistress with unabating fire
That makes me woo thee,
Whether I will or no.

Give me the cup, O passionless planet!
Thou'rt too full of divine treachery!
Forever flaunt thine immortal parade
And let me die!

Dr. Boles put down the moon poems and said, "You obviously placed your mother on a pedestal, comparing her to the unattainable moon. She represented a god figure in your life. What we must do is to expose her feet of clay. She was a victim of her own upbringing and probably did the best she could under the circumstances. She saw that you were always fed and decently clothed. She washed your clothes, darned your socks, and sewed on missing buttons, but there was a great arid area in which no emotional seeds could germinate.

"You felt she always acted in your best interest. That was not true, Gean. There are props that are missing from your emotional structure that she, as the only functioning parent, didn't provide and for which we now have to find substitutes. Your father, who was one of the missing pieces, might have supplied the needed components, but he was shut out of your life by your mother. I think, before we are through, you are going to see both your mother and your father in a different light. In therapy, it isn't mandatory to learn to hate your mother—contrary to popular belief—but your evaluation of both your parents and your feelings about them will change as your understanding increases of the roles they played in your life."

20

Friendship, Work, and Escape

Dr. Boles opened the next session by asking me some questions. "Did you develop any deep friendships with other young men your age? There must have been someone with whom you felt a special rapport."

I thought a little, and then some of my earlier acquaintances began to emerge from the shadows. The first boy for whom I formed a strong emotional and physical attachment was Frederick. He attended the high school, but I can't remember how we became friends. From the very beginning of our friendship he adopted a protective attitude toward me. He was big-boned, with a rugged frame, and I was smaller and more delicate, so I welcomed the support of strong arms. Both in the throes of puberty with hormones running rampant through our bodies, we often masturbated together. It was always a disappointment that Frederick never touched me affectionately or allowed me to touch him in that way, and it seemed only a physical release devoid of sentiment. I wanted to reach out to Frederick and would have welcomed a hug, but on only one occasion did he ever voice his feelings.

It happened one afternoon, when I was spending the day with Frederick and his family at their cottage on Owasco Lake. Frederick and I were in his canoe. He usually did the paddling, and I sat in the bottom of the boat with my head against his knees. Suddenly he stopped paddling, leaned forward, and tenderly ran his fingers through my hair. His voice was low and husky as he almost whispered, "Gean...you know, if you were a girl, I could really neck with you."

146

I was thrilled at his words, but did nothing to indicate how deeply affected I was. It was a warm and spontaneous gesture he never repeated. Since I did not follow up this opening—if it was that—the incident passed without further comment, but still lives for me.

One day at the Auburn High School, one of the seniors, Stewart Rowe, introduced himself to me. He wanted to congratulate me on something I had written for the school magazine. He invited me to his house, and we became close friends. He must have sensed how my sex life was developing, but although he was gay, he made no attempt to influence my behavior. He frequently invited another boy my age, Louis Savage, to join us, and they introduced me to the intricacies of tie-dyeing. They amused themselves by clowning around (what would later to be termed camping) and calling each other girl names. I wanted to belong and be a part of this, but some part of me held back. I felt awkward and uncomfortable and could not let go of my hestitation.

In public, Stewart always acted as straight as possible, but Louis was effeminate and openly powdered his nose on the street. This sort of behavior distressed me greatly as it seemd totally unnecessary. The taunts that Louis endured from classmates bothered me, and I decided to take him in tow and try to straighten him out. I invited him to my home and introduced him to my family, who politely accepted him as my friend. In long discussions with Louis I tried to change his self-image. I wanted to convince him it was useless to be a rebel and flout what society has decided is "manly" behavior. I worked on his walk and tried to eliminate his willowy and languid posture. I also pointed out the importance of not powdering his nose in public. I struggled diligently to reshape his attidues and behavior, to make him appear more masculine.

At first, he tried to please me, but I really accomplished little, for he quickly slipped back into his old ways. He needed the mannerisms to have an identity, and the derisive gibes of schoolmates bothered him very little. Unfortunately, I found myself being shunned by my classmates because of his company. The cliché "birds of a feather" became a popular phrase to describe my friendship with Louis. My position with my peers was none too secure, and rather than have the favorable impression I had made through my writing go down the drain, I finally abandoned my efforts to remake Louis and left him to his own devices.

In 1924, Stewart introduced me to another acquaintance of his, Everett Beach. A pianist in his late twenties, he played in a local movie house for the afternoon shows. This was before talkies, and all films were silent. On several occasions he invited me to sit at his side in the theater and turn the pages. When Everett was free to choose his accompaniment he provided colorful backgrounds from Grieg, Saint-Saëns, Brahms, and Chopin. If the shadowy figures on the screen could have heard, I am sure they would have been startled by the caliber of Everett's musical interpretation of their moods and movements. The audiences responded with enthusiasm, but the theater manager was of a different mind. He had been accustomed to the hackneyed, run-of-the-mill pianists who plodded along with little variation. When Everett used Debussy's "Golliwog's Cake Walk" for an active portion of a film, it was the last straw for the manager, who told Everett that he was being replaced by someone less "avant-garde."

Before Everett left his position in the movie house, he invited me to have tea and cake at a coffee shop nearby. During our conversation he mentioned that he had been invited to a farm in the vicinity for a weekend to attend a study session of the Baha'i, the religious sect that had spread from the Middle East. He could bring a guest and said he would like me to accompany him. Everett was, of course, an adult, much older than I. He was physically unattractive, but had such a winning personality that he captivated everyone and was a delightful person to be with. He had been to my home, met my family, and spent the night there.

After the religious study session, we all had an early supper, and Everett and I took a long walk in the lush countryside. It had been a delightful outing, and the hosts had been warm and gracious. When it came time to retire, I discovered that Everett and I would be sharing a double bed for the night, and I bowed to the arrangement as all that circumstances would allow.

When the lights were out, I was surprised to find Everett making amorous advances. Not to hurt his feelings, I did not protest, but his behavior seemed so uncharacteristic I was at a loss to know what to do. My silence seemed to give consent, and his lovemaking proceeded to its conclusion. In spite of my seeming to be only attracted to men, this had not been the enjoyable thing I had expected such sex would be. I kept thinking, Is this all there is? If I only have sex with men, is this what I have to look forward to? My own feelings had been overlooked, and I tossed and turned, unable to sleep.

The following morning I tried to look at Everett, but could not. I tried to speak with him, but words would not come. He looked truly concerned when he realized how deeply disturbed I was. I could not tell him that I felt betrayed, because it would sound melodramatic. How could I make him understand that what to him was a natural and loving expression had had a totally different effect on me? I was determined not to be with him any longer until I could sort out my feelings. I called my sister and explained that something I had had at dinner must have disagreed with me. I wanted to be at home and asked her to come out and pick me up.

It was weeks before I spoke again with Everett. The friendship continued, but I viewed it in a different light and it was irreparably changed. I never mentioned our evening in the country, or his behavior, and as time and circumstances separated us, we gradually drifted completely apart.

Another friendship that developed in high school and deepened through the years was with another student, Robert. We had many things in common. Our musical likes and dislikes paralleled each other, and our taste for literature had an uncanny similarity.

We loved going through the Sunday *New York Times Book Review* together and vied with each other in checking out the latest books in the library. We both seemed to have simultaneously discovered *Ivanhoe, King Arthur and the Knights of the Round Table, Moby Dick,* and *Robinson Crusoe.* We chuckled over the whimsy of A. A. Milne's Pooh and loved to quote portions of Lewis Carroll, as when the White Queen said to Alice, "It's nonsense to say you can't do the impossible. Why just this morning, I did six impossible things before breakfast," or, "Sometimes you have to run as fast as you can to stay in the same place." Oscar Wilde gave us great delight with his witty plays filled with vivid imagery. Tales of the macabre and the occult held a certain fascination for us, too, amply supplied by Edgar Allan Poe and Bram Stoker.

After having exhausted classical literature, we whiled away many hours with Zane Grey's rugged Western sagas. When Edgar Rice Burroughs began his Tarzan series, I fantasized about the virile, scantily clad jungle man, but Robert was merely entertained.

However, we did share a devotion to poetry. We cut our eyeteeth on Byron, Shelley, Wordsworth, and Keats, but we eventually moved on to the rich and poignant verse of Walt Whitman, Rupert Brooke, Emily Dickinson, Edna St. Vincent Millay, and Elizabeth Barrett

Browning. As time went on, we added Countee Cullen to our long list of favorites.

Voracious reading increased my vocabulary much more than did the classroom or textbooks. Robert and I used to play a little word game each day to add as many new useful words to our vocabulary as we could. I have always been grateful for that exercise.

Robert was as totally uninterested in sports as I was, so we found ourselves participating in many of the same nonsports activities throughout our school years. We appeared in many school plays together and were both members of the debating team. Other than his statement that the male physique had greater appeal for him than the female, there was no indication that Robert was, or ever would be, gay. I told him frankly how my sexual interests seemed to be centered, and though he indicated that my sharing of this information did not threaten or diminish our friendship, he showed no interest in physical contact. I felt that some affectionate response would have made the relationship more complete, but I was intimidated by Robert's avoidance of overt sexual contact. Since I valued his friendship highly, I contented myself with having him as a buddy and nothing more.

One day Robert and I noticed an ad in the local paper for a young man to answer telephone inquiries on weekends. No salary or hours were given, only a telephone number. Earning extra cash was difficult in Auburn, so Robert suggested I should check it out, and we might work alternate weekends. It turned out that Ray Trumbull, who operated a local one-man all-night taxi service, felt he was losing business by not having anyone to pick up calls while he was out in his taxi, and he was offering $4 a night for someone to man the phone from 8 P.M. to 8 A.M. Ray was a bachelor in his early forties whose office was his furnished room where he lived. When Ray interviewed me there, I found these surroundings quite unbusinesslike, but the salary was too tempting to turn down, and I decided to try it out.

When I reported for duty on Saturday, Ray told me that I should feel free to lie down on his double bed when I felt sleepy, as long as I awakened to answer the phone next to the bed. I had one call for taxi service about 9 P.M., and Ray's call to find out about the pickup; after that—total silence. About 2 A.M. Ray came in, took off all his clothes, and lay down in the bed beside me. I pretended to be asleep, and he snuggled close to me. By this time I was aware that he had an erection, and I cursed myself for not sizing up the picture from the beginning—that the telephone answering "job" was merely a ploy to provide company for the night.

When Ray realized that he would get no response from me, he moved to the far side of the bed and stayed there for the balance of the night. The following morning when Ray paid me, I told him that I would not be continuing the job. I gave as a reason that my health might suffer from interrupted sleep. We shook hands, and I left.

Although I found Ray's behavior distasteful and I wanted out of an unpleasant situation, I could not help feeling pity for a gay man who found it necessary to play this dangerous game with minors just to make physical contact with another male. But when I told Robert about what had happened, he was furious. "We can't let him get away with something like this! He should be exposed. We should warn others about falling into his trap!"

I said I felt that the situation did not warrant going off the deep end. I did not consider Ray a "criminal" and believed he was actually quite harmless. He was, in a sense, a victim of the sexual needs that drove him into risky encounters, which, shallow as they were, gave him a semblance of human contact.

Months later, some enterprising muckrakers in Auburn circulated a mimeographed "scandal sheet" in which Ray's activity was exposed, along with other juicy items about the "perverts" who operated more openly in Auburn. This fed the fires of prejudice in a small town of thirty-six thousand people and made the entire consciously gay population, at most twenty-five or thirty people, so fearful and uptight that they withdrew more deeply into their closets. Unfortunately, communities like Auburn only become aware of gays when they break the law, with all the accompanying notoriety. Scandal dominates the proceedings and the innocent are lumped with the guilty by biased and ignorant townspeople.

I went on to another, very different friendship. I was active in the Baptist church, and at one of the social gatherings I met Bertha Ames, a woman in her late forties who taught school in Auburn. She found me an eager conversationalist, and when I sat down at the piano to do some improvisations, she began to take an active interest in my musical education. She had a nephew who was a fine piano teacher; she brought us together and arranged for me to study with him. In addition to financing my instruction, she also provided a piano in my house on which to practice.

My mother had some doubts about this new friendship with Bertha, the disparity in our ages making her cast a jaundiced eye on the woman's attention to me. When Bertha purchased a car and invited me to luncheons at country wayside inns, my mother no longer hid her displeasure and made some sharp and disparaging remarks:

"After all, Bertha Ames is old enough to be your *mother!* What does she want to be running around with a boy your age for? If she invites you to any more luncheons, she's going to have to ask me along to chaperon!"

I realized that Bertha's attention to me upset my mother, but I felt her objections were uncalled for. The woman was the soul of generosity, and if there was any ulterior motive in her actions, she never gave a sign that she expected anything more than the pleasure of my company. She brought so much color and variety into my life that I was deeply grateful. She also entertained me at her cottage on Owasco Lake and spent hours teaching me to swim and the fine points of croquet. We canoed along the shores of the lake and explored the inland waterways. It could have been romantic under different circumstances, but only the most prurient could read anything like that into our behavior. Bertha never gave any sign that she was dissatisfied with our platonic relationship. With her warm and generous nature, she seemed the soul of selfless giving.

In the summer, during vacation, I always tried to take a job that would give me a little extra spending money. One such job was cleaning up the debris from a two-story building that had been altered to provide a showroom for used cars and a gasoline filling station. When the building was shipshape, I worked with oil and polish on the cruddy old jalopies that were to occupy the showroom, in an effort to turn "sow's ears into silk purses." I became quite accomplished at these transformations and pleased my employer to the extent that he offered me a steady job. I was determined to finish school, however, and I turned it down.

The last day I worked at the garage, I was pumping gasoline, and my final customer was a handsome young man in a sports car with an out-of-state license plate. He asked for directions to the next town, and as I placed his change in his hand, he gave me a ravishing smile. He took my hand and squeezed it warmly as he pressed a dollar bill into it, saying, "You have been so helpful. Thank you...boy."

In those days, tips were not so commonplace and I was flabbergasted and also captivated by his charm.

WHIMSY

He only called me "boy"
And passed along—
But in my heart, for joy
There was a song.

He only called me "boy"
And went his way
Heedless of the day
And of my joy.

He only called me "boy"
My name, he knew it—never.
He only called me "boy"
But I'll remember him forever.

During the summer of 1925, I answered another ad in the local paper. This one, seeking a general helper around the Morrisons' summer home on Owasco Lake, proved legitimate. Mr. Morrison interviewed me himself, and I found him quite affable, if a bit reserved. He explained that I would assist with the gardening, help the cook, and make myself generally useful. Since their summer place was about ten miles from Auburn and I had no means of transportation, I would have to live there. This would mean two months of isolation with little outside diversion or amusement. It seemed like a lonely prospect for an entire summer, but nothing else had materialized and I had to give it a try.

The first day with the Morrisons at the lake, I was surprised to discover that in spite of their wealth and position, they had never wired the rambling two-story mansion for electricity! I had to use candlelight in my bedroom. This precluded any reading at night, as I was not about to emulate Abraham Lincoln. To this day, I shudder to think of the danger of fire there. There was a well-stocked icehouse, and part of my work was transferring ice to the icebox, as well as chopping wood for the kitchen stove. I was not used to all this heavy manual labor, but it did develop my biceps, along with calluses and blisters. The other staff consisted solely of a black cook and housekeeper, Margaret. We hit it off famously and made a top-notch team.

Mrs. Morrison was different from her husband. She established a definite climate in which the roles of mistress and servant were sharply defined. She early decided to utilize my services in a capacity not mentioned when I was interviewed by her husband. She began training me in proper table settings and the rudiments of serving. This extended my working day considerably, but I did not object because I had nothing else to occupy my time. I proved to be an apt pupil, and in no time at all I was virtually the Morrison butler, without livery, of course.

One evening an unexpected couple arrived as the other guests were about to be seated. Mrs. Morrison gave me some hurried, last-minute instructions, and I quickly assembled the matching china, silver, and glassware. But there was no time to wash them before I placed them on the table. The pieces had not been used recently, but at a quick glance they appeared to be presentable, so with time of the essence, I put them in place.

The dinner went well enough, but as I approached the last-minute settings, I was horrified to see a telltale ring building up on the plate. The liquid from the food had merged with unseen dust, and I trembled at the thought of what Madame Morrison would say, or do. I bustled about, filling wineglasses and trying my best to divert attention until I could remove the offending dishware. All the agonizing I did with Margaret in the kitchen over Madame's reaction was for naught. Mrs. Morrison never observed the faux pas, and I was never reprimanded. The balance of the summer went off without further incident. As I parted company with them, both Mr. and Mrs. Morrison commented on the quality of my service and offered additional employment in the city whenever I was available.

During the fall of 1925, a stock company set up shop in one of the local theaters. Stewart, who had graduated from high school in 1924, had found no steady work in Auburn, so he lost no time in making the acquaintance of the stage manager, Jean Burton. Stewart loved performing and offered his services to do walk-on parts. He became friendly with the leading man, Myron Calvin, and learned that he and Burton shared quarters in New York City. They both were gay, and they invited Stewart to look them up when he visited the city. A little later these two gentlemen affected both Stewart's life and mine.

My senior year, in 1925, proved to be the most rewarding of all the time spent in school. I threw myself into every activity, and only as prom time approached did I realize that I didn't have a date for this important event. This was a problem, since I had never dated a girl during all my time in school. At the last moment, my resourceful buddy Robert made a package deal for himself and me with two female classmates.

It was an honor when I was asked to compose the school song. I did not know how to put it on paper, as it was improvised at the piano. Again Robert came to the rescue and enlisted the services of a student who could sit with me and write out the notes. The student, ill at ease all during our music sessions, later confided to Robert that he had been afraid I would make a pass at him! This had never entered my mind, and it was a shock that anyone would harbor such an idea. I certainly had no reputation that would foster such fears, and I decided this music student was perhaps not too sure of his own masculinity.

Graduation was one of those rare times one wants to prolong indefinitely. I was on the scholastic honor roll, and it was a thrill to hear the glee club and school orchestra do my song. But it all was part of things coming to a close. I had to begin to think of what kind of future I wanted. I knew it had to be somewhere away from Auburn. Of that, I was sure!

Stewart had departed for New York City. I corresponded with him regularly and learned that he had found a niche for himself as desk clerk in an actors' club in New York City. He spoke glowingly of how rich his life had become in the big city, and how fulfilled he felt. He said that I could come down and share a place with him, anytime I wanted to.

I thought about making the break from home and the narrow confines of life in Auburn, and the idea of moving to New York City intrigued me and terrified me at the same time. Having a friend there would at least ease the transition, and I began to secretly get myself ready to make the move. I knew, however, I would never be able to convince my mother that the move was the right one for me.

I had taken a job at Hanlon's, the finest jewelry shop in Auburn, as a stock boy. By diligence, I was shortly promoted to full-time salesman. I continued at Hanlon's through the holiday season because the only other clerk had taken ill at the busiest time of the year. Hanlon was so grateful for my help that he gave me a handsome bonus—a little nest egg to help me leave Auburn. When I told Hanlon that I was considering leaving for New York City, he offered me a hefty raise to make me change my mind. I expressed my appreciation, but I assured him it was only a matter of time before I left.

Dr. Boles had been quiet, but at this point he broke in. He almost demanded, "How *did* you get away from your mother, Gean?"

I replied that, to this day, I did not know how I had done it. But instead of asking her permission, or even getting into a long discussion about it, I made a flat announcement that I had decided to go to New York City. I saw the pain in my mother's eyes, but by self-hypnosis I shut it out of my consciousness. I saw the tears that filled her eyes when I spoke of leaving, but I stuck to my resolve. Even when she said, "Losing you is like tearing away part of my being!" my answer was, "Mother, you're not losing me. I'm only going to be three hundred miles away, and I'll come back for visits, often."

I boarded the New York sleeping car in Auburn on March 20, 1927, the night before the spring equinox, and to the clackety-clack of the rails, I tried to sleep. Instead of sleeping, I grew wider awake. To give witness to my escape, and to the symbolic rebirth burgeoning within me, I wrote down one last poem on the swaying train before the memory of the words in my head could fade away.

21

Introduction to "the Life"

Even to a sympathetic listener such as Dr. Boles, it was difficult to describe my feelings as I stepped off the train in New York that spring morning of 1927. I had made the break; now it was up to me to prove that the move had been wise. Grand Central Terminal was a cavernous labyrinth and I hoped that Stewart would meet me as he had promised, and that he would find me in the maze of corridors that stretched in every direction. My train had arrived ahead of schedule and Stewart was late. When he saw me, he ran up, hugged me, grabbed my bag, and we took off.

My first ride in a subway startled and confused me. We rushed to the platform, so I barely had a chance to make out what station it was before we were rattling off on our deafening ride. I thought, It will take me years to sort out this crazy system! I was accustomed to buses that required a signal from the passenger to stop, and I was totally unprepared for the mad dash that everyone made for the exits every time the train pulled into a station. Every man, woman, and child was in such a hurry, it seemed that their lives depended on getting on or off. Almost before I knew it, Stewart was hollering in my ear, "86th Street—our station!"

In a moment we were above ground and walking toward the apartment on West 85th Street that I was to share with Stewart and the two actors he had met in Auburn. One of them, Jean Burton, greeted us at the door and ushered us into the two-bedroom furnished apartment I would be calling home. My "bedroom" was one of the smallest I had ever seen dignified by that term, but it did contain a single studio couch, a chest of drawers, and a chair. It also gave me some sense of privacy to have a room to myself, regardless of size. Stewart had the other bedroom, and Jean and Myron shared a double convertible sofa in the living room.

After lunch, Stewart suggested sight-seeing, and we boarded an open-topped double-decker bus that went south on Riverside Drive, over to Fifth Avenue, and down to Washington Square in Greenwich Village. Even though it cost ten cents, twice as much as the subway, it was worth it to travel in the open air. Whenever possible, this would be my transportation whatever the expense!

My bedroom was usurped my first weekend on 85th Street. Myron asked me, as a personal favor, to share my bed with one of two young men from Hartford who would be visiting them. Myron and Jean had been good enough to let me live in their place for modest rent, so as it was only for two nights, I agreed.

My weekend roommate, Arthur Hays, proved a personable fellow, of slim build and well-behaved. He was obviously quite smitten with Myron, but with Jean Burton keeping a jealous, watchful eye on Myron, there was little opportunity for them to share any intimacy.

Since my bed was a single one, close contact with Arthur was unavoidable. We both tried to ignore the circumstances, and when we had settled down for the night, he turned to me and said, "Gean, you're a nice kid, and it's sweet of you to let me double up in your single bed like this. You know I'm really mad for Myron, but it is very frustrating, because we can never get together with Jean's eagle eye. I don't see much point in coming to New York under these circumstances, do you? Give me a nice sisterly kiss—not one of those wet, open-mouth things. I hate those, don't you? Good night, sweetie." And he dropped off to sleep.

The following day Arthur and his Hartford buddy, Teddy Caswell, asked me to accompany them to the Broadway theater district. As we passed Loew's New York Roof, a movie house that, in gay circles, had acquired a reputation for its sexual activity in the upper balcony, Arthur pointed to its marquee that listed a film he wanted to see. Teddy drew back in mock horror. Placing his hand on his hip, he tossed his head and, in high falsetto, fairly screamed, "Lis-sen, Laura, you're not going to get me into that place!"

Every passerby turned to look and either snickered derisively or gave him a look of utter disgust. I was so embarrassed I wanted the sidewalk to open and swallow me. As soon as I could, I took leave of Arthur and Teddy and headed back uptown by myself. This was New York, and granted there was greater freedom, but there was little observable tolerance from the general public for behavior that went beyond the bounds of the "acceptable." I did not want to be consigned to the ranks of the stereotyped "fairies" and from now on would have to give serious thought to my choice of companions.

I could scarcely wait for Monday morning to begin my hunt for a job. Stewart had provided a street map of the city, and with the general knowledge that Fifth Avenue was the dividing line between east and west, and that diminishing street numbers meant I was traveling south, I set out on my own. I found an employment agency easily, and before the end of the first day, I had been accepted by the Duke Power Company as an office boy. I was not aware, at first, of how prestigious the Duke interests were, and how vast a network they formed.

After a few days in the General Office, I was assigned to Anthony Drexel Biddle Jr.'s suite, to devote my time and attention to that gentleman's far-flung interests. Mr. Biddle was currently promoting a young French boxer. My duties revolved around keeping track of newspaper notices and clipping them for scrapbooks. At all times I was treated as a member of the team by "Tony" Biddle. Despite his wealth and social position, he was warm and considerate in all his dealings with me. The night of the big bout at Madison Square Garden, I sat in a ringside seat with the Biddle party and had to witness Tony Biddle's hopeful lose the fight. After his defeat the young boxer quickly retired to the oblivion from which Biddle had taken him, and my office duties turned to other projects that Biddle was promoting.

One of the things I most eagerly looked forward to in New York was the opportunity to see the Broadway shows. Stewart had already alerted me to the bargain basement for theater tickets in Grey's Drugstore. "Never pay the prices at the theater box office," he cautioned. "Grey's has a slew of shows every day, and there is bound to be something there for you at half-price or less."

With my first paycheck, I made a beeline for Grey's and it was an exciting experience. The shows were listed with ticket prices and were hawked by barkers on a raised platform. Ticket purchasers milled about surveying the board in pursuit of the best bargain available. Grey's kept many shows alive that might not have survived the critical slaughter of opening-night reviews.

Most of the shows on the board were unknown to me, but I finally selected a little musical entitled *Judy*.

It was my first Broadway show and for that reason alone it will always be memorable. There is nothing to compare to attending a live Broadway performance: when the lights go down and the orchestra strikes up the overture, exhilaration takes over. Even if the show proves to be a turkey, nothing matches the glow of anticipation before the curtain rises. That evening, *Judy* turned out to be a pleasant little production with several hummable tunes by Charles Rosoff, although Leo Robin's rhymes—for example "Judy, who d'ya love?"—were not destined for immortality. The cast performed with a spirited and winning enthusiasm.

Although *Judy* was my first Broadway show, it was only one of over two hundred attractions on Broadway in 1927, when the theater was at its peak. I was able to see actresses who were to become theater legends, Helen Hayes in *Coquette,* Jane Cowl in *The Road to Rome,* Barbara Stanwyck in *Burlesque,* Claudette Colbert in *The Barker,* and Katherine Cornell in *The Letter.* A veritable feast of talent was on display, and it was always a toss-up in choosing what I wanted to see or could afford. Many times it meant skipping a meal, but the joy that theater going provided helped me to ignore the hunger pangs. I quickly learned that Theatre Guild productions were always of superior quality—fine plays with superb casts. I was fortunate enough to see *The Brothers Karamazov* with Alfred Lunt, Lynn Fontanne, and Edward G. Robinson. I could not resist the appeal of *Dracula,* which introduced the daddy of all vampires, Bela Lugosi.

At some point I discovered Eva Le Gallienne's Civic Repertory Theatre on 14th Street, where outstanding plays were offered at low admission. Miss Le Gallienne included another young actress in her company, Josephine Hutchinson, and I recall how touching their portrayal was in *The Cradle Song.* Rumor has it that Ms. Le Gallienne had more than a theatrical partnership with Ms. Hutchinson, but in those days, any hint of lesbian interest would have destroyed both their careers. It didn't stop the stories from circulating about Ms. Le Gallienne, however. One such told of a gentleman who became so enamored of the actress that he attended every performance. Finally in a fit of uncontrollable ardor, he made his way back to the star's dressing room where he threw himself at her feet and in a voice throbbing with passion exclaimed, "Oh, Miss Le Gallienne, I want you for my wife!" To which Ms. Le Gallienne is said to have replied, "But I don't even know your wife."

The show in 1927 that will always live in my memory is *Show Boat.* Florenz Ziegfeld brought it into the theater bearing his name along with Jerome Kern's glorious score and the superb cast of Edna May Oliver, Charles Winninger, Howard Marsh, Norma Terris, Jules Bledsoe, and Helen Morgan. Bledsoe and Morgan became toasts of the town with their rich renditions of "Ol' Man River" and "Bill." *Show Boat* has had many revivals, in 1932 with the great Paul Robeson, and again in 1946 with fine casts. Many years later, in 1994, the definitive revival by Harold Prince brought a superbly produced *Show Boat* to Broadway, which in spite of its opulent splendor will never tarnish the memory of the performance I saw in 1927.

The theater continued its lush days into 1928 and 1929 with productions topping the 250 mark. Mae West's talent was finally recognized with *Diamond Lil.* Helen Morgan followed her successful run in *Show Boat* with another hit, *Sweet Adeline,* and the sparkling humor of the British comedienne Beatrice Lillie was welcomed by appreciative audiences in several musicals. Miss Lillie has always had a strong appeal for gay people and has probably done more than anyone to establish the word *camp* as a gay expression.

With the advent of talking pictures, the theater by 1930 began to feel the impact. The number of productions grew less and less. Vaudeville, a popular entertainment, finally faded out, and stock companies also began to shrivel and die on the vine.

In spite of the limitations placed on their activities, Arthur continued to visit Myron at our 85th Street apartment, in the vain hope that they would have some private time together. On one of those occasions, Arthur came into New York only to discover that Myron had gotten an unexpected call for work and was not at home. I volunteered to walk with Arthur so he could unburden himself over the disappointment. We headed up the Drive and had gone a little above 96th Street when suddenly we were accosted by two self-appointed "vigilante" plainclothes types. The burly men forced us against a stone wall, and without a word they frisked us in a professional manner. One of them pulled a small compact from Arthur's jacket and, tossing it over the wall, sneeringly commented, "You don't need this, dear. You're pretty enough!"

The other man found nothing so "incriminating" in my pockets, but as if to satisfy his sense of domination, pressed me even harder against the wall, muttering, "I'd like to throw you fuckin' fags over the wall! Get out of our park and stay out!"

They released their hold on us and literally shoved us toward the street. With a final threatening gesture they shouted their parting shot: "If you're looking for something to suck, get your ass down to 42nd Street, where you belong!"

The encounter had been so sudden it unnerved me completely. The humiliation was so overpowering I couldn't speak. Tears of frustration over the injustice of the attack welled up in my eyes. At first, I began to blame Arthur, because nothing of this nature had ever happened to me before when I walked alone on the Drive. He did wear lavender, a shirt and tie combination that in those days was a dead giveaway, and he carried a compact! For my own protection, I would be careful in my choice of companions.

Arthur himself was surprisingly complacent about the entire incident. Perhaps he had had similar experiences before; in any case he dismissed the matter as just another example of "homophobia." He added that so many hated us we had to expect unpleasantness from time to time. This matter-of-fact attitude did little to relieve my sense of hurt and anger, however, and it only strengthened my resolve to choose my companions with even greater care. It was my introduction to the corridor of fear that continually influenced my actions. I became aware that gay people were an endangered species, and every protective device and coloring had to be employed if we were to survive.

Stewart and I had been roommates for about two months when, on one of the rare evenings off that he could spend with me, he said rather impulsively, "There is something I want to show you." We always bantered with each other, and I immediately parried with, "If you show me that thing again, I'll scream!"

"No, not that," he said laughingly. "I want to introduce you to the pastime that engages most people of our sexual persuasion—cruising. I think you're ready for initiation."

We lived only a short distance from Riverside Drive, and as Stewart explained, this was prime cruising territory. We set out about 9 P.M. and strolled leisurely to the Soldiers and Sailors Monument at 90th Street. In spite of the balmy evening, there did not seem to be much activity. We saw a few young men engaged in mating preliminaries, but they seemed to tire of the charade and did not continue their pursuit to an ultimate withdrawal into the thick shrubbery, or even to an exchange of addresses.

Stewart was impatient with how badly things were going and

muttered, "It's a slow night. Usually this place is wild! Nothing much is going to happen, so let's head home."

Only a block away, however, two young men greeted us and we stopped to chat with them. They both had heavy German accents, but were friendly and apologized for having to leave us. They explained that their jobs required them to be early risers but that they would like to see us again. One of the men, whose name was Kurt, seemed drawn to me, and as he shook my hand, I felt his thumb scratch my palm vigorously. He said he would call as they got on a bus.

A few days later Kurt did call and invited me to have dinner with him. I had a few misgivings, but since I was trying to adjust to the demands of "the life," I felt I should be open to all experiences that came my way.

Our dinner at one of the old German rathskellers in Yorkville on the Upper East Side was pleasant and a novelty for me. Kurt monopolized the conversation, about his home life and upbringing in Berlin. I tried to introduce something about my own background, but he did not seem in any way curious about my life, and after a while I ceased trying to include myself. When we finished our dessert, he suggested we go back to his place. As we entered the apartment, Kurt mentioned that he shared it with Eric, whom I had met on the Drive. There was no sign of Eric, so I assumed he had absented himself purposely.

Kurt poured a drink for us and told me to make myself "comfortable." He was gradually stripping off clothing as he talked, and taking my cue from him, I did the same. He motioned toward the bedroom and said, "Let's relax in there. I hope you like opera. I have a wonderful record collection."

I had finally stripped down to my shorts, and I expected that when Kurt joined me on the bed, there would be an affectionate prelude to whatever else would happen. I was seriously mistaken. Kurt's every move seemed planned, and he was not wasting time with affectionate overtures. As he stepped through the door, he was completely nude and had a formidable erection. He moved quickly to the phonograph and put a record on the turntable; I recognized it as *Tosca*. Then he came to the bed and impatiently stripped off my shorts, muttering, "We don't need these," and unceremoniously flipped me over on my stomach.

Completely unprepared for this turn of events, I only had time to think, What have I gotten myself into? Kurt, on the other hand, was very sure of his objective and, spitting on his hands, rubbed the saliva on himself and without a word mounted me.

What followed was the most excruciating pain I have ever felt in my life. As Kurt continued to force himself into my body, my panicky thoughts ran wild: Is this the initiation rite for all queer young men? Is this what every young woman who gives up her virginity is made to endure? I even recalled a woman once saying, "Is giving birth painful? Why, it's like trying to get a baby grand piano through a transom."

The music of *Tosca* rose and fell, and I moaned piteously as Kurt's agonizing thrusts became more intense, but he seemed oblivious to my pain and only viewed my protests as expressions of pleasure! I knew now with sickening certainty that I was dealing with a totally insensitive clod who had no thought other than to satisfy his own raging desire. I could not endure this nightmare any longer, and, with all the force I could muster, screamed, "*Stop it!* I can't take any more!"

My outburst stopped Kurt in midair. I rolled to the side of the bed away from him and retrieved my shorts. As quickly as I could, I put on the rest of my clothes, ignoring the blood that was staining my underwear, and made for the door. There, I paused only long enough to look back at Kurt, who continued to stare at me in blank amazement. The strains of the aria "Vissi d'arte" loosened my tears, and they began to roll down my face. Broken and bitter, I spat out, "What you have done to me tonight I'll remember to my dying day!"

At home, I eased my posterior into a warm bath. It was still extremely painful, but more than bodily pain, I felt anger and resentment for the violation I had suffered from Kurt. My first follow-up from "cruising" had been a disaster. I had been humiliated and abused, and my sheer helplessness to ever right this wrong brought a fresh flood of tears. I kept asking myself, is this what 'the life' is all about? If it is, then it's not for me!

Not until much later did I learn that many men find extreme pleasure from this form of intercourse. Yet, tenderness and concern for the partner's comfort are still a prerequisite. This had been totally lacking in my unfortunate introductory experience, which so traumatized me I never considered trying it again with anyone, ever.

The following day when I spoke with Stewart about the evening's events, he was sympathetic, but also realistic. "Gean, accepting dinner invitations usually places you under obligation. Unfortunately, the benefactor often feels you 'owe' him, and it almost always involves some form of sex. The guy you tangled with was way out of line. What he did to you amounts to rape! The anal method he used we call 'browning,' and it is never done without proper lubrication.

"Usually a partner will ask *you* what you want to do and will be guided by your wishes. The other type of oral sex is called Frenching. Why, I will never know, because the French didn't originate it. I'm sure they did it in ancient Greece, and in Sodom and Gomorrah. Speaking of Sodom, see how much religion has influenced our laws when they used the word *sodomy* to cover all the 'unnatural' sex acts!

"In this life you'll encounter all kinds of men. Some are sweet and tender, and some are thoughtless and brutish, like your Teutonic friend. I am not your fairy godmother. I have no magic wand to wave to make every one you meet a Prince Charming. You're on your own and have to defend your right to draw the line at what you think is appropriate. The choice should always be yours to agree or not, and when it isn't, you don't play! You are only eighteen years old! It takes time, but you will learn. The good times, with the good ones, you treasure. The rest—forget them!"

Three months had passed, and I was beginning to acquire the big-city tempo. I began to run for subways and buses like every other New Yorker. It had taken time to heal physically from my sexual experience because I had been too embarrassed to see a doctor for treatment. But although I had succeeded in restoring my body, I still harbored grim memories. I longed for a piano. I needed this outlet as a means of expression.

One day as I walked along 42nd Street and gazed at the store windows, I decided I would be deprived no longer. It seemed such a simple matter to have the piano and pay for it "on time," as the salesman at Wurlitzer's easily convinced me.

The following day when the little studio upright was delivered, I spent several hours going over music I had brought with me but had not had a chance to play since arriving in the city. Stewart sang "Rose of Washington Square," which he had done in drag at a local Auburn talent show with me as his accompanist. Both Jean and Myron had gone out of town for an engagement, so Stewart and I had the place to ourselves, more so than we realized at that moment.

That evening about six, our doorbell rang and Stewart answered it. It was the superintendent, and he asked to see Jean Burton. Stewart explained that Jean was out of town for an indefinite period. The super then delivered the bombshell: no rent had been paid for three months! Even though Stewart and I had faithfully turned our share over to Jean, he had obviously pocketed it and skipped. We looked in Jean's closet and discovered that both he and Myron had taken every stitch of their clothing with them and apparently had no intention of returning. The super was surprisingly understanding about our predicament, but he said that since he had received no rent on the apartment for three months, he would have to ask us to vacate the premises, unless we would assume the entire rent for the place. Stewart and I looked at each other. Neither of us could manage to take on that much responsibility for rent, so it meant doing some house hunting immediately.

Much to our surprise, the super graciously offered to give us a few days until we could relocate. This was of some help, but another problem was staring me in the face, the piano! With the uncertainty about where I would be living I couldn't move it, and I could not leave it in the apartment. Stewart tried to assure me that if I didn't continue paying, the piano company would take it back under a repossess order. I wasn't so sure that this would be accomplished without great difficulty, but while I was agonizing over my prospects, the doorbell rang again.

This time, I answered the door. I fully expected that the super had returned to tell us that we would have to be out by sundown the following day. My fears were unfounded. A total stranger stood in the doorway and flashed an official badge as he asked to see Jean Burton. I invited him in and introduced myself and Stewart. He gave us his name, an unusual one, Jay Zee, and explained the reason for his visit. He was officially assigned to the vice squad, but he also doubled in brass as a probation officer. It seems that Jean had in some way tangled with the law and was obligated to report to a probation officer regularly. This he had failed to do.

We then told Mr. Zee of our dilemma regarding rent money paid to Burton, with which he had absconded. Quite to our surprise, Zee appeared sympathetic, and after assuring him that we knew nothing of Jean's whereabouts, he gave us a phone number where he could be reached and left.

Stewart set out the following day and found a double furnished room for us on 85th Street across from where we lived. It would be a simple matter to transfer our belongings.

With the problem of living quarters resolved, I girded myself in preparation for my bout with the piano company. After I had told my story and asked them to repossess the piano, they coldly refused to do any such thing. They said I was obliged to live up to the terms of my contract and there was nothing they could do. When I announced that I was vacating the premises immediately and would not be responsible for the safety of their instrument, they altered their tone somewhat. They said they would pick up the piano, but added ominously that I had not heard the last of it.

And indeed I hadn't. The next day I was served with a summons to appear at corporate headquarters for a hearing. The document, looking very official, gave me a sinking feeling. The only person whom I could turn to who had official status was Jay Zee. I called him and told him what had happened. He bucked me up considerably when he chuckled and said, "Relax, kid. I'll cover that hearing with you. It will be all right. Trust me."

When I got to the hearing, Jay was already there. He slapped me on the back and said breezily, "Come on, kid, let's get this thing over with!"

The long stream of questions bore mostly on my character and my age.

"Did you sign the agreement and state your age as twenty-one?"

"Yes."

"What is your legal age?"

"Eighteen."

"You lied about your age and obtained property under false pretenses. This will blacklist you for credit for the rest of your life throughout the United States. Do you understand that?"

After initially identifying himself, Jay had stood quietly by during the interrogation, but at this point he spoke up and his voice fairly crackled as he took command. "That's enough with the 'credit' bullshit. It isn't the first time someone has lied about age, and it won't be the last. The kid is under age and you can't do anything about him, so stop with the harassment. Just be glad you got your piano back in good condition and call it a day!"

His firm, authoritative manner swung the balance in my favor. The spokesman for the piano company closed the book on my case, said there would be no further questions, and that I was free to go.

As we were leaving the hearing, Jay told me of his assignment for the evening. He had to cover a disturbance that occurred almost nightly at a Childs Restaurant at Fifth Avenue and 48th Street. It seems that after the dinner hour the restaurant was taken over by flamboyant gays. They wore makeup and women's jewelry and occasionally a fancy hat. They conversed in loud tones, sometimes broke into song, and behaved in what was considered a "disorderly" manner. The management was beside itself because regular customers were being frightened away by the bizarre behavior. Repeated raids by uniformed police had no lasting effect, for as the offending participants were carted off in the patrol wagon, a new group seemed to take their place.

Jay asked me to join him on his tour of observation, and my curiosity got the better of me, so I agreed to accompany him. I figured it was the same as having police protection. The evening was a revelation! I have never seen anything quite like it, before or since. This garishly dressed group acted as though they owned the place; they were totally without inhibitions and behaved in a public place as they would at a private party. I tried to use the men's room, but it had been converted into a "powder room" and was such a shambles I retreated as quickly as possible. Jay took in the scene quite calmly and seemed amused by the more outrageous antics. I felt distinctly uncomfortable and was vastly relieved that at least there was no accompanying excitement like a police raid. Things gradually wound down after midnight, and the crowd broke up.

This "gay rebellion," however, petered out almost as abruptly as it had started. Apparently tired of their defiant display, the participants all went back into their closets, and those wild goings-on are now only a footnote in gay history.

Another footnote concerns Jay Zee. He kept in touch with us and ultimately rented a single room in the house where we lived. He never attempted to socialize with us, but from hints that he pointedly dropped, he was unmistakably gay. I will always be greatful for the strong support he provided at a time when I really needed a helping hand.

22

The Village and Romance

Stewart was gregarious. He loved to socialize and he loved parties. One Saturday evening shortly after we had moved to our new room on 85th Street, he assembled a group of gay friends for fun and frolic. By midnight, the loud and boisterous gathering had turned into a no-holds-barred affair. It was probably the nearest thing to an orgy that I will ever witness. I was really out of it because I didn't drink or otherwise participate. I noticed another young man did not seem to feel a part of it either. He was quietly on the sidelines, pensively observing. His name was René Ferraris, and because we seemed to share the same attitude about the activity all around us, I was drawn to him. He took my hand in his and said, "Gean, I don't think you'll get much sleep in this place tonight. I live in the Village, and you're welcome to come down to my place, if you want to."

I surveyed the hectic activity on every side, and I realized that what René had said was becoming more evident by the minute. I also wondered if an ulterior motive was behind his invitation. But I was willing to try anything for more peace and quiet.

We slipped out and hailed a cab to take us to René's place at 20 West 8th Street. I was grateful to René for the oasis his room provided. After making me comfortable for the night, he kissed me tenderly on the forehead and whispered, "Good night; sweet dreams."

In the morning we had breakfast in a little place on 8th Street, and René took me on a tour of the Village. The bohemian atmosphere captivated me, and when René revealed that there would be a basement vacancy in his building, I was determined to persuade Stewart to make another move, to the place I had been looking for all my life—Greenwich Village.

Stewart required no arm-twisting to make the move to the Village. On our floor, at the front of our building, was a little restaurant called the Cotton Boll. As we had no cooking facilities, we ate our dinner there, night after night. Stewart had many friends with whom he tried to arrange dates for me, but aside from René, who was never a romantic interest but who had proven himself a good friend, none of them appealed to me. I was fast becoming a "problem child" to Stewart as I noticeably withdrew from making gay contacts.

Almost as a last resort, Stewart took me one evening to a party that an old friend, Harold Wilson, was giving. The guests were a motley group, some already paired off, and some on the prowl seeking a connection. Toward the middle of the evening a tall, attractive young man walked through the door. His brooding look was rugged and yet sensitive. I looked up, and as my gaze caught his, the chemistry of instant mutual attraction took over. He came up to me, and when the host handed him a drink, he sat down and started to talk.

His name was Paul and he told me he was an opera buff. He requested my company at the Met the following week, for performances of *Cavalleria Rusticana* and *Pagliacci*. He apologized for their well-worn familiarity, but I told him that my knowledge of opera was limited, principally recordings of *Madame Butterfly* and *Traviata* that my grandmother had played for me as a little boy. He declared that "Cav" and "Pag" would be excellent choices for introducing me to grand opera. I didn't share Paul's enthusiasm for opera, but as an outsider in gay life, I welcomed the warmth and sincerity that made me feel included. But I also felt, with some cynicism, that he was feeding me a line and I would never hear from him again.

When the pay phone in our hall rang the next evening and I heard Paul's voice on the phone, my knees turned to jelly, and I could scarcely answer his friendly salutation.

"Hi, Gean. This is Paul. Remember me? It was so dumb of me not to ask you to have dinner with me before the opera. Can you make it?" I mumbled my assent, and he went on, "Meet me at Ruth Garner's Little Tavern on West 47th Street at 6:30 P.M. That should give us time to make the Met at eight. It will be nice to see you. Bye."

As I hung up the receiver, I steadied myself and tried to analyze my feelings. This had all the earmarks of an important event in my life, an introduction to the most important of human relationships.

Deep inside I savored the exhilaration that Paul's invitation had given me and began to count the hours until I could explore this new and inviting offer of friendship.

That Saturday evening proved to be everything I'd hoped for. It was my first visit to the charm of the Little Tavern and my first live performance of opera. And it was at the invitation of someone I was drawn to. It was new and overwhelming, and because I was overcome by the novelty of it all, I may have seemed detached, but the impression it made was quite indescribable.

After the performance we went to Paul's place on East 45th Street for a nightcap. He explained that he shared the apartment with a younger sister, but that she was away for the weekend. As we would have the place to ourselves, he proposed that I spend the night with him. I was so drawn to this tall, warm, outgoing person I did not want the evening to end, and I readily accepted the invitation.

Paul drew a bath for me, helped me out of my clothes, and after the bath, literally picked me up and carried me to the bedroom. When he finished his bath, he joined me and gently and tenderly took me in his arms and held me close. Neither of us said a word, but the outpouring of feeling was a mutual expression of total communication and caring. As the waves of emotion brought us ever closer to a climax, I realized that this was what I had been waiting for all my life. This was the communion of body and spirit that I knew should exist but which I had never experienced. It was all so right, so good and so natural. I felt years of tension and indecision slip away, and in the haven of Paul's embrace, for the first time I sensed the warm glow of complete fulfillment.

I spent more and more nights with Paul. The attraction we had for each other seemed to grow deeper each time we were together, and I realized that I had fallen in love.

Living in a Village basement can have its problems, too, as I learned. Stewart and I shared a large studio couch, and one evening I awakened suddenly and touched Stewart's arm to get his attention. I had heard a scratching noise, and switching on the lamp by our bed, I realized, terror-stricken, what had made the sound. Right above our heads, near the ceiling, on a broad pipe that went the length of the room, crouched an enormous rat. I clutched Stewart's arm and whispered tensely, "What are we going to do?"

He was surprisingly calm and, with an assurance he may not have felt, said quietly, "There's nothing we can do tonight. We can't knock it down, and I don't want to corner it, because rats put up a nasty fight if cornered. Tomorrow I'll go out and get the biggest trap I can find, and that will be the end of 'Esmerelda.'"

In spite of my fright, I couldn't help but be amused by the name he had given the rat. I said, "How do you know it's female?" His quick reply was, "I don't know if it's male or female. I guess that really would only be of interest to another rat. Meanwhile, Esmerelda's days are numbered!"

We slept very little the rest of the night, and Esmerelda had retreated to her lair in the walls. True to his word, Stewart did set an enormous baited trap and left it on the floor. The following night Esmerelda was caught, but not without a struggle. For hours the rodent thrashed about, carrying the trap, until finally succumbing toward dawn.

Although it may have been a childish reaction, I felt uncomfortable in the basement from then on. I was getting disenchanted with this kind of life in the Village. I didn't want to ask Stewart to move again, but that we never saw the sun and the premises were dark and damp constantly irked me. I had grown accustomed to the ambience of Village eating places and I would particularly miss the daily breakfast across the street, where we were joined almost every day by the reigning queen of the nightclubs, Texas Guinan. Texas lived directly over the restaurant and, as regulars, gave us her usual hearty greeting of "Hello, sucker!"

However, a bad case of tonsillitis made up my mind for me. My doctor advised me to have a tonsillectomy when the inflammation had subsided. He also recommended that I look for other living quarters immediately.

I discussed the state of my health with my employer, Mr. Biddle, and he offered to have his physician do the surgery. When I explained that I preferred to have the operation done in Auburn, he even arranged for my transportation and said he would take care of all the hospital expense. He added that when I came back, he wanted to enroll me in school to prepare me for a position in the accounting department of Duke Power Company. He said he felt I had too much potential to waste my time as an office boy, and he wanted to get me started on a solid career. I was overcome by his concern for my future, and his generosity, and I promised to contact him as soon as I returned.

Meanwhile, my future was a topic of discussion in other quarters as well. Paul had a piano in his apartment, and after I had played for him, he felt I had too much musical talent to ignore. He argued that in spite of Biddle's magnanimity, I would never be happy doing the humdrum routines of accountancy. He urged me to develop my life to take advantage of God-given gifts and explore those avenues where I could be creative. I was greatly encouraged by his belief in me, and I was torn between the sense of security a solid business background would bring and the yearning to express my artistic desires in the competitive and highly insecure world of music.

After the operation, I spent some time with my family in Auburn and particularly enjoyed seeing my grandmother. Shortly after I returned to New York, she suffered a massive cerebral hemorrhage, so I have always been grateful to have been with that dear and wonderful woman, whom I knew and loved so dearly, just before she died.

When Dr. Boles signaled that our time was up, he was almost apologetic. "I always hate to stop your story. It's like a serial, *The Perils of Pauline* or *The Exploits of Elaine*, the agonizing suspense about what will happen to the person lashed to the tracks with the locomotive bearing down on her. You seemed to view every situation as a 'temporary' one; that somehow, somewhere, someday, you would achieve a sense of permanence and stability."

I had to admit that everything had felt temporary in those days. While I certainly valued my separation from Auburn, and my mother, the umbilical cord had never really been severed. I lived in a constant state of anxiety that I would be drawn back to the nest.

At the next session with Dr. Boles, I had something amusing to tell him. In a movie house men's room recently, I had seen scrawled on the wall, "My mother made me a homosexual." Underneath it some wag had scrawled in the mordant humor of gay people, "If I furnish the yarn, will she make me one, too?" Dr. Boles chuckled but asked me to continue my narrative.

With Paul's encouragement, I worked to develop my musical abilities, or at least experiment with them and see how far they would take me. Therefore, I went to Mr. Biddle and thanked him for everything he had done. We talked at length about my musical aspirations, and how I planned to pursue them. He encouraged my effort. Although disappointed by my turning down his offer of an accountancy internship with Duke Power, he wished me well, and we shook hands warmly. When the economic depression settled in a few years later, I could have easily lost the job when all the big corporations curtailed their staffs.

Paul knew a young woman, Giovanna Coviello, who worked as a cashier to support her vocal training. The general convenience store that employed her was in a new upper-class housing development, Tudor City, at the eastern end of 42nd Street overlooking the East River. Giovanna arranged for me to be a part-time evening cashier in the store, which gave me an income but left the daytime hours for my music. Our having similar musical interests would make the association with Giovanna an interesting one, I thought. What I didn't realize was that Giovanna also had an amorous interest in Paul, and when she finally became aware that I was a competitor for Paul's affection, our relationship became strained. I managed to hold on to the job, however, and made whatever concessions were necessary to placate Giovanna.

The evening hours working were enlivened by another coworker at Tudor City, Marge Costas, an ex-burlesque queen, slightly past her prime, who answered the telephone for orders and occasionally waited on customers. Her answering the phone with "Hello, store?" must have left callers bewildered. Had they reached the store or a busy line with another person also asking if this was the store? I asked why she raised her voice on *store?* Marge said, "It makes for more interesting conversation." In answering questions about merchandise the store carried, she always added, "And stainisipis on the orphan-aside." When I asked her if it was pig latin, she said it had no meaning whatsoever, but she liked it.

When her phone wasn't ringing, she sold papers and cigarettes to customers. She would give a beatific smile to all the males and, running the words together so that they were barely distinguishable, inquire, "Did-you-pull-your-pud-this-morning?" When they looked puzzled, she quickly said, "Did you get up early this morning? You look a little tired. You should take better care of yourself."

Marge regaled me with stories of life on the road—her romances with male admirers and one brush with a lesbian proposition. Approached while taking a shower, Marge yelled at the top of her voice, "You want to do *what* to me?" The startled lesbian made a precipitous exit, Marge reported.

In the rooming house where she lived, Marge had several gay young men as neighbors. They used to congregate in her room and delight in trying on her old burlesque costumes. One of the men, Ronnie, loved wearing her feather boa. He would toss it around his neck, strike a pose, and say, "I think I'll go out now and do a street scene," which always broke Marge up, even as she imitated him for our benefit.

She obviously enjoyed the company of gay men, and she obviously recognized that I was one without my telling her. She was also very firmly anchored in her own sexual preferences and would lecture me on the total satisfaction of straight sex: "Nothing can be a substitute for a man loving a woman. You can play around all you like with other men, but eventually you must find yourself a girl you hit it off with. That's the way to find real happiness."

I could have said, "Did that work for you, Marge?" but I never did. I just enjoyed her company, without ever taking her advice.

Paul located a furnished room for me on East 48th Street, which was within walking distance of the job. Using his piano for practice, as soon as I could, I began instruction with Ralph Leopold, a concert artist celebrated for his brilliant piano transcriptions of the Wagner *Ring* operas. I threw myself into it, but something in Leopold's approach intimidated me. I became discouraged in not measuring up to his expectations. I changed teachers twice, but there was always an element of dissatisfaction. I finally came to the painful conclusion that I was not "concert material," and that loving music was not enough to make it a career.

At this point, I felt that composition might be more suitable for me, so I enrolled in a course at Juilliard. These classes presented a whole new set of problems. I had never before encountered such ferocious competitiveness, and I was simply not equipped to handle it. I stuck it out for a full term, but it was one of my worst years. My self-esteem was devastated, and I felt overwhelmed and defeated. I left Juilliard feeling I knew less about composition than when I'd entered, from the stress in the classes. Through it all, Paul was loyal and supportive. He believed in me, although I had lost a sense of my own worth. But when the building where Paul lived on 45th Street was slated for demolition, he moved to Sunnyside in Queens. He had to sacrifice the piano, due to inadequate space. This was the coup de grâce, and I took it as a sign: my pursuit of a career in music had been an exercise in futility.

I talked with Paul about what I should do. I toyed with the thought of approaching Mr. Biddle again, but although my morale was at a low ebb, my pride dictated some other route back to the business world.

When Paul moved to Sunnyside, I had the opportunity to share an apartment close by in Queens with two young men. As I traveled back and forth to Manhattan on the Queens elevated subway, I noticed the sign of an employment agency, and acting on a hunch, I paid them a visit. Much to my surprise, they had an opening in the executive offices of Paramount Pictures on Times Square. The position called for typing ability, and as I had no experience at all, I was doubtful that I would be accepted. But I went anyway. In the interview I took a typing test; if I had been judged solely on that, I would never have landed the job. Apparently the personnel manager felt I had potential and was willing to give me a chance.

My boss turned out to be a genial Irishman, Larry Flynn, who was desperately in need of a dependable assistant. He informed me that we were a two-man unit, concerned with travel arrangements for all company personnel, including the stars themselves.

I took a deep breath and plunged in. Fortunately I quickly learned the complicated network of rail lines crisscrossing the country. This was 1929, and plane travel was a thing of the future.

It was a good thing that I could adapt, for after only a few weeks on the job, I was forced to assume all the duties of the department when my boss was taken ill. For a wild and woolly six weeks I was totally on my own, and I had run-ins with everyone from the company president on down. Paramount survived, however, and so did I. Larry Flynn had tears of gratitude in his eyes when he came back to his desk. I think he never forgot my yeomanly handling of his job and mine.

Nineteen twenty-nine ended with dire distress in business. The stock market crash in October sent shock waves throughout industry. It certainly had an impact on me. My starting salary had been $25 per week, but with the economy shaken by the Wall Street debacle, I had to take a 10 percent cut in salary. This happened after my trial by fire and only added to my sense of insecurity.

I suffered a worse blow in 1929 when Paul learned that he had tested positive for tuberculosis, a disease virtually hereditary in his family, and which he had long feared would surface. His first concern was for me, and he made arrangements for an immediate exam to learn if I had any contagion. I was given a clean bill of health, as was his sister, Phyllis. But the doctor who treated Paul said that his health made it mandatory for Paul to leave New York City at once for a better climate. All of this happened so suddenly that I was at a loss to adjust to it. I had become accustomed to leaning on Paul. He was the rock of stability on which I depended when the turbulence got too strong to bear. I wanted to join him in his plans to go to New Mexico, but he overruled it. He had slim financial resources and faced an uncertain future. He felt I would be ill-advised to abandon a job that showed promise to cast my lot with him under such doubtful circumstances.

After Paul's departure I discovered how deep was the void his leaving created. I had not taken into account how lost I would feel without his reassuring presence. Without Paul, I no longer had a source of strength upon which to draw when my reserves were depleted.

As the days lengthened into weeks, I began to receive frantic appeals from Paul for money. Only then did I begin to be aware of the extent of his own insecurity. As a native New Yorker in a wholly new environment among strangers, he felt frightened and alone. Many of these fears must surely have plagued him before he left, but he had bravely concealed them.

At first, I tried to help Paul. But when his pleas were repeated time and again, I had to stop. I had no savings of my own, and a salary of $22.50 per week left me nothing more I could send. I told him how much it pained me not to be able to help him, but he returned my letters unopened. I smarted from this rejection. I knew his desperation at this turn of events in his life. I realized with deep regret that for all practical purposes, our friendship was ended by conditions beyond our control. Still, I was wracked with guilt over abandoning the man with whom I had shared my first real love. I shall always be grateful to Paul for showing me the validity of a gay relationship. It had fulfilled a dream and would shape my emotional life from then on.

Nevertheless, I still felt bitter about having to abandon Paul, and this was not improved by a phone call from Paul's sister, Phyllis. She asked me to meet her at the Hotel Winslow, where she shared a room with another young woman. I had known from the very beginning of my friendship with Paul that Phyllis would have relished a romantic attachment with me. I had no wish to become a part of some cockeyed family triangle, and the whole thing had been much too awkward for me to even acknowledge. Because my feelings were centered totally on Paul, I never encouraged any of Phyllis's overtures, even though they were obvious. On the other hand, I never knew if she was aware of my relationship with Paul, if she felt any jealousy, or exactly how she rationalized my indifference. This time I had no idea why Phyllis wanted to see me, but the prospect of more complications made me apprehensive. I dreaded the thought of having to deal with some emotional showdown.

When I arrived at the Winslow, I found Phyllis alone in her room. She had been drinking heavily and was wearing only a robe. She threw her arms around me and gave me a passionate kiss and without further ado began to remove my clothes. I was totally unprepared for a seduction, and I tried to protest. She was not to be put off, however, and persisted in her plan and clumsily maneuvered me toward the bed. I attempted to reason with her:

"Phyllis, Phyllis, listen to me! This isn't getting us anywhere. It's not what I want, and I don't think you want it either."

She continued her advances doggedly and muttered thickly, "You don't fool me! I know about my brother, but you're not that way! You and I could make beautiful music together!" With that, she grabbed me again and bit my earlobe so hard I was sure it was bleeding. I stifled a cry of pain and pushed her away. Though unnerved, I pulled myself together and said, as calmly as I could, "I want to forget this ever happened. And you'd better forget any romantic notions you may have about me. You're the sister of someone dear to me, and I'm only interested in you as a friend. Do you understand? Life is complicated enough without forcing issues that will get you nowhere."

As I started to dress, Phyllis crumpled into a heap on the floor and started to cry. She looked up at me and, between sobs, said, "You won't be able to leave. This is a woman's floor, and there's a house curfew. You'll have to explain what you're doing on this floor after hours. You might as well stay here all night. I don't want you to get into trouble with the house. Stay here with me...please!"

Her warnings and tears all seemed to me transparent devices to keep me there. I wondered if the house rules were rigidly enforced, but they did not stop me from leaving. My only thought was to get away from the disagreeable scene as quickly as possible.

Once down the elevator and out into the night air, I managed to lose the sensation of holding my breath. As soon as I got home, I took a hot shower and tried to wash away the evening. In spite of my annoyance, I did feel sorry for Phyllis. I knew that rejection is always painful, and I didn't welcome the role of the heavy with which she had burdened me. Unfortunately, it is often only by unwelcome confrontation that we are forced to bear witness to our true sexual identity. I hoped that eventually this episode would raise her understanding of her brother's sexual orientation as well as mine.

A few weeks later, I moved back to Manhattan. Three young men I knew had taken an apartment on Hudson Street and needed a fourth to meet their rent. I was glad to leave Sunnyside, with its mixed bag of memories, and it was good to be back in the Village again.

One evening late in December 1929, a mutual friend brought a young man to our Hudson Street apartment for a social call. That night, when I greeted Bruhs Mero, I had no way of knowing that he was destined to become the centerpiece of my existence, the one who would change my entire life.

23

Reality and Recovery

The sessions with Dr. Boles had taken me far back in my life; for months I virtually lived in the past. By now I had retraced my life from childhood to the threshold of the greatest adventure of my life—my partnership with Bruhs.

Late in the afternoon one October day, as I opened the door to our apartment on Riverside Drive, I was rudely awakened to the fact that this was not 1929 but 1953. Our place was a shambles, the contents of every overturned drawer littering the floor. Bruhs and I had been the victims of something that was fast becoming commonplace—a break-in! In the center of the room, two large valises had been partially packed with loot, as if the marauders had been frightened off. But they must have worked fast; they had managed to make off with most of our valuables. All small easily concealed items—cameras, watches, jewelry—were taken and after locating a small amount of cash, they had hunted frantically for more, without success.

My first thought, after the initial shock, was of Topandy. She was quite old by now and with impaired hearing and eyesight. She was no deterrent to intruders. The thieves had obviously not harmed her once they saw she was no threat, and she did not seem to have been traumatized by their intrusion. In fact she may have slept through the whole affair. I was grateful for that, at least. As soon as the police were called, they sent a man to check it out. The officer said a large number of such burglaries had occurred lately and held out little hope of catching the miscreants or recovering any of the stolen property.

When Bruhs arrived, I met him at the front door and tried to break the news to him easily by being offhand about it. "Take a deep breath before you look around," I said. "We wuz robbed, buddy!"

It took time to erase the ugly feeling such a violation of privacy brings with it. We were dismayed to learn that theft insurance was a false assurance, since much of the loss turned out to be uncovered when the claim was finally settled. The seemingly unending red tape, plus the depreciation calculated on the original value, made for tiny awards; the whole matter of "protection" was laughable. One might well question who receives more "protection," the insured or the insurer?

In those years we did make something of Christmas and the holidays. Howard and Grant, partners for many years, whose friendship with us dated back to the 1930s, always invited us to their home on Christmas Eve, and on New Year's Eve we always invited a group of friends to our place on the Drive to ring out the old and ring in the New Year. There was always the hope that the misfortunes of one year would be transformed into good luck in the year to come.

Perhaps it is just as well that we have no crystal ball to peek into the future, because 1954 did not usher in happiness for our household. Early in January, we were awakened one Saturday morning by strange little noises from Topandy. She was standing with her head in the corner and trembling like a leaf. Under her was a puddle. We knew she must be in serious trouble because she had never lost control before and had never soiled the house in any way. We felt her nose; it was very warm. She seemed unwilling to lie down, perhaps for fear that she could not get up again. We had to get her to a vet as quickly as possible. Dr. McKellar had taken care of her since she was a puppy; unfortunately, his office was on West 12th Street in the Village, which meant a long trip from Riverside Drive. Then we looked out the window to find a blizzard. Two feet of snow had piled up against the door, and the wind had blown even higher drifts. We would never find a cab in weather like that, so it would have to be the subway. As soon as we were dressed, we bundled her up and put her in her carrying case and started our slow trek, taking turns tugging her carrier up the 79th Street hill to the IRT station.

When Dr. McKellar examined Topandy, he confirmed our worst fears. She would require a hysterectomy. But, due to her age, the outcome of such an operation was uncertain, and the duration of any benefit derived was equally unpredictable. He suggested we leave Topandy with him and go home to think about what to do. Meanwhile, he would make her as comfortable as possible and wait for our decision. We knew the only other option was to put her to sleep.

Two very sober guys trudged through the snow without the carrying case and entered the silent house. We went through the motions of preparing a meal, but neither of us felt like eating. After lunch, we tried to read, but somehow we couldn't focus on the pages. About 4 P.M. Bruhs heaved a sigh and, looking straight at me for the first time that day, said, "I don't think we should put her through that. We don't know if she would survive in any case, or how long we'd have her if she did. I don't think we have a choice. Shall I call Dr. McKellar?"

I nodded in assent.

Giving our decision to the doctor over the phone, Bruhs asked that Topandy be cremated and the ashes delivered to us. The words had an awful finality. As he hung up the receiver, he turned to me, and without another word, we both threw our arms around each other and cried.

We quietly held each other until our tears had subsided. I took Bruhs by the hand and led him over to the piano.

"I have a melody, and a title, 'Let's Try Again,'" I said. "Do you want to see what you can do with it?"

Bruhs began haltingly, but finally had the words:

LET'S TRY AGAIN

Lyrics by Bruhs Mero; music by Gean Harwood

> Let's try again,
> Not cry again,
> Over the things that are past.
>
> No sighs again, or good-byes again,
> Let's try to make our love last.
>
> For love is a shy thing
> So easy to lose.
> Won't always come back again
> When you choose.
>
> Let's try again,
> Not lie again.
> As lovers may sometimes do.
> Let's try to start anew.

Ever since I'd started therapy with Dr. Boles because of my prostate discomfort, Bruhs and I had been sleeping in separate beds. We had had almost no sexual contact and had ignored each other's emotional needs. But as I became more deeply involved with the therapy that opened up hidden passages in my life, my thinking began to change, and my awareness of Bruhs was heightened. I began to have a totally new perspective on the gift of love that Bruhs and I shared.

More important, the loss we suffered in the robbery, and especially in losing our much-loved pet, was a catalyst bringing us both face-to-face with what common loss means. Things that had held us together had been taken away, but our realization that we belonged to each other and belonged together had been reborn. This sense of mutuality sparked our revival of interest not only in each other but in our surroundings. We experienced renewed creativity. We even revamped the apartment and started refinishing our furniture.

The huge Steinway square piano that filled one end of the living room had long been admired by Robert Fairchild, a master piano craftsman. In his showroom he featured upright pianos that had been reconditioned and altered by use of a mirror at the top, which reduced the height and gave the illusion of its being a smaller piano. We arranged a trade-in of the mellow old Steinway for one of these new-styled instruments by Fairchild. The "new" piano had excellent tone and fitted nicely into one corner of the living room, occupying one-third the space the square piano had taken up.

Changing instruments inspired me, and in three short months Bruhs and I added several new songs to our collection. The first we called, "Love Me" and every ballad we wrote echoed the reawakening we were experiencing, none more vividly than the second new song, "From Now On."

This was followed by another ballad, with which we will always identify ourselves.

IT'S ONLY MY HEART

Lyrics by Bruhs Mero; music by Gean Harwood

If you hear me calling, it's only my heart.
Please be still, O my heart, please be still.
Though my eyes are cloudy, it's only my heart.
Please don't cry, O my heart, please don't cry.

Loving you dearly, I'll always be there,
Waiting for some way to show I still care.

If memories haunt you, it's only my heart,
Yes, it's only my heart that you hear.
And why am I saying, it's only my heart,
When it's all I can give, just my heart.

(Reprise for last half of chorus)

The things that I dream of may never come true,
But I'll keep dreaming—in dreams I have you.
So if I've a feeling, it's only my heart
That keeps calling for you night and day.
I'll go right on saying, it's only my heart,
For it's all I can give, just my heart.

By 1954, gay people had to have become aware of the devastating impact of Sen. Joseph McCarthy's campaign to root out homosexuals, along with Communists, from government. Since 1950, McCarthy, with his associate Roy Cohn (not publicly revealed to be gay himself until after his death) had engaged in an anticommunist witch-hunt in the federal government, and even before that, the House Un-American Activities Committee had done the same in the entertainment industry. No one was safe. Guilt by association and trial without jury had become standard practice in the late 1940s. Civil liberties suffered and the trail of shattered careers grew longer and longer.

The troublesome national scene had a tremendous impact on the two of us. We were demoralized by the turn of events and felt powerless to fight back because there was no gay community and no organized gay resistance to the evils of McCarthyism. While the ACLU and other progressives protested, no gay person raised a voice to stem the hysteria that spread like wildfire and inflamed the redneck know-nothings both in and out of government.

So we were ill prepared to face the crises that developed in our private lives about this time. Declining support from the U.S. Export-Import Bank meant the government of Israel had to curtail the activities of its Supply Mission. The Letters of Credit section in which Bruhs worked was phased out, and Bruhs was terminated with only one week's notice and no severance pay. Since he had been employed by a foreign government, he was covered by neither U.S. social security nor New York State unemployment insurance. He was able to retain only his health insurance for the balance of the year, fortunate in view of an accident he suffered shortly after leaving the Israeli Mission.

Two friends of long standing, Monroe and David, had been living in San Francisco, but Monroe had come back East to visit his mother in New York. When he learned that Bruhs was at liberty, he suggested that they rent bicycles to ride in Central Park. The sun was shining brightly as they started out, but as the skies clouded over, a light rain began to fall. Bruhs and Monroe decided to head back; as Bruhs swerved to avoid a cab, his wheels skidded—as he hit the curb, he instinctively stuck out his right arm to break the fall. His right shoulder took the brunt of the impact, and on the way home his arm began to swell and change color.

As soon as he arrived at our apartment, Bruhs tried to contact the family physician assigned by his Health Insurance Plan (HIP) center. The doctor was unavailable, and after Bruhs stressed the urgency of the situation, the office promised Bruhs they would locate the doctor and get back to him. The hours dragged on, and finally at 5 P.M. when he had received no word from the doctor, Bruhs called the HIP center on 79th Street and pleaded with them to do something. They said that the arm should be x-rayed as soon as possible and told him to go to the HIP lab on 55th Street immediately. The X ray showed a triple fracture of the shoulder. We took a cab back to the HIP center where the orthopedist, after looking at the X ray, immediately arranged for a room at the Hospital for Joint Diseases. We hurried home to assemble a few of Bruhs's personal items, and shortly before midnight at the hospital I saw Bruhs set up in traction, then I headed home.

His hospital stay was notable for the strange manner in which he was treated by the hospital staff. Each day at mealtime a tray was placed before him just below chin level. He could not feed himself, and if he had not been assisted by the ambulatory patients, he could have starved the first few days.

But then, one day Bruhs had a surprise visitor in the hospital— his niece Joan, whom he had not seen for a long time. Several years before, she had visited our place on the Drive and had brought with her a young man named Ron Field, who went on to become a noted Broadway choreographer. Both Joan and Ron were only fifteen at the time, students at New York City's High School of Performing Arts. As Ron looked at the photos of Bruhs and me together, the young man gave us searching looks and appeared to be on the verge of asking an important question. The words never came to his lips, however, and we could only guess at what lay behind his grave and quizzical manner.

Joan's visit to the hospital was very fortunate because thereafter she came every day and fed Bruhs. She alerted other family members and they filled in when necessary. Bruhs couldn't wait to leave the hospital, and he immediately canceled his contract with HIP. He had been so badly handled that he never wanted their services again.

Late in 1954, Bruhs's therapist, Arthur Mann, left the city for a better job. Before Arthur left, he recommended a new therapist, but try as he might, Bruhs never found any of the empathy Arthur had provided. Bruhs was always agitated when he returned from a private session with Philip Ginnetti, who also taught psychology at Columbia University.

One day Mr. Ginnetti asked to meet me, and we arranged to talk. It was brief, but I could see why this opinionated man irritated Bruhs so much. During my visit, I suggested that men were selective in choosing a sexual partner and looked for a definite type with whom to make love. Ginnetti totally rejected my premise. He stated flatly that as long as someone was a member of the opposite sex, it did not matter to a heterosexual man what the other person looked like. He added that the man could perform without regard to "type." And, he insisted, in this respect gay men were no different from straight men.

Seeing how inflexible he was, I could sympathize with Bruhs's problems in working with this man. I suspected that the rituals and subtleties of choosing a mate were foreign to Ginnetti. I excused myself as soon as I could before my intense dislike led to an angry exchange. Maybe this was a device to deliberately provoke a response from me. If it was, I chose not to play games and ignored it.

Bruhs continued doggedly with Ginnetti for some time, always feeling that if they did not hit it off, it was his fault rather than the therapist's. But he did finally give up and took a long rest from struggles with therapy.

As for me, I suspended my visits to Dr. Boles, not because of any disagreement but for other reasons. For some time I had been aware of the sense of peace and tranquillity that seemed to envelope our friend Lenny after his partner had introduced him to Christian Science, and I was impressed and curious. My therapy had done wonders for me in working out psychological blocks, but the physical pain remained, and I wanted to find out what had brought so much peace of mind to my friends and had effected healing in so many others.

Our meeting with Andy in the 1930s and how deeply his philosophical discussions affected us has already been recounted. The interest that he had awakened in us in Rosicrucian teaching had led us to acquire the entire works of the Rosicrucian teacher and mentor Max Heindel. The principal text is an extraordinary treatise, *The Rosicrucian Cosmo-Conception,* a vast compendium on the occult, planetary influences, the structure of physical and spiritual bodies, and the laws of cause and effect. It gave us answers to why we all are here and left us with a lasting conception of life as a process of learning the lessons of our experience and using that knowledge to improve not only our own lives but the lives of others. The pursuit of knowledge places the seeker on an upward spiral that has as its ultimate goal the awareness that God dwells within us and that we are One with Him.

As eager as he had been to study Rosicrucian philosophy with me, Bruhs showed no interest in investigating Christian Science. In fact, he was so opposed to the whole idea that he felt we would separate permanently if I chose to join Christian Science. I realized that for the first time in many years I would be exploring new texts, such as *Science and Health,* with others. I would miss the spirited discussions Bruhs and I always had when we were involved in joint projects. Bruhs remained adamant in his opposition up to the day of my initial attendance at a Science service. Only then did he reconsider and soften his opposition. At almost the last moment, he wished me well in my search for truth and also assured me, to my everlasting relief, that my action would not end our relationship.

24

Stasis and Changes

As 1955 rolled on, things began to brighten for us. Bruhs followed up on an ad he saw in the *New York Times* and, subtracting a few years from his age, managed to convince the department supervisor that he was qualified for a job at the *Journal of Commerce*, a publication designed to give accurate information for those using steamship lines for cargo or passenger service. It carried sailing and arrival listings for every line serving all the ports of the world. This was a time when shipping flourished, so daily updates were indispensable. Keeping track of this vast shipping network was an enormous job, calling for intense concentration, precision, and accuracy. After Bruhs had handled the Ship Card Desk for a week, the supervisor realized that Bruhs was well organized, a perfectionist prepared to give the job his complete attention, and a tremendous asset.

It seems that those who had operated the Ship Card Desk in the past had made devastating errors in the scheduling, and the steamship lines appreciated the *Journal's* now having a competent and conscientious person handling their crucial information, which provided the paper's main source of income. The *Journal's* advertising and promotion manager, impressed by Bruhs's performance, felt Bruhs should be rewarded by a promotion to a position in advertising.

When the steamship lines heard of the proposed transfer, they feared a return to the old hit-or-miss method of handling their notices, but Bruhs assured them that he would properly train his replacement. This satisfied them, and before long, Bruhs assumed his duties in an entirely different phase of the paper's operation. His training in department store advertising, which had provided his income during the early years of our relationship, had made him familiar with printer's terms. He had done layouts for Arnold

Constable and Gimbels, all of which helped give him confidence and the feeling he wasn't a complete novice. There were hosts of details to master, but Bruhs worked hard and was soon competent in his new job.

In fact, his work was outstanding in the new department. He had a friendly, cooperative teammate relationship with his superior, the advertising and promotion manager. Bruhs was shocked to learn one day that the paper was firing his boss and putting Bruhs in charge of the department. It was one thing to be an assistant, but to be suddenly elevated to running the show is quite another matter. Furthermore, Bruhs was dismayed by the paper's action in using him to replace his boss and felt distinctly guilty about it. He had many misgivings about the added responsibility of the managerial post, but felt that the paper's confidence in him could not be turned aside. He took a deep breath and prepared to confront this new challenge.

As for me, I took the next city civil service promotion exam at the first opportunity and became a senior clerk. With reasonable effort and preparation I was at the top of the list. My promotion improved my income and moved me one more rung up the bureaucratic ladder. I valued the security of a civil service position and knew I could ultimately equal or even exceed the salary I had earned in private industry, without the competitive hassle.

The tenants who shared our basement floor on the Drive were constantly changing. For a time, a young stage electrician and amateur photographer occupied the apartment next to ours. He took many photos of us, which we still have. We speculated about his sexual preference. We thought he might be gay, which would explain his interest in us. But when he married and brought his bride to live in the apartment, we decided that his interest was part of his search for different subjects for his avocation.

The next tenant was a colorful, friendly woman who used a nom de plume, Rob Roye, for the plays she was writing. I never read any of them. Occasionally, when we heard the sound of a typewriter, we thought, Rob Roye is at work on a play!—but it always turned out to be the letter-writing frenzy that seized her periodically. She regularly attended meetings of the Women's Press Club, but that seemed to be the extent of her literary interests. We never learned where she got money for rent and sustenance.

Rob Roye fancied herself a gourmet cook and often fixed little snacks, which she brought to our door with the admonishment, "Eat it while it's hot!" But to her credit, she never invaded our privacy, except occasionally when she asked to show her friends what she termed our "house beautiful." About that time, there was a play on Broadway called, *House Beautiful*, so bad that Dorothy Parker wrote a one-line review: *"House Beautiful* is *Play Lousy."* Rob Roye's description of our apartment amused us, but, of course, compared to the shambles in which she functioned, our place was a showcase for the furniture that Bruhs crafted, and for the many photos that lined the walls.

Her own motley assortment of memorabilia and furniture made a magnificent clutter and would have provided an ideal setting for a murder mystery. Each time we stepped into her apartment, she would wave her arms apologetically at all the clutter, but with a certain defiance, saying, "When I get things rearranged, the jumble will disappear!" But nothing ever did disappear.

We speculated about Rob Roye's emotional life, as, I am sure, she did about ours. Bruhs and I had an ongoing relationship that was pretty obvious, but we never saw her with any companion, male or female. We surmised that she was an eccentric virgin who had never known any fulfillment except in her writing.

The rest of the 1950s had a sameness that blurs them completely, without emotional peaks or valleys. We had a large circle of friends whom we visited and occasionally entertained at our place. We often caught fleeting glimpses of our other next-door neighbors, Ben Gazzara and Janice Rule, when they were between pictures. A bright young man named Gary Smith, who became a successful TV producer, lived in our building for a while and would always say hello when we met at the mailboxes.

We saw plays and movies, but avoided dance recitals. They were too difficult for Bruhs to handle. When he watched others doing what he longed to do, his feeling of loss was simply unbearable. He felt an enormous sense of personal deprivation when others moved about on a stage, and he strongly believed that his life had ended when he could no longer dance. Nothing served as a substitute, and nothing ever filled that aching void. The fact that he had fought back from a crippling illness, had successfully rehabilitated himself and carved out a new career, never stood in his mind as noteworthy. From his creative mind and hands had come many useful and ornamental pieces of furniture, and his lyrics certainly added meaning to the songs we created together. But none of these things ever compensated for his loss of creative movement. Bruhs once said, "If I had stopped dancing of my own choice, that would be different. But to have it snatched away from me by a cruel twist of fate is hard for me to bear. Dancing was my life. Without it, I feel nothing but emptiness."

The next upheaval in our lives came in 1962, when we were notified that the building in which we lived was to be demolished. We were given a few months' grace in which to find another place to live, and a small allowance for moving. Our rent on the Drive for two large rooms was $55 per month, including gas and electricity, and was covered by rent control. Few, if any, other rent-controlled apartments were available. We searched the neighborhood and found an apartment on West 78th Street, just off the Drive. But the current occupants were embroiled in some disagreement with the landlord and refused to show the apartment.

Another matter to consider was the piano. We decided to sell it and placed an ad in the *New York Times*. We had two responses, only one of which appeared promising, until the buyer haggled too much over the price. We didn't want to give the piano away and it looked for a time as though we would be forced to move it. Suddenly, one day Rob Roye approached us and asked us point-blank: "Do you have any objection to selling the piano to me?"

She didn't play herself—could she afford such an expensive luxury? We had our doubts. But she was insistent and gave us our price without question.

Because we were coming down to the wire—the date we had promised we would be out—we finally had to settle for a three-room apartment in a four-story whitestone building on West 79th Street between Amsterdam and Columbus. The rooms were large, with high ceilings, but there was no elevator and a two-flight walk up to negotiate each day; this was fortunately no longer a problem for Bruhs. We knew we would miss the convenience of our place on the Drive, with only five steps down to the basement. In addition, the rent on the new apartment, which had been completely renovated with air-conditioning, was $175 a month, and gas and electricity were extra.

We had lived on the Drive for eighteen years, and the thought of packing up the accumulation of those years staggered us. Having a few weeks' latitude before beginning the backbreaking task, we decided we should take a vacation. I juggled my vacation with a coworker, and Bruhs managed to work out with the paper a two-weeks' leave that coincided with mine. On the spur of the moment, we purchased a round-trip air-and-hotel combination for Miami Beach, because our friends, the sisters Shirley and May Frank, had forsaken New York for a more tranquil existence there in Florida. We selected the Hotel Raleigh on the waterfront near them at 18th Street. Having missed their warm companionship, we relished spending time with them.

The Florida trip fell between the latter part of August and early September. We discovered that Miami Beach weather in August was very tropical, to which we had to accustom ourselves. But frequent dips in the Raleigh pool and air-conditioned rooms kept us comfortable. We relaxed completely and tried to forget the household move that faced us.

We had also completely overlooked that hurricanes hit Miami Beach mostly in September. For days we got warnings about a tropical storm, Donna, forming in the Caribbean. Then the warnings became an all-out hurricane watch. There were squalls and brisk winds, then a deceptive calm as the eye of the hurricane moved in. This was a brief respite, and suddenly all hell broke loose as we were hit with the full ferocity of the back side of the storm.

At first we thought we could stick it out in our room, but since it faced the ocean, each blast of wind made the whole building shudder. The hurricane winds—nearly 150 miles per hour—drove against the structure with such power we felt any moment the entire wall would be blown in and we would be crushed. The walls became porous under this onslaught, and in no time the rugs were saturated with water. The storm built to such a crescendo we headed for the lobby, where we found most of the other guests. The manager provided sandwiches and coffee for everyone. He tried to make light of the situation, but it was difficult to ignore the pails standing about, rapidly filling with water that steadily dripped from the ceiling. It was hard to bring levity to this miserable turn of events. It was one awful way to spend a vacation, and we vowed never to chance ourselves knowingly to such an ordeal again.

By early the following day, Donna had spent much of her fury and slowly moved on to the northeast. Our belongings had fared better than we had imagined. Since there was no telephone service, we went to see Shirley and May and were relieved to find that although they had been alarmed, they had come through it well. We arranged for a flight back to New York and toured the area to survey the damage. The Raleigh pool, which we had enjoyed so much, was awash with palm branches and dead fish swept in from the ocean. Beachfront Collins Avenue was a shambles of broken glass, wires, and branches. At the corner of Lincoln Road a huge electric sign was twisted into a grotesque corkscrew. Donna had overnight transformed this tropical paradise into a mass of debris, and we wanted to get away as soon as possible.

In the late afternoon we headed back to the hotel to pack our belongings. At the entrance, I ducked to avoid a flying palmetto bug, and my head collided with a steel pole that supported the canopy, miraculously still standing. The blow made me see stars, and I could feel my head beginning to swell. Bruhs steered me into the building and found ice to apply to the bruise. I developed a splitting headache and Bruhs was stuck with the dual job of packer and nurse. We finally boarded the plane to return home. As they were closing the doors, one of the stewardesses addressed another as "Donna." I almost screamed, "Let me off. I won't fly with anyone named Donna!"

On the flight north, there was still a great deal of turbulence. Even in New York we found another day of torrential rains and high winds. But we started packing for our change of apartments.

From the start, our two-year tenure at 79th Street was horrendous. Our first electric bill was exorbitant and totally unrelated to our use. We complained to the utility company but got no satisfaction. Turning off every appliance in the apartment, we found that the meter in the basement was still showing current being used, proof that the wiring was faulty. We finally got an engineer from the utility, Con Ed, to confirm that we were paying for electricity in some other apartment. Rewiring meant expense for the landlord, which did not endear us to him.

Our first winter spent on 79th Street was dreadfully uncomfortable due to a lack of heat and hot water. We were in despair and bemoaned our choice of the apartment. However, our repeated complaints finally moved the landlord to upgrade the heating plant, at considerable cost.

In the spring, things did improve as far as heat was concerned. Unfortunately, we then began to notice the paint on the bedroom walls was starting to bulge and crack. Either there was water seeping through the walls or the pipes were leaking. The landlord gave our complaints no attention whatsoever and called us "nit-picking troublemakers."

The stay on 79th Street was not totally joyless. Bruhs and I joined Lenny and his partner on a delightful trip to Canada. We traveled up the Saguenay River and spent several days exploring Quebec on our return. It was a rediscovery for Bruhs, for he had once made the trip with a dancing partner, but for me it was the first time that I had been outside the United States. We both had been so harried by our apartment's problems that it was a joy just to relax among new sights.

Back in New York, we learned that a six-foot Mason and Hamlin grand piano that we had ordered would be delivered the following day. I had grown so hungry for the touch of a keyboard that Bruhs decided I should no longer be deprived. He arranged for us to make the purchase along with one by his niece from a dealer in White Plains, and the double sale gave us an excellent discount. With the piano finally in place, I touched the keys for the first time in months and savored the depth and beauty of the instrument's tone: I wept.

Another event is linked to that apartment on 79th Street only because that is where we lived at the time it happened. It was the horrified silence that fell on us all on November 22, 1963, when the news reports of President Kennedy's assassination came over the office radio. We watched the funeral on TV that weekend, grief-stricken. I can still see the stark, heroic figure of Jacqueline Kennedy, and the faces of the Kennedy children, as they walked through the nightmare that had engulfed them. Bruhs and I were numb. We felt a personal loss, not felt since Franklin Roosevelt's death, at this senseless act of violence.

When the time came to sign a new lease on our apartment, the owner announced the rent would be increased to $250. He added that if we didn't remain as tenants, we would have to repaint the entire apartment in a "light" color before we left. He quoted a "law" that legitimized his claim and ignored our protest that the paint had been applied by the previous owner and was in any case not dark. When we notified him that we were not staying, he was adamant about the painting. When I asked him to specify the "law" he claimed to quote, he became hysterical. I realized that we were dealing with an unreasonable man who might easily withhold most of our security deposit when we moved out. With great reluctance I drafted a letter on my New York City Building Department stationery which informed the owner that after a careful check of the building laws, the ordinance to which he referred did not exist. In addition, I asked one of our housing inspectors to examine the premises to verify the condition of the walls, and to document that the damage did not occur through our negligence as tenants.

I might add that we learned that the owner was gay. One might think that this would have made him a little more sensitive to our problems as his tenants, whom I am sure he recognized as a gay couple. Apparently where only the profit motive dominates, it doesn't make any difference whether the landlord is gay or straight. The owner wrote a petulant and vituperative letter to my commissioner about me in which he demanded my removal for overstepping my authority in writing him an "intimidating" letter. The commissioner called me in to show me the landlord's letter and to go through the motions of a reprimand. He found my letter to the owner informative, not threatening. He did deplore my use of department stationery in a "personal" matter, however, and said that a censure would go into my record. My standing in the department was in no way impaired by the incident, and I knew that the citations for code violations, which I was instrumental in slapping on the building, would be a source of irritation to the landlord for months, while he struggled to get them remedied.

We began apartment hunting in earnest, searching for new quarters on Manhattan's East Side. In the Gramercy Park area several new high-rise apartments offered inducements in the form of rent concessions. We finally selected a spacious, well-equipped studio on Third Avenue at 18th Street. There was only one catch— our apartment was on the ground floor, and as the workmen were focusing their complete attention on finishing the upper floors, there was a question as to exactly when our space could be occupied. Once again I sought the help of a building inspector in my department, who persuaded the owner to alter the completion schedule to give our apartment priority and have it ready when we needed it. I was grateful to be able to call on the clout of the Building Department to help us in our dilemma.

25

Retirement

As one grows older, there is an increasing resistance to change. Bruhs and I were nearing sixty, and another shift to a new location was irksome and troubling. We had not yet learned that what seems permanent is not. Permanence itself is an illusion. We must accept that all things change constantly, and we must let ourselves flow with this. Although we had been residents of the City's West Side for many years, we tried to make living on the totally different East Side an adventure.

There were new shops to explore, new restaurants to try, quiet spots in which to relax. Although we did not possess one of the keys to Gramercy Park, it was a joy to have this charming reminder of the past, untouched by the urban turmoil at its gates. We were delighted to visit the Players Club or look in on the cool serenity of the Gramercy Hotel lobby, among the reminders of a gentler day.

The Mason and Hamlin grand piano had such a glorious tone that it was an inspiration, and I took up again the music I had used for Bruhs in his performances. I always had a forlorn hope that in repeating those familiar pieces I would reawaken in Bruhs some remembrance of the movements he had done to them. But his memory of the dances refused to surface, and the wished-for sharing of this part of what we had created together seemed to be permanently denied us.

We expanded our social activities and saw more of our friends. Bruhs's niece Diane had moved to Philadelphia with her husband and two sons, and we visited them there frequently. Whenever she came to the city, we went to plays together and sat up far into the night discussing books. She had a perceptive sense of the characters in James Baldwin's *Another Country*, on a homoerotic theme, and

Christopher Isherwood's *A Single Man*. Bruhs and I never openly declared our relationship, but we sensed that Diane knew of it, and it seemed in no way to affect her warm and attentive attitude toward us. Other members of Bruhs's family, as well, must surely have known of it, but I felt totally accepted as a member of the family.

The *Journal of Commerce* decided to move their offices from Varick Street above Canal to Wall Street in the financial district far downtown. Bruhs had to pack all the pamphlets and brochures with which he worked. This was a backbreaking job, so he asked me to help, for pay. While I was not as proficient as he in packing the voluminous materials, I did at least provide personal support. No sooner was the move completed, however, than Bruhs learned that a managerial retrenchment would affect him. He lost his office assistant and was forced to operate as a one-man department. The pressure on Bruhs became increasingly heavy, and in a short time his health began to show the stress. The management of the paper promised to improve his working conditions, but never did. Finally, on the advice of his physician, Bruhs resigned from the *Journal of Commerce* for self-preservation.

In the aftermath, in August of 1969, Bruhs developed an extensive case of shingles. The doctor who attended him found it was the most severe case he had ever seen—it virtually circled Bruhs's torso. The ailment was painfully prolonged and took weeks to subside. During this, Bruhs missed two important events. Richard, a nephew of whom he was very fond, was married; Bruhs was bitterly disappointed that he could not attend the wedding. That same month we lost one of our dearest friends. Shirley Frank's warm heart finally gave out. Bruhs's inability to attend Shirley's funeral also weighed heavily on him.

An extraordinary occurrence had taken place in June, one that was to have a staggering and permanent impact on every gay person in America. A deputy inspector and seven New York City policemen again raided a gay bar in Greenwich Village, called Stonewall. However, this time a valiant group of transvestites (more generally known as drag queens), weary of the hassling they constantly received from the police, stood up to them and fought back. A violent confrontation ensued. But, contrary to the usual outcome, the gay men and women, albeit battered and bruised, emerged victorious. The police retreated and did not return. In gay history, this is comparable to the Battle of Bunker Hill. It marked the beginning of the gay liberation movement! Gay activists gradually emerged to organize public demonstrations for gay rights. A new gay pride slowly spread, and a sense of gay community. This burgeoning gay self-esteem was triggered by the smashing breakthrough of Stonewall.

Throughout our years together, Bruhs and I had clung to the imagined safety of the closet and had striven to be as inconspicuous as possible. We strictly avoided obviously gay people. Now, suddenly, the remarkable courage displayed by those we had always shunned demanded that we completely reverse our thinking about "flamboyance." We realized that when the chips were down, the very people with whom we had felt uncomfortable had stood up for us as well as themselves. They were our brothers. As we had lived with adversity, we knew we must learn to accept diversity. Yet although we were deeply moved by what happened at Stonewall, we two still lacked the courage to openly declare our sexual identity. It would take more than a decade for us to open the closet door fully and join our gay brothers and sisters in affirming the validity of our gay lives.

In May of 1970, Bruhs's brother Bill died. He had been of enormous help to Bruhs in his dance career and in 1943 had borne the major burden of the expenses in Bruhs's long illness. Bill had been a strong supporter of Israel, but the day of Bill's funeral in New York coincided with the Salute to Israel Parade, and the traffic we encountered caused such agonizing delays in getting to Bill's service we almost missed it. Then in 1971, Bruhs lost another brother, Gilbert, who had been thoughtful and caring of Bruhs and me over the years. Two props had been knocked from under Bruhs and he was devastated.

In 1971, other problems began to surface. Bruhs realized that the nest egg he had so carefully nurtured was dwindling away now that he was unemployed, and with no source of new income, it would shortly disappear. He tried a variety of jobs, but they proved too stressful to continue beyond a few weeks. Since it would be two years before he could apply for social security, we both knew that some solution had to be found, and quickly.

Through promotions I had gotten steady raises at my job, and my salary was sufficient to carry both of us. Bruhs, however, was adamant about maintaining his independence; he was totally unwilling to allow me to assume complete charge of our expenses. Under the circumstances, only one option was available to him. We made inquiries about public assistance, and eventually we had to visit the Social Service office on West 14th Street to make a formal application.

We were totally unprepared for the intimidating atmosphere we encountered. A security guard literally pushed us against the wall with other hapless applicants and barked a command: "Get over there and stay in line!"

We waited for what seemed hours before we were admitted to an area that held scores of would-be applicants, most of whom looked frail and defeated. I turned to Bruhs and said, "This procedure appears to be only for the stouthearted. Do you want to give it up?"

His reply was short and to the point: "I don't really have an alternative. We've gotten by the 'tiger at the gates,' and maybe the rest won't be too bad. If you'll stick with me, I want to try to see it through."

When Bruhs's number was finally called, we sat down with a young woman who was a part of a sadly understaffed group of interviewers. She was understandably impatient and intoned her routine questions in a totally impersonal manner, until she arrived at the subject of financial assets. When I explained that I had opened a joint account with my funds for our convenience, in the amount of $1,000, she exploded: "I can't take your application! If you have that much money, we can't do anything for you!" She threw the application back at us.

Having come this far, I was not about to be shot down by a clerk. I asked to speak to a supervisor, and grudgingly the young woman escorted us to the floor above. Fortunately, the supervisor proved to be a soft-spoken and sensitive person. She struck me as a motherly type. She patiently outlined the department regulations, explaining that a joint account could be considered entirely the property of a welfare applicant, and as such, it exceeded the allowable amount of a "burial reserve"—$500. Even her parting words were friendly: "Use up that joint account for your expenses, and when it's gone, come back and we'll process your application. Goodbye and good luck." We followed her advice, and the following day we closed the bank account in preparation for Bruhs's reapplying.

The second problem we faced was totally different. In the latter part of 1971, I became aware of a tremor in my right arm, at times so severe I couldn't sign my name. If I placed my work on top of a filing cabinet at the office, I could elevate my arm and control the shaking long enough to complete writing. This was not only highly inconvenient, but it caused me great anxiety.

Through my employment by the City of New York, I was still enrolled in the HIP (Health Insurance Plan), and I went there for an examination. My physician referred me to a neurologist, who ordered an encephalogram, which measures neurological activity of the brain. For the procedure needles were inserted into my scalp by a callous and disinterested technician. She seemed totally unmindful of the extreme discomfort I was experiencing.

When I saw the doctor for a report, he examined the encephalogram. He completely unsettled me by asking, "Have you had any convulsions recently?" The discomfort I had suffered from the nurse administering the test had had a direct effect on the resulting graph, which seemed to show possible brain damage, but I didn't immediately make that connection. The doctor added an additional dark note that, based on the findings, it might be necessary to do an angiogram, a more complicated test, with certain risks. By now, my peace of mind was fast ebbing away, and I felt I should give some thought to the future. In consulting the neurologist, he was noncommittal as to the possible cause of my condition. He said I could have had an injury or be under stress on the job. I could not recall any injury that would account for such a condition. I began to collect data on retiring from work. I estimated that with vacation and terminal-leave allowances, I could leave my job in August of 1971 and still be on full salary until January 1972. At that time I could start receiving my pension and my social security. Once I had it figured out, I couldn't wait to file my retirement papers, and so I set the machinery in motion.

In June of 1971, I discovered that my accumulated sick-leave time plus vacation would permit me to stop working six months before my actual retirement date and still draw full salary until then. One of my coworkers, Alberta Hall, was also due to retire, and the office decided to throw a joint retirement party for us. Bruhs was invited, which pleased me enormously. When we arrived at the restaurant in the City Hall area, it was already festive. We were handed tumblers of scotch, and by the time I was called upon to speak, I was totally ossified. My remarks were met with tumultuous applause, but I have no idea what I said. Later I was told that I generously sprinkled my speech with colorful profanities, the likes of which I had never been known to use. When the affair ended, I was grateful that Bruhs was there to see me home; I would never have made it under my own power. I also learned the valuable lesson that, if liquor could completely disorient me, it would be best to avoid it in the future. Accordingly, from that day to this I have not touched a drop of hard liquor, although I do now enjoy a little wine.

By January of 1972 my retirement from the civil service was in effect. Now I could accompany Bruhs to the 14th Street Social Services office to reapply for public assistance. On this visit we learned that he belonged in a different district and his application had to be filed at the East 34th Street office. The difference between the 14th Street and the 34th Street offices was like night and day! We were interviewed by a courteous person, sensitive to Bruhs's needs, who arranged for an immediate emergency cash allowance for him. A follow-up appointment by a staff social worker registered Bruhs also in the aid-to-disabled category. This was accomplished through the acceptance of a detailed report from Bruhs's doctor. Additional automatic benefits, including medicaid and food stamps, were all part of the package. What had seemed at first like a dismal descent into the nether world of welfare in the end gave Bruhs some positive feelings about the step he had taken and lessened the depression he had suffered at having to resign under pressure and being unable to hold subsequent jobs. We didn't talk about his welfare support to friends because of its stigma, but it let Bruhs feel he was a fully contributing member of our partnership. This feeling alone made the travail less significant, and it worked to his future advantage, for when he reached age sixty-two, he was able to go from aid to disabled to social security disability, with greatly increased benefits.

In the meantime there was a change of neurologists at my HIP center. The newly assigned specialist reviewed my case and asked me to repeat the encephalogram. This time I had the test with an entirely different technician, under relaxed circumstances, and the results were a complete reversal of the initial findings. There was no evidence whatsoever of brain damage, and I was able to draw a deep breath of relief and abandoned the thought that my days were numbered. The shaking arm was diagnosed as an "intention" tremor and was amenable to physical therapy. Bruhs took me in hand and together we employed the Bess Mensendieck exercise technique.

We still enlivened our existence by entertaining at home regularly. Our nights were brightened by the thoughtfulness of our friend Milton. He constantly remembered us with Broadway theater tickets, and we went to most of the concert halls in the city.

In March of 1973, Bruhs was hospitalized for an operation on his nose to correct a deviated septum, and he had only barely recovered when he was called to Richmond, Virginia, for the funeral of his oldest brother, Lou. Bruhs now had only two brothers left.

When in early 1974 Bruhs learned that he had glaucoma and began eyedrop therapy, we felt that we owed it to ourselves to take a trip. We had been mostly out of the city only for trips to Auburn to celebrate my mother's birthday. Bruhs's favorite niece, Diane, had developed multiple sclerosis, and her husband had asked for a divorce. She had moved from Philadelphia to Florida, near Coral Gables, and encouraged us to visit her there.

When she met us at the plane in Miami, we were struck by the change in her. She greeted us warmly enough, but we detected an undercurrent of tension that was noticeable and disturbing. She introduced us to her friend Larry, who from that point on seemed always to be around. We recognized that he had become an important person in her life. She constantly deferred to him and hung on every word he uttered. I won't say we took an instant dislike to the man, but we were put off by his Rotarian welcome and reacted to his overblown cordiality with distrust. We were hardly surprised to learn he had been a lecturer at the Dale Carnegie Institute.

The following morning, Diane confessed she was subject to frequent bouts of depression, due to her illness and the divorce. She said she leaned heavily on Larry. He had become indispensable, and she could not imagine functioning without him. She also mentioned that after she had invited us, she had been tempted to call us back and tell us not to come because, in her present state, she doubted her ability to cope with guests. All this did not make us too comfortable. But we were there. Since it was silly to pick up and leave, we would just have to make the best of what might well be a difficult situation.

I was accustomed to giving Bruhs the eyedrops for his glaucoma. We always excused ourselves and left the room to do the eyedrop routine. After a week of observing us and the attention I paid Bruhs, Diane called him aside and said, "Larry finds it quite unnatural for one man to be so attentive to another. I do, too! I wonder if there isn't some way you could be a little less obvious with those eyedrops!" Bruhs was flabbergasted by her comment, and when he told me what she had said, I hit the ceiling: "The crust of that guy! Who the hell is he to tell us what we can do with some eyedrops?" I let out a string of four-letter words and slumped in a chair.

We both voiced the same thought: What had happened to Diane's lovely nature? Was this all due to Larry's insensitivity? I felt like packing our bags and leaving then and there, but Bruhs calmed me down and said, "If we leave now, Diane would be hurt." He also pointed out that we were not in New York, and transportation was a problem. We had planned to spend two weeks, and two weeks it would be.

I found it hard to be civil to Larry after that, but he seemed undaunted. We spent our time at Diane's piano and wrote a song entitled "Say You're Here to Stay," certainly ironic considering the way we felt about our visit. At times Larry offered suggestions for the lyrics, and as he fancied himself a singer, he often chimed in on a chorus. But, however hard he used his plastic amiability, we were not buying it.

In fact, the high spot of the visit to Diane was the lunch we had at the Miami Beach Carriage House with Bruhs's sister-in-law Esther, the widow of Bruhs's brother Bill. She maintained the tradition started by Bill in assisting Bruhs generously. When we returned to New York, Bruhs found an urgent notice to report to social security to make an application for benefits. His dual applications for regular social security and social security disability were accepted, and we looked forward to Bruhs's having a steady income unmarred by bureaucratic red tape and the stigma of welfare.

26

Mothers and Sons

My mother's birthday fell on September 14. In 1974 we went to Auburn to celebrate her ninety-eighth birthday, in 1975, her ninety-ninth and in 1976, her one hundredth. Her alertness had not noticeably deteriorated. In spite of poor eyesight, two hip fractures, and her advanced age, she maintained her intelligent participation in all the activity around her, and her comments on current events and reminiscences of her past were lucid.

I had mixed feelings about the visits to Auburn. I wanted to show my concern for the family's welfare, as well as pay proper respect to my mother, especially at her advanced age. But although I had visited almost every year since leaving in 1927, practically fifty years before, I no longer felt a deep connection to the Auburn family. Going there no longer meant going "home"; I had become merely an interested observer. My therapy had awakened me to the fact that Bruhs was my family and New York City was my home.

I have always been grateful to my sister and brother for caring for my mother. My brother had a strong sense of duty about it, but my sister chafed under that burden at times. Neither of them had ever married, due largely to my mother's manipulative interference. Because of this, they never had households of their own. I was thankful that I had escaped from the narrow confines of that household and could enjoy the freedom to live my life in a community that embraced thousands of gay men and women. But that meant each leave-taking from the family was fraught with guilt that I was permitted to enjoy something they could only yearn for.

My sister would have preferred to live by herself and said so many times. My brother, after attempts at dating were frustrated by our mother, had resigned himself to being my mother's primary caretaker. I reflected on the emotional emptiness of both their lives, but was powerless to change this. In Auburn, my brother ran his floral business, and my sister relished her job as assistant county clerk. The sadness of leave-taking diminished over the years almost to the vanishing point, but my greatest regret was that I could never tell any member of my family exactly what my relationship was with Bruhs, or how its quality filled my life and made it complete.

After her one hundredth birthday, my mother's health went into a steady decline. My brother and sister put her in the hospital as, due to their own aging, they could no longer cope with her care. When the doctor felt she could be discharged, he recommended a rehabilitation facility attached to the hospital.

The day my mother was released, she expected my brother and sister to take her home. When she was merely transferred to another building in the complex, she was bewildered. She wailed piteously, "Why aren't you taking me home? I want to go to my home!"

My sister tried to reason with her. "Mother, you need special care that we can't give you at home. You'll be better off here, much better."

Mother was not to be placated, however. As they turned to leave, she shook her finger at them, crying, "You're abandoning me! After all I've done for you all these years, you turn your back on your own mother! How can you walk off and leave me? I won't forget this!"

True to her word, although they visited her every day for two years, she never again recognized them as her son and daughter, simply as well-meaning, kindly strangers. She seemed to have wiped them out of her memory completely. The effect on both of them was traumatic. After their years of diligent care, to be summarily dismissed in this manner was acutely painful.

When Bruhs and I visited my mother, on the other hand, she recognized us and spoke to us by name. She knew we lived in New York and had traveled to see her. As I looked at the frail little woman in the bed, I could see a wistful look come into her eyes as she said, "Why don't my other son and daughter ever come to visit me? I know they live right here in Auburn, but they never come."

I took her hand in mine and said quietly, "Mother, dear, they were both here today to see you."

Her reply was one of genuine puzzlement. "Why didn't they speak to me? I want so much to see them!"

On one of our visits she turned to me and said, "Gean, how old was Bruhs when we adopted him? I think he must have been about four." Our relationship was something that she may not have understood, but, since it existed, it must have a conventional explanation. I could not help but reflect on the many times my mother had visited us in New York, sometimes staying for a month at a time. She could not have been blind to how close her son was to another man, and how much they seemed to mean to each other. She obviously did accept the unspoken commitment that our relationship had demonstrated. Once there was a misunderstanding over how she had prepared a meal. She took umbrage at a remark Bruhs had made that unintentionally seemed to disparage her culinary capability, a sensitive subject. After she was mollified, she said to me, "You know, I would never say or do anything to come between you and Bruhs. You are closer than brothers, and I would never do anything to separate you."

When I took my retirement, my mother had felt it was time to get me back into the nest with her other aging brood. She had put it very casually: "Now you and Bruhs can come back to Auburn and live with us. It is your home and I know Norris and Marie would love to have you both."

She must have realized that this was wishful thinking, and that we would never leave New York. We could not turn our back on the city that was woven into the fabric of our lives, where so many experiences that could not have happened elsewhere had shaped our lives. With all its faults, we were not about to forsake the city we loved for a stagnant backwater town.

In the city, meanwhile, the season of concerts and the theater was launched with the advent of fall, and one needed a calendar to keep track of the openings (and closings). Theatergoing and the exchange of dinners with friends helped to brighten our lives through much of the 1970s. The holidays always added a festive note, with a variety of celebrations, and time passed pleasantly.

But, after the New Year, the reality of the ills to which we humans are subject would come sharply back into focus. However carefully I planned entertaining diversions, some reminder of human fragility seemed always to surface. With the shift to social security, Bruhs had lost his medicaid coverage, and he enrolled again in HIP. He developed what seemed to be a kidney infection, and he found it necessary to see a urologist. In spite of antibiotics the condition persisted, returning at frequent intervals.

When Bruhs had rejoined HIP, he began to use their mental health coverage as well as the physicals done by the so-called family physician assigned to him. The psychiatric social workers who saw patients in the Mental Health Division regularly put their notes in the patient's folder, to be seen by the examining physicians. In view of how doctors sometimes abused this information, this was a questionable procedure. As a case in point, after his kidney infection diagnosis, Bruhs made an appointment for a complete physical with a Dr. Cantor, a physician he chose at random from the HIP roster. When Bruhs arrived for the appointment, the doctor instructed him to go into another room and take off his clothes while the doctor looked through Bruhs's chart. Cantor had covered only a few pages when he suddenly jumped up and stormed into the adjoining room where Bruhs was waiting. The doctor waved the chart in the air as he fairly bellowed, "Put your clothes back on! I'm not going to examine you! You had a physical two weeks ago! There is nothing wrong with you but your nervous anxiety...and *stop it!*"

Bruhs was so taken aback by this unprofessional exhibition he was speechless. He dressed hurriedly and came out to where I was waiting. He was practically incoherent. That evening he wrote a lengthy letter to the HIP medical director outlining the entire situation. He explained what may have appeared in the chart as a "complete physical" was, in reality, only a cursory examination done in connection with a request for an intravenous pyelogram for the suspected kidney infection. He pointed out Dr. Cantor's unprofessional outburst and his misdiagnosis based on information from a hasty and inaccurate review of the mental health reports.

The medical director did reply, but staunchly defended Dr. Cantor and praised his professional qualifications, at no time acknowledging that Bruhs had been badly treated. He closed with the remark that another family doctor would be assigned, if requested. At an open meeting at HIP a few weeks later, Bruhs stood up, identified himself, and asked the medical director, who was taking questions from the floor, what HIP's definition of preventive medicine was. The director, who no doubt recalled Bruhs's name from his letter, with ill-concealed annoyance and a patronizing air, snapped, "Mr. Mero, if you don't know the meaning of preventive medicine, look it up in the dictionary."

Bruhs requested an appointment with the urologist for problems with the prostate. This doctor also proved to be quite inept at putting a patient at ease and closed the interview with a blunt prediction that Bruhs would shortly require surgery. Several months elapsed before Bruhs saw his new family physician at HIP. In the meantime, he tried various herbal remedies on his own. When the doctor examined him and looked in the chart for the urologist's report, his face darkened, and with a gesture of impatience he exploded, "I don't know why you are stalling with this thing! How do you know it isn't cancer?"

His bluntness so shocked Bruhs that again he was speechless. After sober consideration he once more wrote the medical director about this new confrontation he had experienced. This did have an effect, due perhaps in part to a duplicate copy this time sent to the HIP public relations director. The family doctor did receive some sort of reprimand from his superiors, and when Bruhs attempted to see him, he announced curtly, "I can no longer treat you. You have to see another doctor." Bruhs began to question whether his enrollment in HIP was totally ill-advised. Still in limbo about the condition of his health, he decided to temporarily postpone any surgery.

At this time, Lee, one of Bruhs's two remaining brothers, was hospitalized at Sloan Kettering for cancer of the bladder. Lee's wife, Leonore, of whom we were very fond, stayed at our apartment to be near her husband. We gave her what moral support we could. After repeated and protracted hospital stays, Lee died in November of 1976.

To lift Bruhs from his doldrums, I subscribed to a season of the New York City Opera. The first production was Richard Strauss's *Salomé*; it brought back memories of the many times Bruhs had danced to that score with Sandor and Sorel back in the 1930s. The opera season included *Turandot* and the premiere of Korngold's *Die tote Stadt,* both handsomely staged and superbly performed. The New York City Opera had rapidly gained recognition for its innovative programming and splendid performances and was at the forefront of outstanding opera companies. We had been boosters of the New York City Opera since their beginnings in the 1940s. At their first home in the old Mecca Temple Building on 55th Street, they mounted a striking Menotti's *Medium* with Marie Powers, so successful it went on to Broadway. After that, a stunning production of *Pellèas and Mèlisande* brought the legendary Maggie Teyte out of retirement to sing the role of Melisande. These were followed by *Tales of Hoffman, Die Fledermaus, Der Rosenkavalier,* and *The Love for*

Three Oranges, all a credit to the imagination and vision of the New York City Opera director, Julius Rudel. Neither Bruhs nor I were ever opera buffs, but we liked that the New York City Opera concentrated on the freshness and novelty of the material, rather then on big names for the principal roles. The operas that had the most appeal for us were always done by New York City Opera, not the Metropolitan Opera. The Met clung to standard fare, such as *Rigoletto, Aida, Cavalleria Rusticana.* Only in recent years has the Met broken with its traditions to follow the New York City Opera's innovative lead by presenting productions of Britten's *Peter Grimes* and Richard Strauss's *Die Frau ohne Schatten,* for example.

In January of 1979 my mother had her final release from her dreary bedridden existence. I remember the icy roads to her funeral; only a few longtime friends who could brave the stormy weather attended. Looking at my mother's peaceful countenance, I felt only relief that all traces of pain and suffering had been wiped away by the skilled hands of those who had prepared her. I could not shed a tear. I looked at my sister and brother and noticed they were dry-eyed. For them there must have been mixed feelings; relief at their release from the responsibilities of her long illness temporarily surmounted the realization of the awful separation that they would experience.

The weather made it impossible to open a grave, and we were spared the heartrending ritual of seeing our mother lowered into the ground. But this only reinforced my convictions about cremation, which I believe immediately releases the soul to continue its journey to the stars, vastly preferable to years of moldering in an earthbound grave.

Bruhs had very much wanted to come with me to Auburn, to be with me and feel a part of the family. I was afraid, however, that the strain of all the details surrounding my mother's death would only increase his already elevated blood pressure, and I insisted that he remain in New York.

My stay in Auburn lasted barely two weeks. My brother and sister needed assistance in straightening out our mother's affairs. I could see the void that her passing was leaving in their lives. While they had had to focus on their common interest in caring for her, they were able to communicate with each other. Without that, they were already becoming almost strangers under the same roof.

On Christmas Day of the same year, I received a call from my brother, telling me that my sister was in the hospital and that the doctor doubted her recovery. I could tell from Norris's voice that he felt an insecurity bordering on panic. When I offered to come up to be with him, he was overjoyed.

Auburn had become quite inaccessible due to the discontinuation of direct rail or bus service. There was a tiring five-hour train ride to Syracuse, then a taxi to the bus station for a local bus from Syracuse to Auburn. In the past, either Marie or Norris had driven the twenty-six miles to Syracuse to meet me in a car I had given them. But as his age increased and his insecurity mounted, Norris became fearful of driving even in the only moderately busy streets of Auburn, and the thought of the heavy traffic of Syracuse terrified him. I resigned myself to the bus.

Once in Auburn I could see how Norris's insecurity had grown. He gradually disclosed his difficulties, foremost among them his inability at mathematics. Terrors lurked in every bank statement that required reconciliation, and simply writing checks to pay bills became an impossible hurdle. My suggestions for variations in our daily menu were seized upon as if by a drowning man clutching at straws. Each day his dependence deepened, and I could see that he looked to me for answers about his future if our sister did not survive. This uncharacteristic dependence troubled me greatly. It brought him closer than we had ever been before, and he shared private moments of his life with me that he had never revealed. He spoke quite frankly of how many times my mother had intervened when he was on the verge of developing a serious attraction to another woman. She was obviously determined to keep my brother and sister in her home regardless of how deeply it might restrict their emotional lives. Although Norris and Marie harbored resentment, they had somehow seemed compelled to accept this infringement of their liberty.

Norris also spoke of an incident from when he was about fourteen. My mother was convinced that my father was consorting with prostitutes, who were no doubt diseased, and she feared the contamination to such a degree that she locked him out of her bedroom. My father was forced to bunk with my brother as no other beds were available. One evening during this forced sleeping arrangement, my brother became aware that his genitals were being fondled. As it continued, a wave of revulsion swept over him. I could see that even as he recalled the incident he was shaken, and his voice sank to a pained whisper as he said, "Imagine my own father doing that!"

I recognized how much this had disturbed Norris, but hearing it, I felt closer to my father than ever before. I knew I could never convince Norris that my father's motives were not licentious but rather a gesture generated by a desperate sense of loneliness and isolation. I think it was an attempt on my father's part to offset some of the sexual prudishness that my mother had instilled in all her children. He may have wanted to show Norris that it is all right to share affection sexually if it is done with tenderness and love. I knew that my view of the incident was of course colored by my sexual orientation, but I felt my attitude was much healthier than my brother's, who could only see my father's actions as an abhorrent "molestation." My father was a decent man who loved his children and would never harm them in any way. When I saw how deeply affected Norris was by this incident, I decided it would be next to impossible for him to accept my sexual pattern, and felt that I would never be able to reveal my true self to him.

Furthermore, the new closeness to my brother had built-in hazards that gave me a sinking sense of being trapped in a situation from which I would never be able to extricate myself. Norris and I visited the hospital every day, but my sister remained comatose and unaware of our presence. As each day passed, it grew increasingly evident that I would have to force the issue and make a break somehow, but I was at a loss to know how to make any plan for leaving Auburn. I had spoken on the telephone with Bruhs on New Year's Day, and he made no effort to hide his discontent. His frequent letters, too, expressed his unhappiness over our continued separation.

By January 29, I had almost abandoned all hope of getting back to New York City when the hospital called us to report that Marie was being discharged that same day. She had unaccountably rallied sufficiently for the hospital to shift her from critical to custodial care and take her off medicare.

Norris and I made it to the hospital in record time, and I accompanied Marie in the ambulance back to the house. The hospital provided visiting nurse service for some days, and Norris took charge of preparing meals. Fortunately for me, Marie's recuperation was rapid, and by early February I could leave without too many pangs of conscience. My brother's condition was disquieting, but the attention I had given him seemed to have served a purpose, and I was confident that soon my sister would be able to manage affairs for both of them. It was time to resume my life in my own home with the person who meant the most to me.

Bruhs's birthday on February 15, 1980 had a special significance for us that year. We were reunited, and the enforced separation brought us a renewed sense of belonging to each other, and the comfort of knowing that we would share whatever lay ahead in the 1980s.

27

Family Visit

The lease that we held jointly on the Third Avenue apartment had come up for renewal in 1977. At that time, my sister and brother from Auburn begged me to assist them in caring for my mother, and persuaded me to leave New York City for an indefinite time to lend a hand upstate. On the advice of well-meaning members of our tenants' association, Bruhs then had my name removed from the lease, which would qualify him for a rent-increase exemption. It seemed sensible at the time, and it did save Bruhs a lot over a number of years.

However, my stay in Auburn turned out to be brief. When I returned, the agreeable superintendent, who also functioned as manager of the building, had left, and the main office flatly refused to reinstate me as a leaseholder. I had no choice but to remain an "occupant" without leaseholding privileges of renewal, and with the prospect of eviction if anything happened to Bruhs.

In 1980 the building on Third Avenue changed from a rental property to a cooperative. The tenants' association worked diligently to prevent the conversion, but in July it became a fait accompli and we were all faced with the question of whether to buy or remain as rental tenants. Our own decision was officially Bruhs's to make, as he was the leaseholder, but we agonized over it together. The "insider's" price for our studio was approximately $40,000, with a carrying charge of $270 per month, plus a utility assessment of $35. We remembered only too well the stock market crash of 1929 and the predicament that forced co-op owners to walk away from their property when they could neither meet carrying charges nor sell their apartments. We feared a replay of this situation due to the unpredictable state of the economy. Anticipating the unreliability of

Reaganomics, we felt the bubble could burst at any moment and send our life savings down the drain.

With Bruhs's rent-increase exemption the current rent was pegged at $270 including utilities, and we reasoned it was best to remain rental tenants under the protection of a noneviction law that covered senior citizens. We could not foresee the condo/co-op mania that would sweep the city, with ballooning housing prices. In any case, the insider's price on the apartment was offered for a very limited time, and when that had expired, we were left without an option to buy at that price. Yet even though I was not on the lease, I felt reasonably secure in our setup.

However, as Bruhs's health deteriorated, I began to regret that we had not bought our home to provide a secure roof over our heads. "If wishes were horses, beggars could ride," "don't cry over spilt milk," and other clichés came to mind as I became the proverbial Monday-morning quarterback. That we did not buy the apartment will probably remain one of the greatest mistakes of my life, but I finally had to stop torturing myself and become reconciled to a wait-and-see attitude.

Several pleasant surprises in 1980 helped us to forget our troublesome housing situation. We had a visit from a grandnephew, Diane's son, Ken Mogul. He brought with him a young man, Ralph, whom he introduced as his lover, and we all had an outpouring of previously unrevealed facts about our lives. The many times we visited Diane we had, of course, seen Ken, but there was never a hint of the direction his emotional life was taking. He sometimes seemed morose and withdrawn, with no wish to communicate, but he was obviously popular with his peers, both boys and girls. We thought he suffered from some problem related to being a teenager. It never occurred to us that he might be experiencing confusion about his sexual instincts. He had always accepted us as his two uncles, but gradually, as he matured a bit, he began to realize that we must be a gay couple. When he approached his mother about it, she said she was aware of what our relationship was and neither approved nor disapproved. She was not reconciled to the idea of her son being gay, however, and since Ken's father and she were divorced, she consulted her "mentor," Larry, about the problem. This was the same man who back in 1974 when we visited Diane in Florida had been so disturbed by the attention I gave Bruhs for his glaucoma medication. He was the perfect one to give advice to the parent of a gay person! After some deliberation Larry pronounced that Ken should be identified as a "bisexual," which would have less stigma attached to it. Diane seemed willing to accept this terminology, and Ken proceeded to live his life as he chose, regardless of how others categorized him.

When Ken and Ralph joined us for a brunch two weeks later, Ken told us that they had gone to Philadelphia together and he had introduced Ralph to his father as his lover. The father, who had created quite a scene several years before when he had discovered a "love letter" to Ken from another boy, did an about-face and took the news quite calmly. He was pleasant to Ralph and assured Ken that he would gladly assist Ken financially to finish his education. Ken's father seemed content with whatever made his son happy and at peace with himself.

At another brunch, where we were Ken and Ralph's guests, we had a lively discussion about *Metropolitan Life* by Fran Lebowitz, whose ascerbic wit they greatly admired in spite of her less than positive comments on gay life. Bruhs and I could see from their conversation that, aside from their parents, they kept themselves otherwise closeted, conservatively conforming to society's demands in employment, housing, and all other aspects of life. They seemed relatively unmoved by the gay liberation movement, which had gained considerable momentum since the Stonewall uprising of 1969. Strangely enough, they even objected to the term *gay* as applied to homosexuals. We could see reflections of our own attitude over the years, as we clung to the security of our closet. But for them we felt a vague disappointment: at their young age why couldn't they be at the forefront in working for equality for gays? We hoped they might move toward greater militancy, that they would stir our own imagination, and help us change our own stance in the closet. But when this did happen to us later, the impetus would come from an entirely different quarter.

In any case, we were startled one evening to receive a long-distance phone call from Ken's mother, Diane. She had learned that Ken and Ralph had broken up, and Ken was no longer pursuing what had seemed a promising career with a public relations firm. She feared that he might be deeply depressed. She was also distressed because at their last meeting she and Ken had had some bitter words about his life. In the heat of the moment, she had referred to him as "sick" and he had subsequently severed all communications with her. She entreated Bruhs to contact Ken and get what information he could without revealing that it was for her.

When Bruhs finally reached Ken, he seemed in a relatively good frame of mind. He spoke calmly and rather dispassionately about Ralph, saying that they had parted company because he felt Ralph had been using him. At the outset Ken had assumed the total cost of their living arrangements. As time went on, Ralph seemed totally unwilling to share any of the expenses and the burden simply became too much for Ken. Unfortunately, it is not unusual for romance to evaporate under a strain of this kind. I reflected on Bruhs's wisdom in insisting over the years that our financial responsibilities be equally divided. As for the public relations position, Ken said he had left it because it had not lived up to his expectations. He had a growing conviction that he should continue his education, as his father had suggested. He was disappointed this meant leaving New York, but it was unavoidable. Ken may have sensed that Diane was really at the bottom of the phone call from Bruhs, for he added, "I have no wish to speak with my mother. I have nothing else to say to her, and I don't need her neurotic outbursts. She can't help me. I will take my dad up on his offer of assistance and see if I can get my life back on track." Bruhs wished him well and assured him that we cared about him and would always be glad to hear what was happening in his life.

After the 1981 Thanksgiving holiday was over, we had a visit from Richard, another of Bruhs's nephews. We had never known this young man well, but as a child he had stayed overnight with us on Riverside Drive, and without knowing why, we had always felt close to him. Whenever our paths crossed at family gatherings, he had always exhibited a tenderness toward us that touched us deeply. After a tour of duty in the U.S. Air Force he had completed his education and had passed his New York State bar examination to practice law. He opened his office in Schenectady, in the Capital District, because it was convenient for his wife, who was a teacher in nearby Clifton Park. His marriage seemed to be going smoothly, so it was a shock when Richard announced that they had separated earlier that year. Richard had acquired an old colonial house, the Widow Kendall, which dated back to the 1700s, and he had ambitiously embarked on its restoration. His wife still supported work on the house even after the divorce, which had fortunately been amicable.

Bruhs and I had many questions in our minds as to why this split had occurred. We posed the first question: "Did you break up because of differences on the desirability of having children?" Richard answered very positively, "No, it was something far more basic than that, and it is the reason I wanted to talk with you today. Back when I was in high school, I had a crush on a guy—not a girl, mind you, but a guy. Being a very up-front person, I decided to tell my parents. My father was concerned, but my mother was grief-stricken! After much discussion they decided I should see a psychiatrist to 'straighten me out.'

"The psychiatrist gave me reasons why I must consider all options before 'deciding' what my sexual preference should be. But, of course, in those days, if you were homosexual, you were 'sick,' and not very many psychiatrists, if any, would consider any goal except to make you 'normal.' Visits with the psychiatrist basically changed nothing and succeeded only in stifling any honest emotional expression. Later I learned that being gay is set early, and there is little or no latitude for making decisions about it. I finished high school and went on to college, but I was too confused to have any meaningful sex life. What I did have was a miserably lonely existence. I felt like a misfit, and altogether out of it.

"When I finally met Janet, she seemed quite different from other girls I had tried to date. She was sensitive to my moods, and there was enough of a physical attraction to make me think we could make a go of it. We were compatible in many ways and I was sure that marrying her would fix everything.

"For ten years I struggled to make the marriage work. But urges I couldn't control continued to surface. To her credit, Janet showed understanding that I would not have believed she possessed. It was as if she had sensed all along what the real stumbling block in the relationship was, and wanted, as quickly and painlessly as possible, to take whatever steps were necessary to reorganize our lives.

"Whether you know it or not, Uncle Bruhs, you and Gean have always been role models for me. I have admired you both for years. Now that I'm on the threshold of a new life, I need your love and support more than ever. I have a partner, a man younger than I am, with whom I hope to build a lasting relationship. I know I want to be monogamous, and my constant search for transient partners has left me uncomfortable and incomplete. Now that there is just one person in my life, I hope for the kind of fulfillment that you two seem to have experienced in your years together."

He gave us a questioning look, as if to ask our blessing. We both embraced him. Bruhs broke the silence. "Richard, you are a dear boy, even dearer now. You have shared so much with us. Opening your heart to us today has given us a priceless gift. We love you, and from now on we want you always to feel a part of our lives."

When Richard left that day, an enormous gap in our lives had been filled by his expression of care. We had lost many close friends over the years. Those who had not died had moved to distant places. Our circle of close friends had dwindled to four people—Lenny and his partner, and a lesbian couple we had known a long time. We were grateful that Richard's unexpected emergence from nowhere had cast a warm light into the shadowy corners of our growing loneliness.

By mid-1981, our apartment was badly in need of painting, which entailed a lot of tugging and lifting to get it ready for the painters. As a result, Bruhs began to feel disabling pains in his back and right shoulder. When an orthopedist's conventional treatment failed to provide relief, he sought out a chiropractor who had been recommended by friends. After preliminary X rays, Bruhs accepted the doctor's rosy forecast by visiting him regularly. Alas, the chiropractor's predictions only raised false hopes. With months of treatment, Bruhs saw no improvement and decided that his trial of chiropractic was an exercise in futility.

We had both been hearing favorable reports about the treatment of pain by the widely acclaimed oriental technique of acupuncture and were curious about this new approach. We located the Acupuncture Center in the East Eighties. With high hopes Bruhs started on an extended course of treatment. The treatments, however, did not have any effect on Bruhs's pain. Reluctantly, he finally abandoned acupuncture also and returned diligently to his own familiar Mensendieck exercises. He discovered what he had always known, that the Mensendieck technique, while not as exotic or dramatic as other methods, did as a daily discipline lead to solid improvement.

In 1980, my eyes began to be troubled by cataracts. My first effort to postpone the inevitable surgical correction of my eyes' lenses was to read the literature on natural healing. This led me to visit a holistic doctor, who, rather than focusing on specific symptoms, treated the whole body by cell nourishment to correct any imbalance. This theory appeared reasonable, and I entered wholeheartedly into this different approach. The medicines used were homeopathic and as dispensed by the doctor always remained something of a mystery, and I never knew exactly what they were. Part of the treatment meant wearing special pinhole glasses; these did seem to diminish the visual defects caused by the cataracts. I persisted with this holistic approach long beyond the time it was either useful or productive, in the vain hope that I could somehow obtain the desired results.

In my exploration of natural health methods I also learned of an herbal eyewash called eyebright, widely used in Europe and in some cases successful in arresting cataracts and "restoring" vision. When I was finally able to purchase the remedy, I used the solution faithfully every day for over a year, well beyond the period in which improvement should have come. I was so convinced that I was going to be helped that I stubbornly refused to accept that it had no effect. I should have realized that an external eyewash cannot be effective for the lens, which is completely covered by the iris. Cataracts do not form a crust on the surface of the eyeball that can be soaked and made to drop off, whatever testimonials may claim.

In spite of my disappointment with the alternatives, I remained adamantly opposed to surgery. My next effort entailed traveling fifty miles up the Hudson to visit a country doctor about whom I had read in *Prevention* magazine. He was treating cataract patients with combinations of vitamin B_6 and cod-liver oil and reported promising results. The doctor, a licensed ophthalmologist, gave my eyes a thorough examination but dashed my hopes completely when he reported that the cataracts were too advanced to be amenable to his method of treatment.

Bruhs had accompanied me on this futile excursion and he squeezed my hand to bolster my sagging spirits as we made our way back to the train station. He knew how hard I had tried to forestall surgery, but he also realized, as I did, that no further alternatives were available. I would have to face up to having my cataracts removed by surgery.

28

Theatrics

Although the cataracts had noticeably impaired my vision, I tried to keep active. When Milton offered us tickets for Lanford Wilson's play *Fifth of July*, for my birthday, I jumped at the opportunity. We had read reviews but were totally unprepared for the impact the play would have on us. This was the first story we had seen that revolved around a gay man whose dignity was recognized and whose lifestyle was accepted by his whole family. We watched in sheer disbelief as scene after scene unfolded with gay people treated as wholesome and unthreatening. The critics were unanimous in their praise of the play but had mixed opinions about Christopher Reeve in the principal role. Some characterized him as wooden and stilted, but we felt exactly the opposite about his portrayal. He did the role with restraint, but it was all the more powerful because he played it from the inside out, without external dramatics. He made us all painfully aware of the emotions that seethed within him. The scenes with his lover, played beautifully by Jeff Daniels, were deeply touching. *Fifth of July* was a milestone in the theater in that it presented gays as real people, the message everyone sympathetic to gay rights had been trying earnestly to convey for years. Wilson's story, one of our choice memories of the theater in the last thirty years, stirred nascent feelings of gay pride in the heart and mind of every gay person who saw it.

The theater season was in full swing, and Milton offered us tickets to an unusually large number of shows. In most cases, Milton was able to get us seats down front, and even with my limited vision I could make out most of the action onstage. In spite of my vision, the plays were too good to refuse. In quick succession we saw Nicol Williamson's powerful portrayal in *Macbeth* and Suzanne Pleshette, bright and amusing, in *Special Occasions*. This was followed by a lively musical, *Woman of the Year*, in which Lauren Bacall gave a stellar performance, singing and dancing up a storm. The high spot of the evening was a hilarious duet she did with the droll comedienne Marilyn Cooper, entitled "The Grass Is Greener," one of Kander and Ebb's great show-stopping songs.

In May of 1980 two friends, Joyce and Albert Levinson, gave us their tickets for a special event at Avery Fisher Hall, for which they were sponsors. The Film Society of Lincoln Center was devoting an evening to John Huston in tribute to his contribution to motion pictures. Several stars who had worked with Huston reflected on what a privilege that had been, but it was Lauren Bacall who made the evening come alive. She told of her first meeting with Huston, and her husky voice became unsteady and halting: "John Huston, you are a man's man and I am only a woman." To which his smiling reply had been: "That's right. I am a man, and you are a woman. That's the way it's supposed to be, isn't it?" With sly wit and disarming modesty, she had skillfully underscored the genius of John Huston, and the audience erupted with a spontaneous roar of approval.

At the conclusion of the program, which included clips from many of Huston's films, we moved on to the Vivian Beaumont Theater across the plaza, where everyone enjoyed a convivial and well-stocked bar and piles of hors d'oeuvres. Milton was there, and he said he was as surprised as we were to be guests at this glittering affair. He escorted us to the table where John Huston was seated and introduced us as two of his dearest friends. Huston was gracious, and we were impressed by his total lack of pretense or affectation. He seemed enormously moved by the adulation of the group who surrounded him, and his warm, direct manner won everyone's heart.

Milton then brought another legendary figure to us and introduced her. As I took her hand, I became totally unstrung by sheer disbelief. That I was shaking hands with Lillian Gish was simply unreal! I tried to tell her of all the golden moments she had given us through the years, with such classics as *Broken Blossoms* and *Way Down East*. Her smile was tinged with her uniquely wistful, fragile quality. But her voice was strong and rang with conviction: "The film holds the power. It speaks to us with an authority that will not be denied." She repeated the phrase, a summary of her philosophy of the cinema and of her own connection with the powerful film industry: "The film has the power!"

Kevin Brownlow later did a story on Lillian Gish for the March 1984 issue of *American Film* magazine, in which he told of the intense hardships she put herself through in the filming of *Way Down East*. She insisted upon doing the perilous sequences herself, which meant hours out in subfreezing temperatures. Her hands and hair trailed in icy water as she lay on a precarious ice floe that might at any moment break up and submerge her completely. Reading this underscored for me her intense dedication and brought tears to my eyes. I sat down and wrote an impulsive note to Milton Goldman declaring that Lillian Gish should be proclaimed a national treasure. He sent my letter on to Miss Gish, and she sent back an autographed photo expressing her appreciation. This luminescent figure, by the sheer magic of her talent, had an enormous impact on motion pictures for decades.

Our close friend Lenny called us about a new play called *Torch Song Trilogy* he had seen at a studio theater on upper Broadway. Unfortunately, the show had closed the weekend he saw it, but he knew it was scheduled to reopen at Actors' Playhouse, and he gave me the date. I had never seen Lenny so moved by anything in the theater, and he stressed that we must see this play at all costs. I trekked down to the Village the following day and explained to the man in the box office that, due to the condition of my eyes, I would require first-row seats. The first date this was possible was March 22, 1980. I kept my fingers crossed that I would see well enough to sense some of the excitement that Lenny had experienced.

When the night of the performance came, Bruhs guided me to my seat, and as the houselights went down, I caught my breath and waited for *Torch Song* to begin. Lenny's superlatives were right on the mark. As the play unfolded, we were totally immersed in Harvey Fierstein's rich dialogue and the intense, almost relentless sweep of his portrayal of Arnold, the central character. The play—really three plays rolled into one—went on and on, but we were so engrossed that we were oblivious to the passage of time.

When the play was over, we still sat in our seats so much under its spell we could not move. The houselights began to blink insistently to warn playgoers that the house would be dark shortly, and we knew we had to leave the theater. As we got to the street, I could see that Bruhs had been as shaken as I. Wordlessly he gripped my hand, and we got to our house in complete silence.

I was so stirred by what I had seen I found it impossible to sleep. I felt compelled to write to Mr. Fierstein to convey how much his play meant to us.

Dear Harvey Fierstein:

Torch Song Trilogy is by far the most extraordinary experience I have ever had in the theatre. As a writer, you are so articulate, with words apt and trenchant. The dialogue is brilliant. The first and second parts flesh out the characters of Arnold and Ed, but the whole thing comes together in the third part with a devastating impact. Here your perceptive exploration of the relationships that bear on Arnold's life come to full flower. You say the valid things that have for so long needed to be said about gay people's capacity for loving and caring.

Your portrayal of Arnold is a tour de force. It must be an exhausting challenge to meet night after night, but you have projected Arnold as probably no one else could. You have surrounded yourself with a company of performers who are in perfect sync with the emotional currents that make *Trilogy* a pulsating, living entity.

I have spoken with several people who have seen *Trilogy* and who loved it, and we are in agreement about Scene 4 in part 1. You make your point early enough in that scene that the rest of the action that follows is unnecessary. It does a disservice to the play as a whole and cheapens what could only otherwise be considered a masterpiece.

I know you are considering a possible move to Broadway and this must be a thorny problem for you. On Broadway the intimacy of a small house would be lost, the rapport that present audiences seem eager to share with you. However, if you feel you can reach a larger audience and thereby realize a dream, then go for it! As a senior citizen on a limited income and a tight budget I had to think twice about purchasing tickets for a performance at Actors' Playhouse. After seeing *Trilogy* I felt it was money well spent for a very rare evening. I hope to get a paperback copy of *Trilogy* so I can slowly savor your wonderful lines and relive the magical moments of your fascinating work.

My warm good wishes for continued success. You richly deserve to have it all!

Gean Harwood

After breakfast I sent the letter off. As with all the other letters of appreciation I had written over the years, I was satisfied when the words were down on paper. If I got no acknowledgment, it didn't matter. It was enough just to put down my thoughts and send them off.

About this time in the first-run houses, a movie, *Making Love*, dealt with the breakup of a marriage due to the husband's becoming aware that he was gay. It was the first time, to my knowledge, that a film had treated the subject honestly and nonjudgmentally. It got mixed reviews, depending on the critic's prejudices or lack of them. It deserved better notices than it got, for being straightforward and avoiding sensationalism. It was well written and directed and benefited from the performances of Michael Ontkean, Harry Hamlin, and Kate Jackson.

Discussing the film with gay friends, I was surprised at their reactions. Some agreed it was a breakthrough to have gay people portrayed as decent, credible people rather than psychopaths in bizarre, corrupting escapades. Many, however, were critical of the producer's motives and dismissed the entire film as shallow and trivial, feeling that it did little to advance the status of gay people in our society. Perhaps his effort was flawed, but I still felt the producer was to be commended for attempting to portray a gay relationship as a legitimate expression of love between human beings, and not a freak show. It brought the message to Middle America that gay people are indeed people. *Making Love* might be only half a loaf, but in my opinion, better than no bread at all.

Meanwhile, each day the condition of my eyes grew worse. I could no longer read, and in the streets at night the lights were so distorted that I moved through an unbelievable nightmarish phantasmagoria. By May 1, I was so weary of my struggle with my vision that I finally went to the eminent ophthalmologist Dr. Herbert Katzin to make arrangements for a cataract operation. After a complete physical checkup by Dr. Ressler, he booked me for surgery at Manhattan Eye and Ear Hospital. On May 26, 1980, an intraocular lens was transplanted into my right eye; I was released May 29. My sight was so much improved that I cursed myself for so long avoiding the surgery and suffering so needlessly. Frequent visits to Dr. Katzin for follow-up made it possible for me to resume a normal life.

29

Life Out of the Closet

With my new eyes, we saw Sidney Morris' play, *If This Isn't Love,* toward the end of July 1980, dealing with the long-term relationship of two gay men. We were impressed by Morris's dialogue, at times brimming with caustic wit, often touching. The play was heightened by Leslie Iron's directorial expertise.

A few days later we saw Blake Edwards's film *Victor-Victoria.* I thought it great fun, and was particularly pleased by the casual and matter-of-fact way in which gay people were presented. It was refreshing to see an audience encouraged to laugh with, not at, them. Julie Andrews, always a delightful soprano, assayed a decidedly different role. *Victor-Victoria* was sparkling entertainment and I enjoyed it fully as much in subsequent viewings.

Milton made my seventy-fourth birthday a special occasion. He arranged for tickets to a lovely little picture-postcard musical, *Charlotte Sweet.* Before the show we were his guests for dinner at Curtains Up, in the theater district, with photo murals of every star in the theater staring down at us.

Bruhs and I celebrated my seventy-fourth birthday when he took me to hear a poet of the piano, Abbey Simon. On leaving Carnegie Hall that evening I was floating on air. I wrote Mr. Simon a lengthy letter which read in part:

> On December 13th I was privileged to hear you for the first time in recital at Carnegie Hall.
>
> For many years I have frequented the concert halls. I have heard the great, the near-great, and those struggling for recognition, but I have never experienced so completely the kind of musical satisfaction you provided. Everything

you do is beautifully structured and exquisitely articulated. You reveal inner voices in the music.

As a young man I studied piano privately with Sam Lambertson of the Mannes School, but I lacked the stamina, the dedication, and the finances to pursue a career in music. Today I play only for my own amusement. When I hear the perfection that shines through your work, I am aware of your enormous accomplishment in a vast and crowded field of musical endeavor. I am grateful that I had the good fortune to attend your concert and I hope never to miss another.

God bless you and prosper you.

> Sincerely,
> Gean Harwood

I was enormously pleased to receive a reply from Mr. Simon. It reinforced my belief that performers in any field welcome expressions of approval for an artistry that has taken years of effort to perfect:

> Geneva, Switzerland
> January 10, 1983

Dear Mr. Harwood:

Your letter of December 25th has just been mailed to me at my home in Geneva, and I can't tell you how much I appreciate having it.

I am always gratified when I see that someone has understood what I meant to do at the piano and that it "came across" to the audience.

I shall treasure your kind words, and I do hope that the next time I play in New York you will come back stage and introduce yourself so that I can thank you properly in person.

With all good wishes for the New Year,

> Sincerely,
> Abbey Simon

Senior Action in a Gay Environment (SAGE) through Ken Dawson, its executive director, was doing splendid work with a neglected segment of the gay community—its elders. And in 1982 we became a part of that community. Ken had endless energy and vision, and he utilized every branch of the media for promoting SAGE. He arranged TV appearances and was instrumental in securing a prominent place for us in *Silent Pioneers,* the 1985 documentary that was widely distributed. So touchingly did it portray the milieu of gay elders, that it was shown in nursing schools and colleges.

Coming full circle to the beginning of our story, and a few days after the *Village Voice* printed Arthur Bell's interview with us in 1982, we were shopping in a neighborhood supermarket. A young woman approached and, with a pleasant smile, said, "I believe you two gentlemen deserve congratulations. I saw your pictures in the *Voice.* I want to offer you my compliments."

We thanked her, and as she walked away, I turned to Bruhs and said, "How do you like that? A perfect stranger comes up to us, so friendly and matter-of-fact about it all. I just can't believe it!"

As we walked that day down Second Avenue near our home, a portly gentleman, sweeping out of a liquor store, spotted us. His eyes lit up, his face wreathed in a smile. He beamed as he pointed his finger at us. "I know you! You're the two oldest gay men in America!"

This broke us up completely. And it showed us how much one article in a newspaper had affected the public. We also realized that we were "out" now, and there could be no more hiding. This meant people where we lived would know we were gay. We might have to face the landlord and any tenants objecting to living under the same roof as gay people. Memories of the 1930s and my eviction because I was a "fag" surfaced. Fear of hostility was ingrained in us, and we viewed our new open stance with mixed feelings. We had a sense of freedom and a certain elation that came with the revelation, but an equal amount of trepidation could not be ignored.

Shortly after we arrived home that day, the telephone rang. Ken Dawson was checking to see how we were. He was enormously pleased by the article and wanted our permission to use it in SAGE literature. We voiced some of our fears regarding our landlord. Ken was quick to reply, "Don't worry, you're not alone anymore. You have the SAGE family to back you up. If anyone tries to make trouble for you, we'll handle it—with a picket line, if necessary." Ken mentioned that he would like us to meet his assistant, Morgan Gwenwald, for lunch.

We met at a charming little restaurant called Whole Wheat 'N' Wild Berrys, almost opposite our old Dance Gallery at 52 West 10th Street. The old neighborhood cast a nostalgic glow over the lunch with Ken and Morgan. Morgan's warm and outgoing personality was so like the lesbians who had formed our closest circle of friends that we felt we had known her all our lives. The purpose of the lunch was to explore whether we might actively participate in the SAGE outreach efforts. Ken mentioned possible media appearances, which made our heads spin, and we were carried along in anticipation of what our new "openness" would bring us.

I had to visit Dr. Katzin several times. He told me my vision would be better balanced with surgery for the left eye. I was impatient to proceed, and he made arrangements for the second operation in August, 1982. The doctor and his wife turned out to be supporters of SAGE. In a mailing to him, SAGE had included a reprint of the Arthur Bell *Village Voice* story, and much to our surprise, Dr. Katzin knew about our lifestyle. We had initially posed as brothers to give Bruhs free access when I was hospitalized; now this pretense was no longer necessary.

Before the hospital date we had Ken and Morgan for lunch. I wanted to discuss a call we had received from Roger Tuveson about an article he was doing for *Mandate,* a gay magazine. He had read Bell's piece in the *Voice* and wanted to include us in his own article. I knew that each month the magazine featured provocative articles, lurid fiction, and an array of nude male photos. I could not envision the story of our life together in that setting. Ken volunteered to speak to the writer and be present when we were interviewed; as long as we had control over the final article, he felt it would be okay.

One evening in August, Arthur Bell was our guest for dinner. He regaled us with stories about his feuds as a critic with some of the stars, including a classic contretemps with Raquel Welch. The actress had come fresh from her movie triumphs to appear on Broadway. Arthur covered her performance opening night and wrote a one-line review: "Raquel Welch is way out front in the hooter department, but as an actress she runs the gamut from A to B." Welch was furious, and when she saw Arthur next, she let him have it: "How can you be so bitchy? Just because you're gay, you are out to destroy me. Well, you are not going to destroy me! I am a *star* and you are a pathetic hack who wouldn't recognize talent if you fell over it. Take your nasty pen and get out of my life—and stay out!"

Arthur was unflustered by this dressing down. It had happened many times with others. "The fact that I'm gay has nothing to do with what I say in a review," he told her. "I call'em as I see'em. Always have. Always will. In my business I try never to forget a face, but in your case I'll be glad to make an exception. Meanwhile, star-bright, try to lighten up. See you around."

Arthur's candor and his contempt for phoniness had him constantly locking horns with the famous. Arthur seemed to always land on his feet. Looking at this frail man, we were struck by his indomitable courage. In spite of his limited sight, he was a prolific writer, and despite his limp, he covered a great deal of ground pursuing material for his column. His diet, restricted by diabetes, proved troublesome at social functions. But his fiercely independent spirit carried him through, and one got the impression that he had scorn for those who felt sorry for him. Since Arthur was basically a lovable man, seeing all his physical problems at close range made it difficult not to mother him. He made it plain, however, that he would handle everything by himself.

Arthur spoke with great feeling about the Stonewall uprising and declared, "No one is going to put down the drag queens when I'm around! There would have been no gay liberation movement without them!" We had carefully saved an article of his—the devastating piece on Anita Bryant. For several years she had conducted a one-woman crusade against homosexuals. As publicity queen of the Florida Citrus Growers, she had a platform for her ferocious homophobic diatribes. In his article for the *New York Times*, Arthur deftly cut her to shreds by exposing her demagogic prejudices. He was pleased that we considered it worth preserving.

It was appropriate that Arthur wrote for the *Village Voice*, for in truth, he was the voice and conscience of the gay community, in the vanguard of the gay liberation movement. This fragile man was a giant, a tower of strength and conviction in the struggle for gay rights. We were proud to call him our friend.

We were pleased to hear from Ken Dawson about another matter that had been troubling us. Our relations with our landlord had become clouded since the conversion to a co-op, and a number of questions had arisen concerning our rights as tenants. Ken mentioned that he had made arrangements for us to meet with a young lawyer who had worked in the New York State attorney general's office on housing problems. The lawyer, Richard E. Feldman, devoted an hour to our situation and assured us he would lend assistance whenever we needed it. He drafted an affidavit of residency on my claim to tenancy and generally raised our spirits by his warm and helpful manner. Richard also said he would arrange with Tom Stoddard, his gay partner at the time, to draw up our wills, putting our affairs in better order. In settlements of gay estates a gay partner can often be disinherited unless the language of the will is very specific. This valuable connection was another example of how SAGE thoughtfully reached out to help gay elders.

We began to attend the SAGE socials regularly. Mixing with people who shared our likes and interests gave our spirits a lift, and we enjoyed being able to dance together. We had been adopted by the SAGE family and were welcomed warmly.

At one of the socials, Donald Vining introduced himself. A writer, with two volumes of his *Gay Diary* already published, he was interested in interviewing us for an article for *The Advocate*. Part of the gay press, this paper had attracted a large readership nationwide, and we appreciated the opportunity to have our story so widely known. When Donald came to do the interview, he spent hours digging into our past. He followed up with detailed questionnaires that he sent. His competence and his serious, in-depth questioning made us feel that he would produce a fair story of our life together.

In the midst of all this attention, an unpleasant incident brought us down from the stratosphere. We often shopped at a Shopwell supermarket on University Place. On this November day, as we were going about the store picking up items, we became aware of a man with a rather sinister, creepy expression dressed in a long overcoat that reached down to his shoes, and wearing a broad-brimmed fedora. He seemed to turn up in whatever aisle we went to. It became obvious that he was watching us. We went through the checkout, paid for our items, and turned to leave. But the man put out his hand barring the way. He asked us to go to a back room and empty our pockets. For a moment we were speechless. We were being accused of shoplifting, and we were outraged. The man who had stopped us was a security guard, who insisted he had seen Bruhs secrete two packages of cheese in his pockets. Fortunately, Bruhs had the presence of mind to firmly refuse to go to a back room. There it would have been easy for the guard to plant the cheese on Bruhs. The questioning drew curious shoppers and they began to protest that the line was being held up. The manager finally came over and asked us to go to a room adjacent to the checkout for a search. This we refused to do. We suggested that instead he examine our shopping bag, where he would find the cheese in question, as well as the sales slip showing it had been paid for. We offered the manager the opportunity to search us, but in the open. He avoided this, as he was no doubt aware of the penalties imposed for an illegal search. The situation for everyone became more embarrassing by the moment. After some thirty minutes of detention, the manager realized that a stalemate had been reached, and he told us we could leave.

We were both shaken by this incident. Still smarting under the sense of injury, Bruhs wrote a letter to the owner of the grocery chain, describing in vivid detail the events of that day, even down to a detailed description of how the security guard was dressed. Bruhs called Richard Feldman, our lawyer, and read the letter aloud. Richard praised it as direct and to the point. He suggested that we add that a copy had been sent to him. Two days later, Bruhs received a call from the company president's representative. He was solicitous and offered restitution for the anguish and embarrassment caused by the store's employees. He asked what Bruhs would consider an equitable settlement. Bruhs cannily sidestepped a dollar figure, indicating that details would have to be handled through his attorney. The spokesman for the store bridled at "bringing lawyers into the picture," but Bruhs held firm and repeated that his lawyer would be in touch with the store management. Richard did take over and obtained the maximum allowed for an out-of-court settlement. We were once again indebted to Richard for taking the task of negotiating out of our hands.

Sometime in the early 1980s I had sold my Mason and Hamlin because I was not using it. Now, the yen to have a piano in the house again prompted me to visit the Yamaha showroom. Excellent reports about the Yamaha's fine quality were confirmed when I tried the Yamaha forty-two-inch studio piano. The string length provided a resonant bass vastly superior to the other makes, and the treble had a pleasing sonority that satisfied my ear. I was all too easily persuaded when Lenny's partner offered to apply his professional discount to the purchase price. We once again had a piano.

We were inspired to try our hand at composing a new song together. Our change of style surprised us both. Besides our continuing sense of personal commitment, the lyrics had a new meaning for us that could only be explained by a new openness from our association with SAGE. Not intended primarily as a gay song, we wrote:

I'LL NEVER SAY GOOD BYE

Lyrics by Bruhs Mero; music by Gean Harwood

When I was so very young
I thought real love was rare,
But then I found a lover who was true.

Now my heart is his to keep,
I've thrown away the keys
Of all the others that I ever knew.

I'll never leave you, dear.
I always want you near.
You are the part which is my heart.
I'll never say good bye!

No need to wonder why
My love can never die.
I took the chance and found romance,
I'll never say good bye!

Some folks may like to go out and play,
Finding a new love every day,
But I cannot feel that our love is real
Unless we are there to stay.

For you are my answered prayer
I've been seeking everywhere.
Now that you're here,
It's really quite clear,
I'll never say, no, never say good bye!

One Sunday late in February, 1983, a friend of Ken Dawson's, Jed Mattes, called for us and took us to a Mexican restaurant, Caramba. Our other dinner companions were Ken Dawson, Diego Lopez, Fred Hochberg, Ted Hook, and Garry Hunt, an actor whom we remembered seeing in an off-Broadway play, *Naked Highway*. After dinner we went on to Carnegie Hall where we were Jed's guests at our first hearing of the Gay Men's Chorus. The performance was entrancing, and the rich interpretation given each number was deeply impressive. Glorious voices poured out the touching songs with such appeal that tears rolled down my cheeks. I had to pinch myself to believe it was really happening publicly. The many times we have heard the chorus since, their performance has always been musically perfect. But the satisfaction that invariably thrills gay people goes much deeper. We glow with pride that such a fine group so ardently holds a mirror to the world to proclaim the beauty and validity of our love.

To stimulate interest in SAGE activities, their writers' workshop offered prizes for the best essay on growing up gay. When I decided to try, I did not know that there would be formidable competitors, including Donald Vining. Much to my surprise I was awarded third prize, my trophy a cake from the Erotic Bakery—a charming male torso of marzipan, complete in every anatomical detail! It was fun to share the fruits of my victory with friends, although it was hardly a prize I could show off to a maiden aunt, if I had one.

Later that month SAGE celebrated its fifth year of existence with a splendid party for its members. The event at the Palace Club, the former site of Luchow's Restaurant on 14th Street at Union Square, was a plush affair, and the ambience of the club bathed the partygoers in a warm and rosy glow. But we had to leave early to see a performance of *Greater Tuna*. The play lived up to its fine reviews, and the two men who played many roles of both genders gave remarkable performances. However, nothing onstage could make up for Bruhs's disappointment at leaving the SAGE party, and I doubt he has yet forgiven me.

In April, we also went to the Ringling Bros. Barnum & Bailey Circus at Madison Square Garden, a benefit for the Gay Men's Health Crisis. The Garden was filled to capacity with some seventeen thousand gay men and women. They had assembled under one roof in a common effort to assist in the battle against AIDS. My heart swelled with pride and my eyes filled with tears. Even as the performers performed their death-defying feats in the arena, I couldn't take my eyes off the audience. Here at last was an exhibition of gay community spirit and caring, a portent of what a gay community could be. Ironically, this spectacle did not rate one iota of mention in the media!

About this time a long shadow was cast on our future—the

ominous hint of a condition that was to have a marked effect on our lives. Bruhs had become aware that he was having difficulty with his memory. The impairment was slight, but we secured an appointment with a neurologist at HIP. The findings from a CAT scan were not alarming, and the doctor downplayed Bruhs's symptoms, simply labeling the condition "mild dementia." There seems to be little the medical profession can do to ameliorate memory problems. The doctors shied away from a diagnosis of Alzheimer's, but early symptoms so mimicked the dread disease that it was impossible for the patient, or his loved ones, to ignore it. Senility has many stages, and as one observes the inexorable progress of the disease, a feeling of utter helplessness takes over. I suddenly discovered that the foundation of our life's structure was sinking in quicksand, with no means of shoring it up. I tried to conduct myself as though everything were "normal," but the dread of the unknown persisted, gnawing away at my peace of mind. Even when I thought I had relegated the problem to the back burners of consciousness, it would surface to haunt my waking hours and destroy my sleep.

In September, SAGE announced that for their October 7 benefit, they would be offering choice seats to *La Cage aux Folles*. It was the show of the century, but the prices were out of reach for us. We put the announcement to one side and forgot about it until our friend Lenny called and suggested that he and his partner order four seats through SAGE with us as their guests and invited us to join them for dinner at Café des Sports, a charming French restaurant in the West Fifties. Afterward, from our orchestra seats we greeted other SAGE members all around us. When I turned back to Bruhs, he wasn't there. He had gone over to Carol Channing to tell her how much her performances had meant to him. She seemed pleased by his compliments. Seated with Ms. Channing was Jerry Herman, the composer of the score for *La Cage, Hello Dolly, Mame*, and other brilliant musicals. I would have liked to tell him how big a fan of his we had been all the way back to his earliest musical, *Milk and Honey*.

From the moment the curtain went up on *La Cage*, one realized this was a dazzling, once-in-a-lifetime evening at the theater. The esprit de corps of the company was a joy. Through our laughter and tears, the cast held us rapt until the final curtain. Never has an audience seemed the recipient of so much love pouring from a stage across the footlights. With breathtaking sets and spectacular lighting, this show moved at express-train speed. When we were not being serenaded by Jerry Herman's beautiful ballads, "Song on the Sand" or "Look Over There," we were dazzled by the Cagelles, ten boys and two girls skillfully transformed by costume and makeup into twelve girls. They were the most versatile dancers, and they sang their hearts out, as if to say, "Look at me! I'm gay and I'm somebody!"

Parts of the script resembled the film, but in Harvey Fierstein's skilled hands it became a living, human document on people you really cared about. Combined with Herman's magnificent score, the lyrics validated gay lives and gave them the meaning we had known all along they had. George Hearn's stunning performance of Jerry Herman's poignant lyrics "I Am What I Am" seemed to sum up everything gays everywhere had always wished to proclaim to the world. It gave us the stature we felt we had always deserved and offered us the "gay anthem" we had always craved.

At the final curtain the audience erupted in a tumultuous roar of approval. Everyone's throat was hoarse from shouting out praise. The warmth of Dino Georgio and Louis Malkin's after-theater party in their Chelsea duplex was the perfect way to finish that wonderful evening. Everyone had seen the performance and put their stamp of unqualified approval on it.

In November, Pat Snyder had assembled some footage from her documentary on gay elders, *Silent Pioneers,* to screen at a WNET Channel 13 studio, as a fund-raising event for additional money to finish the film. I was invited to speak after the showing. It was the first time I had publicly appeared in the role of gay activist. I did not prepare notes and had no idea what approach I would take. As I began to speak, the words came forth without hesitance or stage fright. Well received by an audience of straight and gay people, I surprised myself. When I returned to my seat, Bruhs stood up and impulsively leaned over to kiss me. I was delighted by his willingness to publicly display his feelings.

Nineteen eighty-three had been a memorable year for many reasons, and we celebrated it at a gala SAGE Social held at the Church Chapel of St. John the Divine, followed by a delightful punch-bowl party given by William Wynkoop and Roy Strickland at Roy's Greenwich Village apartment. We were increasingly involved in the gay community through SAGE, and we welcomed our new roles as activists.

30

The Pace Quickens

On New Year's Day I had a bad cold and could not attend a benefit at Limelight for which SAGE had given us tickets. It was being given to celebrate the opening of a new Gay Community Center—an opportunity to support a good cause and see the newly opened and much-talked-about discotheque on Sixth Avenue and 20th Street. The Limelight building had been an Episcopal church that had had a gifted organist, Lynwood Farnum. I had met Lynwood back in the 1930s in the Andersons' country home near Woodstock, and it had been a delight to subsequently attend a candlelight service in the city to hear Lynwood's ravishing presentation of Bach's organ music. Those days were long past, however, and two enterprising young men had transformed the same church into a strikingly original disco. I finally persuaded Bruhs to go by himself: we should not both be deprived of the opportunity to see the place.

Bruhs found that the Limelight measured up to all its publicity, but was startled when a radio reporter from station WBAI asked him for an interview right then and there. The following Wednesday evening it was put on the air. I was impressed by the way Bruhs fielded the reporter's questions. With his memory problems, Bruhs had increasingly felt compelled to take a backseat. I was proud, though, that he had made the effort to go out alone, and his interview showed he was capable of holding his own without any assistance from me.

SAGE had inaugurated a series of brunches held once a month at various restaurants. The one in February coincided with Bruhs's birthday, and we were guests of SAGE for the occasion at Trilogy in the Village, a restaurant patronized by the gay community. We enjoyed the convivial company so much that we vowed we would be on hand for the next monthly event.

A few days later we were invited to speak at an evening meeting of the Greater Gotham Business Council, a gay businessmen's association. It was actually another fund-raiser for *Silent Pioneers*. After the screening of footage from the film, I took questions from the audience. Afterward a young optometrist who was a member of Dr. Katzin's staff came up to us. In the office Bruhs and I had often speculated about him, but finding him at this meeting confirmed that he was one of us. Another council member, someone we had known for decades, greeted us warmly and exclaimed, "Bruhs and Gean, how great to see you after all these years! You've become activists now! More power to you!"

To maintain the momentum that SAGE had already generated, Ken Dawson notified us in March that he would be bringing a young *New York Times* reporter, Craig Wolff, to our house for an interview. Wolff's questions showed uncommon perception. The brief piece he did about us in the March 25 Sunday edition used only first names, but the article was couched in favorable language and presented a factual picture of the plight of the aging homosexual in our society. However, I resent this term; the fact that heterosexuals are *aging* somehow never receives the same emphasis.

That same month we received another visit from Richard, Bruhs's nephew, whom we now felt we shared as a relative. This time he stayed over with us, and we talked until late into the night, discussing the many ways that partners communicate understanding and contribute to their unfolding of mutual love and respect. We learned much about each other and felt enriched having his presence in our lives. We were reluctant to have him leave, but he could spend only limited time with us. He had already spent years on the restoration of the colonial Widow Kendall House in Schenectady, New York. Given his many commitments Richard had to husband his time very carefully.

The following Sunday in March, Milton gave us tickets for a memorable Martha Graham recital. Bruhs and I were fascinated by the depth and scope of the dances, enhanced by the striking decor of Isamu Noguchi, whose studio we had taken over and transformed into the "Dance Gallery."

The next treat that Milton provided was the opportunity to see Kaye Ballard's one-woman show "Hey, Ma, Kaye Ballard." It was performed at the Promenade, an intimate little playhouse on upper Broadway. From the moment she came on stage she held the audience, and even at intermission the electricity did not subside. We had been immersed in a total theatrical experience.

I wrote to Milton about Kaye's enchantment, and he forwarded the note to the actress. She sent us one of her hand-written notes, with little drawings.

Dear Gean,

Milton Goldman sent your letter to me, so I could share your thoughts about my show!

I was so touched! Thank you—thank you—thank you! I shall always keep your letter!

And thank you for writing to Milton!

My love to you and Bruhs always!

Kaye

x x

P.S. The show closed Sunday!

Later that month, a friend, Joe Smith, suffered a massive stroke. Our friendship with Joe dated back to the 1940s when he attended Bruh's men's dance class and was a charter member of the Nucleus Club. He had proudly displayed his membership card even in the 1980s. When we visited him at Bellevue, we were not even sure he recognized us. He lingered on for a few weeks. Friends assembled in June for a memorial service that fondly recalled this warm and wonderful man.

We lost another good friend that June of 1984. Arthur Bell, responsible for reintroducing us to the public, finally succumbed to an accumulation of ailments that had dogged him for years. At the theater where memorial tributes were being offered, Arthur's brother—who had been present the day Arthur interviewed us for the *Village Voice*—put his arms around us and whispered, "Arthur loved you both and spoke of you often. I know he's pleased that you're here today." The actress Dorothy Loudon, and Vito Russo, author of *The Celluloid Closet,* a book on gay people's portrayal in the movies, both close friends of Arthur's, related amusing incidents that spoke eloquently of Arthur's wit and charm. It was a touching farewell to a noble human being.

Our days seemed filled with sad trips to hospitals and memorial services. Bruhs's nephew Jack Shulman had a condition of the lymph glands that perplexed the doctors at University Hospital. His wife, Jean, Bruhs's niece, had always been warm and caring toward us, accepting our relationship without question. We wanted to give her our moral support, and visiting Jack at every possible opportunity seemed to strengthen her defenses.

On a happier note, in June we participated in the gay pride parade for the first time. Becoming more closely identified with gay rights, we felt we should be a part of this visible expression of pride. We rode in the car of SAGE members Wayne Steinman and Sal Iacullo. Their spirit and dedication were an inspiration to us.

July 1984 was memorable for several reasons. On the twenty-fourth SAGE, in its ever-widening outreach to the media, approached Mark McCain, a reporter for the *Boston Globe,* and invited him to our home on Third Avenue for an interview and pictures. He, too, was interested in our long-term relationship and thought he could convince his editor that our story was newsworthy. It was a pleasant two hours spent in the interview, but it was never published in the conservative *Globe.* We finally chalked it up merely as experience in our public relations effort for SAGE.

However, Ken Dawson had made contact with WNYW Channel 5 in New York and arranged for us to appear on *Midday with Bill Boggs,* a popular television talk show. This was our first experience with TV. On July 27, after five minutes with Bill Boggs we felt completely at ease. His questions were searching but perceptive. He became more and more interested in our lives and what our relationship had meant to us. It was embarrassing for us as prominent people were waiting in the wings—Virginia Appuzo, head of the National Gay Task Force, and David Rothenberg, founder of the Fortune Society. As David took his place on the platform during a commercial break, he smiled at us and remarked, "You're a tough act to follow!"

Bill Boggs's program took phone calls from listeners. One was from a twenty-five-year-old woman, a practicing attorney, who had called to say, "I have always had difficulty dealing with gay people. But today, the two dignified gentlemen on your program have changed my opinion." We found this to be heartwarming.

Richard Feldman, our friend and attorney, was squeezed into the last five minutes and gave a masterful summary of the compelling reasons why the mayor should issue an executive order barring organizations that received subsidies from the City of New York from discriminating against gay people in employment. The Catholic archdiocese had sent its lawyer as a spokesman to offer objections to the proposal, but limited time left the question unresolved.

We were taken completely by surprise when the lawyer for the archdiocese congratulated us. But he asked, "Tell me, in this fifty-four-year relationship, were you celibate?" I almost blurted out, "You have to be kidding!" After a moment I said quietly and firmly, "No, we were not." He frowned. Then his face brightened and with no discernible disapproval he said, "Well, in spite of that, your relationship is a very remarkable one. I congratulate you."

At home the phone was ringing as we opened the door. "I'm so proud of both of you!" said Bruhs's ninety-year-old sister, Anne. We had told no one in the family about the impending date on TV. By sheer accident, Bruhs's niece Jean had happened to catch the program and hurriedly called her mother. This support from a family member, perhaps the most loved and admired by the whole tribe, gave us an enormous boost. Anne's approval gave us further assurance that we were engaged in something worthwhile and inspired us to press on with our efforts for the gay cause.

In August of 1984, Pat Snyder came to see us. She came quickly to the point: "I was impressed by your appearance on the Bill Boggs show. I have been traveling around the country shooting different gay people in different walks of life. I've got some good footage, but there's something missing. Seeing you two on *Midday* I realized what is missing. I need a love story—and you are it! What do you say to working with Lucy Winer and me on developing a sequence on the two of you?"

We had seen some of her takes of the ongoing filming of *Silent Pioneers,* and we felt privileged to be asked to be a part of this promising documentary. Next we had to meet Harvey Marks, the actual producer; he shared Pat's enthusiasm. After a brief conference with Pat and the director, Lucy, we were told shooting would begin on August 23. Transportation would be provided to the location.

When we assembled with the crew at the SAGE office, on West 13th Street, we were struck by everyone's speed and skill. Lucy, working with Pat, had some rough ideas about what they wanted from us, but there was no prepared script. After a few suggestions, Bruhs and I were allowed to wing it. We began in the SAGE office. The crew set up a few props and a record player, and then Bruhs and I were asked to dance together. The camera focused on our feet, and as it came up to our faces, I remarked that we had been loving partners for fifty-four years.

For the next sequence we took to the streets with our shopping cart in tow. Pat and Lucy scouted the neighborhood for the best spot and selected a Village bakery in which to do our shopping. When we had loaded our purchases in the cart, we walked the side streets talking to each other. In a later voice-over, I expressed regret that we could never tell many of those close to us how much our relationship had enriched our lives.

The next day we all went to Central Park West for some interior shots. Pat's friend Mrs. Jimmy Breslin had given the use of her apartment for the filming. Her living room had a grand piano, and Pat asked us to do one of our own songs. We tried several, finally settling on filming "It's Only My Heart."

Afterwards, Bruhs and I sat on a sofa and talked about the Stonewall uprising and the birth of the gay liberation movement. We were able to put forward many of our ideas, particularly our change in thinking about "flamboyance" after the drag queens' heroic stand against police harassment at Stonewall. With enviable defiance, the most garish segment of the gay community had taken up the cudgels that historic night, and we had admired their courage so intensely we were forced to rethink our prejudices.

Occasionally, Lucy would ask a question. She asked one of us to demonstrate the gestures and walk of an "obvious" gay man. Bruhs flatly refused to participate in this, so the demonstration was up to me. I was not at all comfortable about it, but I wanted to be a good sport in spite of my misgivings. It did provide some levity in an otherwise serious segment and did not undermine the sense of dignity we were trying to establish.

When Lucy felt she had exhausted the possibilities of the interior shots, she moved the operation out-of-doors again. We were amused by the deference with which we were treated. The crew, all young lesbians, gave us the attention accorded theater stars. We felt like royalty being carried on silk cushions to our various destinations. In Central Park, when the cameras were set up, we were again briefed by Lucy on what topics we should pursue. She gave us an idea of what she would like, but let us use our own words. The result was a natural exchange of thoughts about our love and what it had meant to both of us. Under Lucy's guidance a portrait of two men who had been in love for over half a century emerged. Moments of lightness kept it from being too sentimental. When Lucy felt she had what she wanted, she called it a wrap and we all packed up.

We had one more recording session on October 6, to get voice levels and voice-overs and expand "It's Only My Heart" to accompany the credits at the end. Then began the delicate and arduous job of cutting for a projected premiere of October 21.

Silent Pioneers was ready for its October 21 gala premiere at the Limelight. Fred Gottschalk, prominently featured in the film, had finally succumbed to his long struggle with cancer. A memorial service was held at noon the day of the premiere. At one point in the film Fred expresses exasperation at the length of time it is taking: "I hope the damned film will be finished soon and not shown posthumously." His prophetic words added a further touch of poignancy to his role in the film.

We had to try to shake off the sadness of Fred's memorial to get into the spirit of the premiere. Over six hundred people assembled for the showing. At the conclusion the audience rose to its feet, shouting approbation. Pat Snyder had arranged to have Bruhs and me come onstage, and as the closing credits rolled and the strains of "It's Only My Heart" were reprised and died away, we were picked up by the spotlights in a live chorus of the song. The crowd went wild with applause. Nothing like this had ever happened to us before, and the love and acceptance that welled up in that throng were overwhelming.

I celebrated my seventy-sixth birthday in an unusual way. Pat Snyder called to tell us that by chance the Museum of Natural History was screening *Silent Pioneers* that day, and the Museum program director, Malcolm Arth, had invited her to be present. She had asked if Bruhs and I could accompany her. Not until we were seated in the auditorium did she mention that the program director had requested that we speak to the audience after the screening. This perturbed me, since I could not measure the reaction of the audience in advance. It appeared to be "straight," predominantly middle-aged women. I was slightly apprehensive about whether they would accept a gay lifestyle presented by gay senior citizens. When we were introduced, there was a restrained ripple of applause, and I dreaded the questions because I feared "morality" would be the paramount issue with this group. Much to my surprise, none of the questions were so loaded. When Bruhs was asked how his family responded to his commitment to me, he repeated his ninety-year-old sister's remark, "I'm so proud of both of you!" There was spontaneous and prolonged applause; Bruhs had won the day. Many came up afterward to shake our hands and tell us how much our protrayal had touched them. A day from which I had expected only crumbs of tolerance had instead become a wonderful birthday gift— the joy of acceptance.

Shortly before, on October 10, we had been guests of SAGE at the Human Rights Campaign Fund dinner at the Waldorf-Astoria. Tommy Tune had given a donation of two thousand dollars to SAGE to cover a table for members. Lily Tomlin contributed her antic talent to the occasion. A posthumous award to Arthur Bell for his tireless work for gay rights was presented by Vito Russo.

On October 12, Amber Hollibaugh had come to our apartment on Third Avenue for an interview. She planned to do a documentary for NYC-TV about Greenwich Village and why it had become a mecca for gay people. She arranged to bring in her camera crew the following Monday to get interior shots and record some of our piano music. This developed into a four-hour session, but we were beginning to feel quite at ease in front of a camera. It was a special joy to work with Amber, a person we greatly admired for her outspoken support of gay rights. We were beginning to enjoy the opportunities for enlarging our work with SAGE.

A phone call from our ophthalmologist soon brought us back to earth. Bruhs had been under a doctor's care for ten years for glaucoma. He used eyedrop medication five times a day to stabilize the pressure in his eyes. Dr. Katzin had now made an appointment for a Yag laser procedure he felt would improve the movement of fluid in Bruhs's eyes. The laser is used to do an iridectomy, which provides a new outlet for fluid, relieving the abnormal sluggishness of the natural ducts. Although this is a surgical procedure, there is little bleeding, and recovery is practically overnight. Even though Bruhs had to hold perfectly still for the laser, the operation went smoothly. We were once again impressed by Dr. Katzin's skill. In Bruhs's case, unfortunately, the abnormality in the ducts persisted and the hoped-for stabilization did not occur. The doctor recommended a second try later. Our severe disappointment was the consequence of our high hopes. We stifled our misgivings and let ourselves be guided by Dr. Katzin.

Ken Dawson was always on the alert to attract new members to

SAGE, and he had a fund-raising party at Van Varner's apartment, to which he invited Bruhs and me. During the evening, I spoke of how great an impact SAGE had had on our lives. When I finished, I was startled to see Bruhs step up for an unaccompanied rendition of one of our songs. He took everyone by surprise and charmed the guests, which loosened several purse strings. Once again Bruhs won the evening.

At a SAGE social later that month we were introduced to a young man, George Chauncey, who explained that he was doing research for a book on gay life in New York City of the 1920s, 1930s, and 1940s and would appreciate an interview. We always enjoyed discussing with younger people our own fateful meeting, and the dissembling gay people had had to practice then.

As luck would have it, the day he came for the interview, we also had a visitor, Bert W., an older friend whom we had not seen since he moved to Florida. During our interview, Bert remained quiet, but when we finished, he began to regale George and us with some of his more bizarre sexual experiences. Although they were colorful and provocative, I have chosen to forget them. Oddly enough, however, the following three limericks he told us that day I remember word for word because of their vivid style and clever rhymes.

Claude, Claude, the cabin boy,
Pernicious little nipper,
Filled his ass
With broken glass
And circumcised the skipper.

Nymphomaniacal Alice
Used a dynamite stick for a phallus
And now her vagina
Is chuggin' in China
And her ass is in Buckingham Palace.

If that naughty old Sappho from Greece
Loved anything more than a piece
'Twas to have her pudenda
Rubbed off by the enda
The little pink nose of her niece.

Because George seemed fascinated by Bert's stories, I began to feel that he would probably give Bert's spicy anecdotes more space than our gentle and committed life story. But I worried needlessly, for when George Chauncey's book, *Gay New York*, was published in 1994, there was no mention of Bert and his escapades and Chauncey gave a detailed description of our life, and even mentioned the novel idea we had had of bringing lesbians and gay men together in our Nucleus Club.

Ken Dawson asked Bruhs and me to stand in for him at a Gay Press Association Conference, which had representatives from every gay periodical in the Northeast. It was part of his plan to give us publicity wherever there was an opportunity to do so. We were warmly received by the press, and the usual indifference of newspaper people was entirely missing. Their empathy encouraged us to talk freely and at length.

Emboldened, I decided to write a letter to NBC Entertainment President, Brandon Tartikoff, to express my concerns over cancellation of *Love, Sidney*, a sitcom starring Tony Randall. After discussing other NBC shows I had appreciated, I told Mr. Tartikoff:

> Losing *Love, Sidney* made me very unhappy. You see, I am a gay man, age 76, and the demise of Sidney Schorr was like losing a member of the family. I thought, at last there was a show about my life style done with dignity, and a person with my affectional preference presented as a human being. Too bad that such a noble experiment had to expire. It is to NBC's credit, however, that the subject has always been handled with sensitivity, as in Richard Jaeckle's performance as a gay detective in *Gimme A Break!* References to gay people in *Cheers* also have been made in a positive manner without denigration.
>
> As a recently uncloseted gay activist I am engaged in the struggle to educate the general public about the positive and stable aspects of gay life as opposed to the too-quickly accepted frivolous stereotypes. NBC's rational attitude in general is appreciated. It is to be hoped that in the future other writers will pick up on the topic and treat it honestly and without sensational overtones. This will make an enor-

mous contribution. We at SAGE are dedicated to the task of seeing that gay people receive no less than honest treatment in media coverage and appraisal by society in general.

Mr. Tartikoff failed to reply. Although one grows accustomed to indifference from network brass, I always hope to awaken a response.

On Christmas Eve, my sister, Marie, phoned; our brother was in the hospital. She reported that he was completely disoriented, and she was uncertain as to his future wellbeing.The holidays had always been celebrated in our home with an effort at yuletide cheer; I could tell by my sister's doleful tone that this year would be somber. Fighting back tears, I was witnessing one more chapter in the dissolution of the Harwood family. The hard facts of change and the ultimate acceptance of conditions one cannot alter pressed in upon me.

31

On the Gay Celebrity Circuit

Milton had given us tickets to the hit musical *My One and Only,* originally opened by Tommy Tune on Broadway. A member of the cast was our friend, Tiger Haynes, and we went backstage to tell him how much we had enjoyed his performance. He embraced us warmly and we went out of the theater together, chatting about old times when we had all worked together in our little Dance Gallery. That was the beginning of Tiger's career, and he had fond memories of those early years.

Also in 1985, arrangements were made for us to appear on the *Phil Donahue Show,* together with Ken Dawson, Ruby Juster, and William Wynkoop, all of SAGE, and from Boston, Buffy Dunker. We attended a briefing at Pat Snyder's apartment to cover the best responses to questions Donahue might ask. The meeting acclimated us to Donahue's staccato interrogation style.

The weather turned frigid, and the boiler in our building was out of order, which meant no heat. The morning of January 21, we were picked up by a limousine and taken to the NBC studios in Rockefeller Center; the warm studio was a relief after our cold apartment. Before the program, Donahue paid us a brief visit to assure us of his support and to ask us to disregard his sometimes gruff and inquisitive manner. He seemed affable in person and we were put more at ease.

That comfortable feeling evaporated shortly, though, for the program was barely under way when a young woman who had stood up to address a question to our panel slumped to the floor in a faint. Studio attendants immediately came to her aid, and she was taken out of the studio. The program went to a commercial, which gave us a brief chance to settle down. I looked at Bruhs and remarked, "I think the fainting was prearranged. Someone wants to disrupt this show because it's giving gay people a chance to be heard on national television." Bruhs nodded in agreement. The show had progressed only moments further when it happened again. This time a man slumped to the floor and had to be carried out by attendants. By this time most of the panel felt there was some kind of put-up job to discredit gay spokespeople. Donahue himself must have suspected foul play, but he treated the incidents as genuine and apologized to the audience for the disruption. He suggested that the change of temperature on entering the warm studio from the extreme cold outside might account for the fainting. But those most affected should have been the panelists under hot lights, and since none of us were experiencing any problems, we agreed that the faintings had to be contrived. Anger and resentment welled up in me, and my morale was devastated. I was completely unstrung and had no idea what questions were asked of me or how I replied.

Another fainting occurred each time the show resumed, but never during a commercial break. Finally, in desperation Donahue ordered the studio cleared, and we finished the show without an audience. To his credit, Donahue remained fully in control of what must have been a trying session for him. Whatever point our appearance might have made was lost in all the confusion, and I felt our golden opportunity to be on this nationwide program had been ruined. He also explained that the show was carried live out of town but was taped for later showing in New York City. Donahue commiserated with us in the waiting room. As a salve to the bitter disappointment we all felt, he assured us that he would have us back at a later date.

The evening paper reported that, as we had suspected, an elaborate hoax had been perpetrated by a professional prankster named Martin Abel. He had organized a group called F.A.I.N.T. (Folks Against Inane Network Television) and had paid several unemployed actors to faint on cue to disrupt a well-publicized show chosen at random; the subject matter of the program had no bearing on their selection. We were relieved to learn that it was not antigay by intent, but it still could not diminish our disappointment over a wasted opportunity to show the public that gay people have ideas and interests unrelated to their sexual preference.

Returning home, we were met with a strange, dank odor and were horrified to see a veritable Niagara of hot water cascading down the living room walls. For a moment we just stared blankly at the water, then we dove for a pail and mop from the kitchen. But King Canute could not have held back the tide, and the two of us struggled with Herculean mopping and sopping for hours. Eventually we learned that the extreme cold had frozen and burst pipes on the sixth floor. When it had run its course, we surveyed the damage. The linen closet was totally saturated; every sheet and towel we owned oozed water. Nor was clothing spared. Worst of all, drawings of Bruhs when he was a dancer were ruined. The rugs were practically afloat and we seemed literally up a creek without a paddle! Toward nightfall there was a knock on the door—the superintendent with an insurance adjuster to handle claims. They promised to have the damage appraised the following day.

Fortunately our bed had ridden out the flood, and as we settled into it for some much-needed rest, Bruhs shook his head sadly and muttered, "How could so many bad things happen in one day?" To which I added: "To two nice people like us!"

The appraisal of damages took days. How does one put a price on irreplaceable works of art? We were adequately reimbursed for our material losses, but there was no remuneration for the hours of backbreaking labor and mental anguish we had undergone.

When we had finally dried out, we were ready to resume our lives. We were excited by a phone call from Philadelphia. Station KYW-TV offered us a one-hour interview on their program, *People Are Talking*. Metroliner tickets would be sent to us. Since the broadcast was scheduled for the morning, we were provided accommodations at Holiday Inn the night before.

The host of *People Are Talking* was the personable Richard Bey. We shared the platform with Gerry Faier from SAGE, and with Buffy Dunker, who had been with us on the ill-fated Donahue show. Members of the audience posed several loaded questions raising "moral" issues. Bible Belt influence was evident in the tone of a question directed to me, which implied that gay people were so morally corrupt they could not expect God's grace to be extended to them. I replied, "Even though you may not be comfortable with the thought, nevertheless I consider myself every bit as much a child of God as you, and He would never deny me His blessing." This question aside, the program went well. There were several healthy expressions of "live and let live," evidence that open-mindedness can flourish in spite of the choke weeds of bigotry.

After the broadcast we were interviewed by a lesbian from the *Philadelphia Gay News*. Her questions were pointed, well thought out, and delivered in a kindly way. She seemed amazed by the years we had had together, setting the tone for her article, with which we were enormously pleased.

Returning aboard the Metroliner, I noticed that Bruhs had a hemorrhage in his left eye, probably related to stress and glaucoma. I thought it should be checked out with Dr. Katzin as soon as possible. His examination revealed little more than that the capillaries were fragile and susceptible to hemorrhaging. The doctor felt, however, that a repeat of the laser procedure would be advisable.

On previous occasions Bruhs had had only minimal discomfort from the laser. But this time he experienced severe pain in his eye, accompanied by nausea. It was a rough night for both of us. At the doctor's office the following morning, the nausea finally erupted into violent and spasmodic retching. The nurses scurried about trying to make him more comfortable. The doctor realized that Bruhs was having an acute glaucoma attack and, after administering medication, instructed me to put drops in Bruhs's eyes every five minutes to bring the pressure down. After a time the retching subsided, and Bruhs was able to lie down and rest. I continued applying the eyedrops for an hour or more. When Dr. Katzin tested the pressure, it had dropped to 28, still higher than it should have been, but the doctor assured us the attack had been caught in time, and with frequent use of the eyedrops, it would stabilize.

The nausea persisted for two days, but by faithfully administering the eyedrops I hoped we were making progress. At the doctor's again on Monday, the pressure was still at 28. Diligent use of the drops had at least held it at that figure, but we were told that the drops would probably eventually bring the pressure down to a more acceptable level. The experience had been scary, but Dr. Katzin's calm and efficiency did much to relieve our anxiety.

I began to feel symptoms of a hernia, confirmed by my family doctor at HIP. A HIP surgeon booked me for an operation at the Cabrini Hospital, just around the corner from where we lived. But having to be hospitalized for several days concerned me, since Bruhs would have to fend for himself while I was away.

The operation was routine. But an irregular heartbeat kept me in the recovery room for seven hours. Bruhs, waiting in my room, was expecting me any moment and became agitated. He started questioning anyone he could collar for information about me. It didn't help him to learn that I was still in the recovery room and that when I would be returned was uncertain. By the time I was brought back to the room, he was beside himself with worry. Even in my groggy state, I could see how upset he was and tried to calm him down. Little by little, he relaxed and told me some of his fears and concerns.

Bruhs was with me all three days I spent in the hospital, and I had several visits from friends at SAGE. My main concern was Bruhs's anxiety at every turn of events. I had to realize eventually that his extreme agitation was symptomatic of the dementia gradually usurping his ability to cope with unexpected emergencies.

Bruhs's memory failure was an ever-increasing concern. I had heard people speak favorably of hypnotherapy and felt it might be helpful. I sent questionnaires to several practitioners and decided on someone I hoped would be the right person for Bruhs. I have no idea whether we selected the best of the several methods used, but Bruhs, for whatever reasons, did not seem amenable to the treatment, and after several ineffectual sessions we abandoned it.

We were introduced to forty representatives of the International Gerontology Conference who were touring the SAGE office and had been shown a version of *Silent Pioneers*. Two young women from Sweden and Denmark earnestly discussed with us the overall impact of the film. The English and Australian representatives gave us invitations to visit them, and we received compliments from the Spanish and Italian members of the group.

To reach as many people as possible with her film, Pat Snyder arranged to show *Silent Pioneers* at schools and libraries. We were asked to appear with the film at Jefferson Market Library in Greenwich Village, together with the film's director, Lucy Winer, to take questions from the audience. The mixed group was enthusiastic and full of questions. Pat Snyder stayed with us for a short while but had to leave early. Pat had a teaching assignment in Barcelona and that evening there was a big farewell party for her and her husband, which we were also attending, at 5 P.M. at Studio 54, the most popular disco of the day.

So much had been happening, and so fast, we had to stop long enough for a deep breath. Up to now in our lives we had been closeted, quiet people. Everything seemed to conspire to bring us more and more into the spotlight.

A Hunter College panel on aging included a screening of *Silent Pioneers* and numerous workshops on gay elders. In the workshop we attended, we met Benay Phillips, administrator of a nursing home in Queens. Not gay herself, she exhibited great sensitivity to the problems of elderly gay people. At the conclusion of the workshop she approached us to shake our hands. "It's a pleasure to meet you two," she said. "I'm the administrator of the Madison-York Residence for Seniors. I'm sure we have gay residents. But they are fearful about disclosing their private lives. I feel it would help our communication to show them *Silent Pioneers*. I'll arrange to screen it, if you two will come to speak to the group afterwards." Her screening of *Silent Pioneers* was well attended. At first I could not determine what effect the film had had on the audience. They were unusually quiet and did not readily communicate their feelings. After a few remarks by the SAGE social worker Michele Schwartz, the floor was turned over to Bruhs and me for a question-and-answer session. Gradually the seniors' reticence evaporated, but their questions were halting and not self-revealing. Nevertheless, at the conclusion they came forward, one by one, to shake our hands and wish us well. I have no way of knowing from their questions how many of the residents were closeted gay people, but obviously something in our demeanor reached them, combined with the actions and events in the film. If it didn't strike a sympathetic chord in their emotional lives, at least it had a positive educational effect. Mrs. Phillips's note of thanks congratulated Bruhs and me on the durability of our relationship, adding that many heterosexual couples would give anything to enjoy what we had together.

June of 1985 was a milestone for us, when we were selected as grand marshals of the gay pride march. We attended the Gay Pride Week proclamation ceremony at City Hall and had our pictures taken with Mayor Koch. In addition, the *New York Native* invited us to a photo session at the Gay Community Center. They wanted pictures of representative gays for a special section to be devoted to Gay Pride Week.

All our activity culminated in the march. The sun shown brightly that Sunday morning, June 30, 1985. At the assembly point on Central Park West, television news reporters talked with us and took our pictures, which we were certain would never make the evening news. Our sense of purpose, our demeanor, and our appraisal of what we considered important topics seemed to fall largely on deaf ears. Almost without exception, the media people were single-minded about what they considered newsworthy material on gay people: their rule of thumb—unless it's bizarre, ignore it. Who among their readers or viewers gave a damn about two guys who had loved each other for fifty-five years? Perhaps if they appeared in drag for the picture!

This raises the question posed in an editorial by Candace Chellew in *The Advocate* of September 6, 1994, which has caused controversy over the appropriate boundaries of gay public behavior. Ms. Chellew makes some strong points; for example: "'Out' does not have to be synonymous with 'outrageous.' At a Gay Pride March, for example, gay people are on display. What image do we wish to project? Do too many groups of the grossly over-dressed or extremely under-dressed represent us? I think they do not. Bigots would love to have this image of decadence perpetuated in the media and we play into their hands by flamboyant behavior.

"Is this to say we should not celebrate our gayness on Gay Pride Day? Absolutely not! There is a time and a place to let ourselves go— a place where we do not limit our self-expression and our group humor. But that place is not in public areas like the streets, where we should be putting our best foot forward. Many 'performances' on Gay Pride Day are exercises in self-indulgent exhibitionism, and have little bearing on the development of a sense of gay community. Instead of awakening a feeling of oneness among us, we are extending the destructive process of separation."

But on June 30, 1985, there was equal indifference shown by reporters toward our co-grand marshals, May and Marion, together for thirty-eight years. Their story, too, lacked media buzz and was not what the reporters thought would interest their public. But we did not allow our cynicism about the media to dampen our enthusiasm, and we were proud to wear our purple sashes emblazoned with "Grand Marshal" in gold letters. As we were about to get into our car for the parade, we each received from Ed Murphy, the unofficial mayor of Greenwich Village, a medallion commemorating the Stonewall uprising of 1969. The Parade Committee had provided big signs for the side of the car giving our names and the number of years we had been together. This proved a revelation to people watching the march. All along the route across Central Park South and down Fifth Avenue, the watchers broke into shouts of approval. Many apparently recognized us from *Silent Pioneers* and called out greetings and congratulations. At the Public Library at 42nd Street, Mayor Koch joined the head of the march, but not before he came over and shook our hands with words of congratulation.

As the march turned at Washington Square to go west to Christopher Street, there must have been thousands of people. When they saw us, they shouted and screamed approval; the sound that enveloped us was totally overwhelming. If we had ever dreamed of being "men of the hour," we really lived it at that moment. By the time we arrived at West Street for the rally, we were tired. Wayne Steinman and Sal Iacullo kept a watchful eye on us. Overcome as we were by the day, we nevertheless came alive again when they brought Harvey Fierstein over to us and offered to take our picture together.

We stayed at the rally to hear what Harvey would say to the throng. With wit and style, Harvey recounted the many reasons to be proud to be gay. The gay community was indeed fortunate to have a man with his unique gifts always ready to do his best for every gay cause. Our friend Amber Hollibaugh was chosen to close the program—her fiery declaration of where we had been in 1969 and where we were now held the crowd to the very end of a long program. When she came down off the platform, we put our arms around her and hugged her, with tears in our eyes, holding each other silently.

Since we were in the Village, we chose Fedora's to finish off the day. Picking our way through crowds as we headed toward West 4th Street, we were greeted on every side. Young gay couples approached us to pose for pictures with them all the way to the restaurant door.

32

SAGE and the Book

A few days after the gay pride parade, we attended a party at our friend Milton Goldman's. He took me aside: "Gean, I've watched all the activities you've been in, and read many of your letters. I think you should consider doing a book about your lives. The gay community would really benefit from your commitment to each other and I'd be glad to help you get it published."

He felt deeply about the idea, and it was touching that he believed I could do it. I had managed letters to the editor, but a book was a whole new ball game. I was flattered, but also intimidated by the effort it would involve. Thanking Milton, I agreed to think it over. As we said good night, he again reminded me of our talk and said, "Let me hear from you, soon."

The seed was planted, and I could, in fact, think of nothing else. I had so much to tell. But how to start? I had kept notes in an abbreviated journal since 1971, but anything before that would have to be dredged up from memory. I wanted so much to do the thing; something in me clamored to do it. I set to work and, my thoughts rushing ahead, found the words to make a beginning.

In August of 1985, Bruhs began the arduous task of typing my handwritten pages. This was especially difficult as I print rather than write script, and I do it all in uppercase letters. This proved disconcerting, as Bruhs was never sure when to capitalize something. To speed the process, I sat with him and guided him through the difficulties.

Bruhs soon complained of severe dizziness. It became so disabling that we went to the HIP Emergency Center. The doctor was unable to determine the cause. He diagnosed the condition as vertigo and gave us a prescription to alleviate the symptoms. I realize now the dizziness was a forerunner of a more complex problem, a telltale sign of a possible stroke, but not recognized as such at the time.

The following day we learned that Bruhs's sister Anne had suffered a stroke and had been taken to University Hospital. When we got to see her, we found her vision and speech noticeably impaired and facial muscles affected. At the end of visiting hours we had to pocket our concern for Anne and fill an engagement at a Gay Friends and Neighbors meeting in upper Manhattan we had promised to address. Murray Kaufman was in charge of the entertainment, and the attendance—nearly one hundred—indicated he had given us a great deal of publicity. Mentioning the stressful events we both were experiencing, I took over the speaking. Bruhs joined me in singing some of our songs later in the evening, which went very well. Afterward men crowded around to shake our hands. Murray, elated by our appearance that evening, put us in a cab. He told us that members had declared this the best meeting they had ever had.

The following week we went to the WBAI Radio Station Studios for an interview with Craig Harris. Our account sketched in the years we had spent together, and spoke at length about SAGE and the changes it had brought to our lives. When the interview was aired two weeks later, SAGE was delighted to have two spokesmen helping to bring the organization to the public's attention.

Our attention was increasingly taken up by politics, centered on David Rothenberg's race for a seat on the New York City Council. He was the first openly gay candidate to run for this office. Highly qualified, he rose head and shoulders above the incumbent. But the gay community, which would have benefited enormously from having a gay man on the council, failed to give him unqualified support. The lack of gay enthusiasm for him shocked us, and when David lost the primary, we realized that the cause of gay rights had taken a beating at the hands of lethargic gays in a position to swing the vote to him. The loss of an opportunity to have an articulate spokesman for gay rights in city office rankled deeply. Mayor Koch was also campaigning for his third term, and we attended a fundraising affair at the Area disco. It gave us an opportunity to view this popular nightspot from the inside, but when we learned that the mayor had bowed to the dictates of the clubhouse and turned his back on David Rothenberg, we lost any interest we might have had in Koch's political campaign.

One of the first plays to deal with AIDS and its impact on gay men opened in May of 1985. *As Is* proved to be a beautifully written, superbly acted and directed piece. The author, William Hoffman, managed skillfully to etch the utter sense of futility that overwhelms the victims, and the agony of devastating changes that the disease forces on everyone caught in its grip. It took weeks for us to shake off the author's shattering picture.

We began to attend events focusing on AIDS. Our friend, George Worthington, got two seats for us at an AIDS benefit at the Metropolitan Opera House, coincidentally on my birthday. This was a milestone in entertainment, to which a panorama of stars of the theatrical world contributed their talents to benefit AIDS.

Only two days later we were invited by SAGE to meet Lily Tomlin after her one-woman show, *The Search for Signs of Intelligent Life in the Universe*. She greeted us like old friends and so disarmed us that I was unable to tell her how closely we had followed her career. No matter how much she put us at ease I became more speechless by the minute, and I tried to compensate by nodding and smiling. I finally stuttered and stammered a few words, deplorable clichés, so that night I wrote her a letter to say all I had wanted to say in person.

The documentary that Amber Hollibaugh had filmed earlier in our apartment was finally aired on NYC Channel 31 in November 1985. *Neighborhood Voices* dealt with the feeling of community that Greenwich Village evoked in gay people. In two of the sequences Bruhs and I talked about our lives together and the special meaning the Village had for us. The film had many poignant passages by four articulate lesbians, who included Audrey Lourde, Sonny Wainwright, and Joan Nestle. The account of passionate loves, creative drives, discriminatory insults, and an overwhelming will to survive fostered by their association with the Village was deeply moving. A warm and vital portrait of gay life emerged from Amber's skillful hands.

That same month, I made the acquaintance of Arlene Kochman, a newcomer to the staff at SAGE. Her skills in social service were being tested in outreach assignments. We accompanied her to a class of Aging in America, Inc. The school was in the Bronx and was hard to find. Unfortunately we knew less about the Bronx than Arlene so we were not much help. When we finally found the school, our presentation followed our pattern. After *Silent Pioneers* Arlene spoke about SAGE to the students, all of them young people interested in geriatrics, then offered them the opportunity to ask questions of her and of us. Such meetings allowed us to exchange views with and relate to many outside our own sometimes insular gay community.

We had one more presentation for SAGE in December. We again accompanied Arlene this time to the Dorchester Senior Center in Brooklyn. Her usual presentation format was altered for the administrator of the Senior Center. This woman was closeted, fearful of disclosure, and chose not to show the film *Silent Pioneers*. Arlene bowed to her wishes. At the Senior Center, the only space available was the adjacent synagogue. But the Orthodox Jews who made up the audience looked upon us as interlopers, and we had entered a sanctified space without the proper covering on our heads. We could immediately sense the tension. Arlene was skillful, but her attempts were not well received by this hostile group. The women were quiet; the men, however, remained obdurate and belligerent, and when Arlene introduced us as a couple who had shared their lives for over fifty years, they fairly bristled with ill-concealed contempt. A man stood up, pointing an accusing finger at us, his voice trembling with rage, to literally spit out his words: "It doesn't make any difference how long you have been together if you have been living in sin! What you do is unnatural. It is an offense to even stand in this holy place and declare yourselves. Have you no shame?"

I certainly felt like Daniel in the lions' den. I was not at all prepared for this type of affront and visibly recoiled. Up to this point Bruhs had been listening quietly, but he rallied to our defense. His voice rang with conviction: "It is unfair to use the term *unnatural* as applied to us! What is 'natural' to you can be 'unnatural' to us! As for sin, who among us is without it? We are not ashamed of our love and we do not have to apologize to anyone for our lives! We have a clear conscience, and we know that God's love extends to us as fully as it does to every other living thing in His universe!"

As I took Bruhs's hand, I could feel him tremble with emotion, and I felt love and gratitude for his eloquent response. The vociferous man muttered something under his breath as he sat down. He seemed nonplussed by Bruhs's vehement retaliation. But before any further confrontations could arise, Arlene offered closing remarks. On the way back to Manhattan, Arlene expressed appreciation for our handling of an unpleasant experience.

In December 1985, Ed McCormack of the *Daily News* phoned to say he had seen the interview of us with Mike Morris on WPIX. He planned to interview two other straight couples for a special Valentine's Day piece. He felt our relationship deserved inclusion, and he asked us to meet him. I was floored: The thought of having our story in the *Daily News* was flabbergasting, and I began to visualize the slant a gay relationship would get in a conservative tabloid, but to my surprise they did a good job.

There was no more delightful way to round out the year than by attending the SAGE annual Christmas social in the parish house of St. John the Divine on Morningside Heights. The carved stone walls lent a special charm to the gathering, and the garlands of holiday greens with their brilliant red bows added warmth and color. They gave every gay person in the hall a sense of belonging in the glow of the occasion. This had been a memorable year for Bruhs and me, and we relished the satisfaction of an active role in the gay community. SAGE had truly changed our lives by giving us purpose, and I had embarked on the greatest creative endeavor of my life—my book.

33

Moving and Performing

In June of 1987 our living arrangements changed drastically. Bruhs's niece Jean told us of an apartment to be vacated in July at Seward Park Cooperative Village on the Lower East Side below Delancey, where we had been on a waiting list for a decade. Jean, who lived in the building, offered to help us obtain the vacant apartment. She persuaded the management that we were rightfully entitled to it, and we were finally offered the apartment. Because of his inability to grasp the situation, I couldn't confer with Bruhs, as I would have liked to, but had to make the decision on my own, and quickly.

Our present living arrangements were extremely vulnerable. Bruhs's health was rapidly deteriorating, and his future was a big question mark. He was the sole leaseholder on Third Avenue, so my tenure in that apartment could be terminated immediately if something happened to him—at that time there was no official recognition of a gay partner's right to keep a rented apartment unless he also was on the lease. Several gay and lesbian leaseholders in the city had adopted their partner to meet the narrow definition of "family" to insure the transfer of their premises if required. The runaway inflation in real estate in New York City made Seward Park seem the best alternative, and a property in both our names would improve my security.

But I did not sufficiently consider the effect of uprooting Bruhs from the familiar surroundings of Gramercy Park. In our twenty-three years of living there, this neighborhood had become thoroughly familiar to him. The psychiatrist at Bellevue was quick to point this out to me and frowned on radical changes of any sort as complicating Bruhs's treatment. I was on the horns of a dilemma. But a decision had to be made, and I opted for Seward Park. I later regretted my decision for several reasons. We had had no difficulty in adjusting to the ethnic makeup in neighborhoods into which we had moved in the past, but this move caused Bruhs to suffer complete disorientation. From the day we moved to the Lower East Side, Bruhs was perplexed even by the route the bus took to reach our house. He got no reassurance at all from my explaining that we must go downtown to reach our new home, some thirty blocks south of our old apartment on Third Avenue.

On the advice of Bruhs's niece we had listed ourselves as "stepbrothers" on the original application in 1977. Jean felt a "family" relationship would have greater influence than "friend" in obtaining an apartment. In any event, we continued with this fiction in signing for the apartment and in speaking with a few apartment neighbors. This was fortunate, for we discovered that the first five floors were occupied by Orthodox Jews who, to our dismay, were for the most part intensely "family oriented" and in any case unfriendly to any non-Orthodox "outsiders." In fact, they viewed every non-Orthodox person as an interloper. Our posing as "brothers" was some protection in an essentially hostile environment. However, this ethnic concentration created a problem for me, and my resentment mounted at this need for pretense; we were retreating back into the "closet."

To notify the Third Avenue landlord of our intentions, our lawyer, Richard Feldman, dictated a letter releasing us from the remaining three months on the lease and allowing us to use our security deposit to cover the last month's rent. There were no problems, since the insider's price of $40,000 had escalated to $150,000, and the apartment's owners were delighted to have the property available for sale.

The move now looming began to overwhelm me: I would have to handle all the details. Bruhs would be unable to cope with any of the arrangements and problems. Luckily, Eugene Weirsman, a nephew of Jean and Jack Shulman's, was a furniture mover. I would be physically unable to do the packing, so regardless of cost, I contracted for the professional service of Eugene's woman associate, an excellent packer.

Bruhs's niece Jean had gotten a key to the new apartment so we could examine it more closely before the move and make a sketchy plan for placing the furniture. The layout included a comfortably large living room, a kitchen that could accommodate a table and chairs, and an adequate bedroom and bath. Venetian blinds had been left on all the windows by the former tenant. There was even a usable telephone. Jean made a list of things in the apartment that were not to be removed. She carefully documented all the repairs needed. With years of dealing with the co-op's maintenance staff, she felt she had prepared us for as smooth a transition as possible. Without her guidance, I would have been totally lost in dealing with a new bureaucracy.

Our packer, Perdue, began dismantling and putting things into boxes. Our friends Vicki and Esther asked to buy our record collection, from which I kept only a few items. They also helped me sell a guitar I had given to Bruhs but which he had never used, as well as a vintage Polaroid camera and a Wollensak tape recorder that, in its day, had been state of the art. Our new SAGE Friendly Visitor, Andy Watson, located a place that would accept our excess books. I tried to reduce in every way possible the things that would have to be packed. Even so, we ended up with fifty cartons. The excitement of packing, plus the trauma of giving up the home we had shared for twenty-three years, did have a profoundly disturbing effect on Bruhs. He wandered about the place aimlessly, wanting to be a part of the work, but totally unable to coordinate his efforts with any success. Fortunately, the mover had recommended doing it in two installments, keeping a bed to sleep on at Third Avenue while we set up living and sleeping arrangements at the new apartment.

A few days before the move I visited the apartment to see how things were going. I discovered that while the place had been freshly painted, the venetian blinds had disappeared, along with the telephone. I paid a workman in advance to cover the concrete closet floors with parquet flooring, which was in place but not finished with moldings as promised. I learned my lesson—not to pay for work in advance. Less than half of Jean's careful cataloging of needed repairs had been done. The maintenance manager's only comment was that it was not co-op policy to furnish venetian blinds, and that if they were taken, he had no way to trace them. As for the phone, he would try to find one, but management had no obligation to replace stolen property.

Seeing little likelihood of getting redress, I tried to shrug it off. In the welter of things not done I was agreeably surprised to see how clean the apartment was. The living room and bedroom floors had been gone over and the kitchen and bathroom washed. I credited maintenance with doing something right, until I learned that Jean had been so horrified by the condition of the place she had hired someone to clean it up for us. I had to conclude that Seward Park maintenance left much to be desired, in efficiency, thoroughness, capability, and agreeableness. It was a blessing to have Jean's thoughtful and loving assistance to smooth out some of the rough spots.

Perdue had been diligently packing at Third Avenue, and the first load was ready on August 25. That same day new locks were installed, with only minor frustration. Three days later we made the second and final move and set up residence in our new home. Jean helped me locate used venetian blinds, and they were in place to provide some privacy for our first night in the new apartment. Near total collapse, with packing boxes piled high about us, we tumbled into bed. For a few hours, at least, we could forget about unpacking and settling in. For now it was enough to know that we were in our new home, for better or for worse. We had a roof over our heads that we could call "ours," and best of all, we had each other.

The apartment was plagued with problems. If I used both ceiling lights in the kitchen at the same time, they invariably blew a fuse. I was never able to get the control lever on the circuit breaker to stay in place. This meant relying on the maintenance crew, but the power outage always seemed to occur late at night, so it was next to impossible to get them until the next day; we often spent the night with no lights at all. Toilet flushing required repeated flushings; from time to time maintenance used a plumber's snake, with indifferent results. Finally, through SAGE, I hired Herbert Hoeger, a versatile jack-of-all-trades, to do the repairs; he made a simple adjustment inside the toilet tank to correct that problem. So much for the expertise of Seward Park maintenance!

It was painful adjusting to life on the Lower East Side—vastly different from that on Third Avenue and 18th Street. Like Bruhs, I felt lost in the new neighborhood and despaired of ever getting acclimated to it. I listened wistfully to the commercial on radio and TV, "Please, Mr. D'Agostino, move closer to me." I always seemed to forget that shops would be closed up tight on Saturdays due to the Jewish Sabbath. I longed for my familiar choice of grocery stores— Sloan's, Food Emporium, Pioneer—and the weekly specials. I had known my way around those stores, where to find what I wanted. The Pathmark supermarket was too far to be of practical use.

However, a large, well-stocked supermarket in our block was operated by the Park Village Co-Op; while prices were often higher than at other stores, their weekly specials evened things out a bit.

It took weeks to unpack the fifty boxes, and Bruhs chafed under the delays, largely due to my inability to find places for the contents. I had planned in advance where the furniture would go, so that was no problem. SAGE sent Jerry Lepow, who skillfully hung pictures and did all sorts of odd jobs. One task, however, was quite difficult—securing a four-foot circular mirror to the wall. We had acquired the mirror back in 1935 when we lived at 66 Fifth Avenue. In each home since, Bruhs had always been able to attach it to the wall, but he could no longer handle such a complicated task. Bruhs's nephew Jack came to our rescue by carefully measuring the wall and getting a friend, an engineer, to do the drilling and hanging. Ironically, Bruhs was able to give the final touch by guiding the hook on the mirror's back into the pin attached to the wall. His sense of accuracy was not lost and he knew he had helped hang the mirror. We all breathed a sigh of relief when it was securely in place.

But I could not overlook the cold fact that Bruhs's condition was worsening. In spite of the good intentions of our family doctor and the psychiatrist at Bellevue, he was losing ground daily. The psychiatrist had prescribed a drug call Haldol for Bruhs. I was skeptical of this drug from the start, but I waited to see exactly what the effects would be. I soon discovered that the drug was inducing hallucinations: Bruhs would wake up during the night blowing at the air. When I asked why he was doing this, he was surprised I couldn't see clouds of dust around the bed. The drug had not reduced his anxiety and I had to request that the doctor discontinue it. The psychiatric methods being used at Bellevue were quite orthodox, so I began to search for alternatives. I felt there must be a system of care that would ultimately furnish some hope.

In the meantime, I tried every social diversion I could manage. Bruhs was by nature gregarious, and social contact did help. With others around he visibly brightened, losing the moribund expression he wore when we were alone, and he became affable and communicative. Therefore, I accepted every opportunity for him to mingle with other people. We participated in another Orientation Group meeting at the Gay Community Center, and the usual warm reception was a tonic for both of us. We were guests at a dinner in the Hotel Roosevelt sponsored by Parents and Friends of Lesbians and

Gays; this was our introduction to P-Flag, a group that has done a remarkable job easing the strain when gays declare their sexual preference—"come out"—to their parents. Present that day also were our friends Wayne and Sal and their newly adopted little girl, Hope. Another of the guests was New York City councilmember Ruth Messinger, who remembered our appearing at the gay rights bill hearing and embraced both of us.

Late in October we attended a gala farewell party at the Saint: Ken Dawson was finally resigning as executive director of SAGE after years of service. The Saint, a psychedelic disco catering to gay people, was a fascinating place, with several levels—the dance floor was way up under the roof, a phantasmagoria of multicolored flashing lights and incessant musical rhythms; it was a little scary for us. The floor was filled with twisting couples gyrating to the savage beat. Given our quieter approach to dance, I couldn't see us becoming a part of this frantic throng, and Bruhs was bewildered. So we watched from the sidelines, then retired to the lower level and the relative quiet of the area around the bar where we found many friends from SAGE, including our Friendly Visitor, Tom Keith, a good friend and talented young actor/playwright.

34

Old Friends and New

Nineteen eighty-eight got off to a good start with a party of Friendly Visitors at Kelly's, a pleasant Village bar. Arlene Kochman had started bringing together the Friendly Visitors with the "Friends at Home"—the way SAGE describes the clients they serve—for a warmly sociable afternoon. We had lunch with drinks and chatted with old friends and new people. René Ferraris, whom I had introduced to SAGE, was there. We had met in 1927, as I already recounted, but over the years our paths had crossed less and less.

Another SAGE-assisted Friend at Home was Howard Sosnicki, a friend since the 1930s. The death of his partner, Grant, in 1978 left him with a great emptiness, complicated by the onset of Parkinson's Disease. I introduced Howard to SAGE and SAGE stepped in to give him support. SAGE members showed him he was not alone and that the quality of his life could improve, further proof of the value of SAGE's ministrations.

In 1988, a warm and empathetic young woman, Ruth Gonsky, began visiting us. She had learned of us through Chris Almvig, from whom she was taking a course on social relationships and aging at the New School for Social Research. Ruth was writing a paper using material from her visits with us. From the start, Bruhs, in particular, responded to her personality and her uncanny perceptiveness. A relative of hers had a condition similar to Bruhs's and she dealt with his moods well. Sometimes a spontaneous embrace proved the most effective way to meet the problem of the moment.

Ruth interviewed and observed us for nine weeks, during which time we met her partner, Hilda. The two women were quite different in temperament, but their personalities complemented each other, and they made an attractive pair. They became like family for us.

One evening we had dinner with them at their home in Brooklyn. The rooms reflected the warmth of the owners, with a comfortable, lived-in quality. We met the rest of their family, two wonderful cats and a cocker spaniel named Honey. The women served dinner on a patio in front of the building, and it was a delightful change to dine alfresco in the balmy Brooklyn night. A gentle breeze stirred the overhanging trees, and the air was so clear we could actually glimpse the stars. So removed from the city hurly-burly, it seemed another world, and we soaked up as much as we could before going back to the canyons of Manhattan.

SAGE had asked us to perform some of our songs at a social. Even though impromptu performances at other places had gone well, I had always declined doing performances at a social because of uncertainty as to how Bruhs would react under the pressure of a performance there. I had also noticed how inattentive the social's audience was when others performed. As I frankly told the Entertainment Committee, I was too attached to our material to waste it on an unappreciative group. But they assured me an appearance by Bruhs and Gean would be enjoyed so much they could guarantee the undivided attention of the audience. Our performance would be recorded by a video camera and we would receive a cassette of the event. This persuaded me.

The performance went surprisingly well. At the beginning I warned the audience they had better pay attention because there would be a quiz at the program's end. We hoped, we told them, that our songs of the 1930s would strike a responsive chord. The audience gave us rapt attention throughout and warm applause at the end. One gentleman sought us out later and, after announcing that he was ninety, paid us a lovely compliment: "I enjoyed your songs so much! They reminded me of Noël Coward. I knew him, and Noël would have been delighted to hear your songs!" Thanking him, I turned to hear my name called by another man, who smiled and opened his arms. It was my therapist of the 1950s, Dr. Boles, whom I had not seen for years. He praised our work and introduced his partner of many years. Dr. Boles was a member of SAGE and had followed our career with interest. That day at the SAGE social, which I had dreaded, proved an unqualified success.

Later in the month Bruhs and I spoke to a group of gay, lesbian, and bisexual youth. We were startled by the turnout, easily eighty young people in their teens and early twenties. They were fully attentive and at the conclusion plied us with thoughtful and provocative questions. One young woman inquired, "What do you think of gay men or women raising a family? I love children and I would like being a parent."

"Here's a simple answer to a complex question," I said. "My personal feelings have always been against having children. I love children, too, as long as they are someone else's. However, if a gay man or woman, living alone or with a partner, feels that life is incomplete without a child and is ready to bear the responsibilities involved, by all means do have one."

A young man with a twinkle in his eye posed a query: "I'm a natural-born flirt. If I'm ever lucky enough to find a steady lover, how can I make the relationship work if I'm drawn to every cute guy I see?"

I smiled and replied, "When you're young, it's normal to have a roving eye. But you're not going to be young forever, and it's a good idea to look down the road and visualize being alone in those later years. If you do find someone with whom you share a community of ideas and goals, you will curb your enthusiasm for every cute guy you see and settle for the stability and comfort only a lasting relationship can bring. Of course you can look at other guys! But keep your priorities and don't bring pain to your partner by playing around. It takes patience and a willingness to compromise to make a relationship work—but it's worth it! Believe me, you're speaking to a guy who knows!"

The bulk of the questions I had to handle myself, aside from sporadic interjections from Bruhs, which usually fell short of the mark. I was impressed by the quality of these young people's inquiries and left with a greatly altered opinion of gay youth. The younger generation has by far a better knowledge of themselves and keener awareness than most of us imagine. The event was a discovery for me as much as for them, and we seemed to bridge the gulf of age with a new measure of respect for each other.

35

Irreparable Ruptures

In April of 1988 SAGE held a spectacular tenth anniversary party in Radio City Music Hall. The great hall was dark; SAGE took over the promenade and mezzanine. Banquet tables laden with floral displays and sparkling goblets on snowy linen filled the lower floor, and the eye traveled up the majestic staircase to the mezzanine where cocktails were served to a milling throng. Shortly after our arrival we were greeted by Ron Alexander of the *New York Times* and posed for a picture. He heard our account of attending the original opening of Radio City Music Hall in the mid-1930s and included it in the article with our pictures in the *Times* the next morning.

At the dining table, we barely noticed how attentive our waiter was. We only sipped our wine, but the glasses were constantly being refilled. I was totally unmindful of the amount of wine we were consuming. We were literally feeling no pain and relished the ravishing singing of Margaret Whiting, enhanced by Peter Howard's accompaniment. When it was time to leave, we felt almost numb and made the trip home in a haze.

A bitter aftermath to our evening of enjoyment, two days later Bruhs suffered a slight stroke. It affected his right upper lip, and his speech became slurred. I thought back to the wine we had consumed at the SAGE party and felt instant guilt. I took Bruhs to a local doctor, but he made light of the wine as a contributing factor. Generally dissatisfied with the doctor's examination, however, and after a talk with Bruhs's niece Jean, we decided a neurologist would give us more reliable information. She recommended Dr. Harold Weinberg. Two days later he did some testing in his office to see if there was brain damage and proposed that we have a more definitive diagnosis from an MRI. This pointed to a succession of slight strokes over time with damage to cells on the right and left sides of the brain. There was no prescribed treatment for the condition, but precautions against recurrence included careful monitoring of blood pressure and abstaining from alcohol in any form. I felt a distinct twinge of guilt at this admonition about alcohol, but since the damage had been done, we had to work toward prevention. The slight droop of Bruhs's lip eventually disappeared, and I made it a point to faithfully follow the regimen of one aspirin a day—and no alcohol!

We attended Ruth Gonsky's final class at the New School, at which she had offered to show *Silent Pioneers*. I could not judge whether Ruth's classmates were gay, but they all enthusiastically endorsed the film. We talked informally after the screening, and although some of the students were more vocal in their support than others, we had evoked a positive reaction from all of them. A week later, Ruth came for her last weekly visit and we were saddened at losing her presence in our household.

A few days later we had a call from Barbara Zellman, a therapist working out of the SAGE office, who had proposed some sessions with us. Her plan was to see us together at first and eventually work into individual sessions. The idea seemed constructive but did not work out well. As long as we were together, Bruhs managed to bring out his thoughts, haltingly at first, but more assuredly as he progressed. After his recurrent phrase of how long we had been partners, Barbara elicited some idea of the extent of his confusion.

Barbara did try one session with me alone. I arranged to leave Bruhs in the SAGE Drop-In Center and thought he would be sufficiently occupied by other people he knew. After a short time, however, he felt abandoned and became agitated. Barbara and I were so engrossed in discussing the problems I was experiencing we lost track of the time until there was a knock on the door. One of the men from the Drop-In Center stood in the doorway with a worried look on his face. He apologized for the interruption but said we must come down and speak with Bruhs because he was in such a state that they didn't know what to do. When I got to Bruhs I was appalled to see that he had experienced total panic and realized that separate sessions were impossible. It also established that Bruhs looked on me as an anchor, his link to reality. Without me in sight, his insecurity multiplied and he lost all sense of where he was. Frightened, he simply could not cope.

Even daily living raised problems. On the advice of an orthopedist, I had purchased a trundle bed with two ultrafirm mattresses.
The doctor felt this would alleviate Bruhs' back pain which caused
him to toss and turn. I looked forward to the improvement our
sleeping in separate beds would provide, but the moment the bed
came into the house, Bruhs loathed it. He refused to even try it and
it took months of persuasion to get him to use it. Two years later, he
was finally resigned to the new bed, but still cursed it daily. In his
mind the switch from a double bed to separate ones was equivalent to
our separation.

We had two final flings at public appearances in 1989. In March
David Collier offered us a spot in his documentary, *For Better or For
Worse*. A day of shooting in the house included scenes of us shaving
and having breakfast. A session at the piano brought out several of
our songs, and Pat Snyder, building on her earlier work with us in
Silent Pioneers, did an in-depth interview. David got some intriguing
footage of us on Times Square, at the Brooklyn Bridge, and in the
Bellevue music therapy sessions. He later took shots of Bruhs in his
nursing home. As a director, David's sensitivity made him easy to
work with. The finished production aired on PBS in 1991 and won
an Academy Award nomination.

We had been promised a return engagement on the Donahue
show after the 1985 fiasco created by Martin Abel and his F.A.I.N.T.
participants. With help from SAGE, the program's producers, two
young women in their thirties, rounded out a panel consisting of
Buffy Dunker, the articulate seventy-year-old Boston lesbian; Ruby
Juster, activist and SAGE Board of Directors member; Barbara
Emmerth, the executive director of SAGE; William Wynkoop and
Roy Strickland, partners for forty years; and myself. When the
producers spoke with me about having Bruhs on the panel, I
advised against it given the unreliability of his responses. I did ask to
have him in the audience and I arranged for Yvonne McDonald,
with whom he felt comfortable, to sit with him.

At the studio, in October, we were disconcerted by two additional
men flown in from Denver, who had no connection with SAGE and
were not partners. One was sixty-two, the other thirty-five. The
producers appeared to fear that it would be a dull show with so many
oldsters so they had augmented the original group. But they
overlooked the topic, which was older gays and their relationships.

Put off by this intrusion of "outsiders," on the air I had little to say beyond underlining the sense of commitment I felt to Bruhs. I pointed out that caring for one's partner with Alzheimer's called for patience, and his tendency to talk back had to be ignored. I remarked that I had to apply to myself Archie Bunker's admonishment to his wife, Edith, to "stifle yourself." Unfortunately, most of the audience apparently had no memory of the Archie Bunker program, *All in the Family.*

One woman in the audience gave us a touching tribute. But another crassly inquired, "When they are so old, what do they *do?*" Others were titillated by the younger Denver man's disclosure that he was bisexual, further evidence that he did not belong on the panel, adding to my discomfort. However, the camera did pick out Bruhs several times during the show, and at one point juxtaposed his image with mine so the audience was aware of our relationship. One hopes exposure of this kind does good things for SAGE, but overall it was less than rewarding for me. I felt I had gone out with a whimper instead of a bang.

Bruhs's deepening dementia was casting a dark and difficult shadow on our lives. Our day often started at 5:30 A.M. when Bruhs awakened ready to begin the day. He could sometimes be persuaded to return to bed to get some more sleep, and having retired the previous night at 1 A.M., I badly needed it. His demeanor and attitude were particularly bad in the morning. On awakening his first words were "God damned son of a bitch!"

I would try to ignore this and other four-letter words that were invading his vocabulary. If I stayed in bed pretending to sleep, I would hear him go into the bathroom and start to wail. When I went to him he would often be on his knees, saying over and over, "O, God, please help me!" This piteous entreaty to the Almighty, repeated again and again, was totally unnerving. I would hold him in my arms and try to reassure him: "God loves you...and He and I will take care of you."

I tried to postpone as long as possible dressing him, the task I most dreaded. He was only dimly aware of the time of day, and the need to dress or undress always mystified and distressed him. He impatiently asked the same question over and over: "Why do I have to do this?" Like a two-year-old, he was never satisfied with the explanation that he had to put clothes on to go out in the street. He put up the same stony resistance every day.

In the morning the trundle bed had to be rolled back in place, and the blankets and pillows put on the closet shelf. At first Bruhs tried to help but his obsessive neatness became too time-consuming. Something that should have taken at most ten minutes, stretched out to thirty, and finally to save time I took over the task myself.

After I had prepared and fed him breakfast, he had to take nutrient supplements and medications. As I started to give them to him, he would look martyred and pathetic. He would take a pill in his mouth and turn it over and over on his tongue, and I practically had to stand on my head to get him to swallow it. This performance was played out three times a day, and I had to muster every bit of patience I could command to get through it without screaming.

His attention span was about five minutes. He could not concentrate on reading, and he had only momentary interest in TV. This left a very long day to fill with almost nothing to provide diversion. A daily trip to the grocery store or the post office would get us outside, but he had great difficulty walking, so we were severely limited as to how far we could go. A pleasant little park was in back of our building, with flowers, shrubs, and shade trees. I would take him there for a change in activity, but after five minutes of sitting he would become restless and fidgety and insist that we move on.

The high spot of the day for both of us became the hour we spent playing and singing our songs. Time was magically rolled back to brighter, happier days. Bruhs used cue sheets and, except for occasional substitutions of words, did a fine job. The doctor explained to me that songs, both lyrics and melody, are recorded in a part of the brain that is seemingly untouched by the disabling dementia, so we made the most of this in our daily routine.

Each Thursday, we attended an hour-long session called Creative Therapy for Seniors at Bellevue. Since Bruhs shared this with me, there was no trauma associated with separation. The group was initially conducted by a music therapist, but when she left Bellevue, our group was going to be disbanded. We had become so attached to each other we felt like family, and at the urging of others in the group I wrote to Dr. Michael Friedman, the Geriatric Clinic director, to ask him to continue our sessions. My letter was successful and aided by Dr. Thomas McRae and our effective social worker, Marilyn Graubert, a new group instructor, Peg Van Brunt, was assigned. Her imaginative approach and enchanting personality widened the scope of activities beyond music. However, the ten-minute exercise period, part of the previous group activity, now had no leader. I offered my services, as I had often taken charge of it for the music therapist. After due observation by the nursing staff, I was deemed qualified.

The other bright spot in our otherwise circumscribed existence was the social given by SAGE once each month. This was a get-together with friendly acquaintances for four pleasant hours. Bruhs loved to dance, and miraculously the aches and pains he experienced in walking disappeared completely on the dance floor. The atmosphere was warm and congenial, an oasis where we could forget the arid desert that otherwise surrounded us daily.

Other nuisances such as shaving and bathing had to be gotten through, and I was always relieved when they had been accomplished. Of course bedtime presented a continuation of the resistance offered earlier in the day. When I watched a little TV for diversion, Bruhs took his only escape—namely, to sleep. Unfortunately, that napping detracted from his regular night sleep and I needed mine desperately. Even if I started getting us ready for bed at 11 P.M. we never got to sleep until one in the morning. It took monumental cajolery to get his clothes off and pajamas on, and to complete his toiletries. I was so exhausted after the evening meal and cleaning up that I frequently dozed off myself and missed the conclusion of the program I was trying to watch. Often after preparing our beds and finally lying down at 1 A.M., I would awake an hour later to discover that Bruhs had not been in bed at all! He spent endless time in the bathroom and was fascinated by taking pieces of toilet paper off the roll, folding them, and placing them in neat little piles. He never explained why he felt compelled to do this. Sometimes I was hard-pressed to replenish the roll, as it seemed to disappear overnight.

Often in the morning or late at night, utter despair would seize Bruhs, and he seemed overcome by conditions beyond his control. Words, lucid and intense, torn out of his inner being, would take shape, and he would cry out, "I'm just going down there! I'll throw myself out the window and go to hell! No one wants me anymore, and everything will be all right for you!"

At times like this my despair almost matched his. I was so perplexed I did not know how to answer, or what to do. Tenderness had no effect whatsoever. As an alternative, I adopted a disciplinary tone. So I usually said, "Jumping out a window is no answer. You might just break your legs, and then you would be in a wheelchair.

You don't want that, do you?" Of course, I realized that any attempt at logic was fruitless, but I had to say something. Sadly, during these episodes there was little that I could do or say to alleviate his distress. I simply had to wait for his anxiety and anger to subside.

I struggled to maintain equilibrium in the face of his desperate outcries or a thousand other disturbing or irritating circumstances. In spite of my own sense of inadequacy, I knew the overpowering frustration that must be consuming Bruhs.

I could not bring myself to consider placing him in an institution. As long as he continued to know me and remember our relationship, I could not consign him to the callous uncertainties of institutional care.

Despite all the bizarre and unpredictable behavior he exhibited in his dementia, at unexpected moments he was almost himself. With tears in his eyes, would turn to me and say tenderly, "I love you. I would never do anything to hurt you."

Most of the time, however, I represented the enemy and the relationship was of captive to captor as he rebelled against the untold discomforts of dressing, undressing, and taking his pills. I asked for divine guidance daily, and I was comforted by the belief that no matter how disabling the dementia can be to the mind, the spirit suffers no impairment. Deep within me I knew that this spirit of the man I loved would someday be free and soar above this transitory misery that held us both captive, and on that day we would resume our journey as full partners. This, together with my firm belief in God's love, enabled me to continue.

These burdens were eased somewhat by other events in 1989. Arlene Kochman assigned another young man to us, Thomas Keith, to act as a Friendly Visitor. From our very first meeting we felt an strong empathy. Something in his calm and outgoing personality had a salutary effect on Bruhs. As we learned more about Tom, his interest in the theater as an actor and playwright, and his avid devotion to all forms of poetry and prose, our friendship with this remarkable young man deepened. Through his caring and attentive devotion, he became an essential part of our life. It was unbelievably comforting just to hear his voice on the phone, and as my problems with Bruhs buffeted me about, Tom became my refuge. It was hard to imagine how I had managed before he entered our lives, and I dared not think how desolate I would be without his reassuring support.

To help with Bruhs's care I obtained the services of Yvonne, who had cared for Bruhs's sister Anne until her death several years before. Later as Bruhs's problems intensified, we had to change to a male attendant and were extremely fortunate that Rupert Blearie, whom we had known through SAGE, was available.

Having Rupert in the house to care for Bruhs, it was good to get away, even briefly, from the situation at home one evening in December to see Tom Keith and Jane Young do their clever play, *Histories of Gladys,* at the Courtyard Playhouse in Greenwich Village. It was a fascinating vehicle for those talented young people and it was made more enjoyable for me by including a song, "I'm Allegedly Yours," written by Bruhs and me.

I wrote a brief review:

THOUGHTS ABOUT *GLADYS*

There is a delectable quality about *Gladys,* its imaginative unpredictability, spiked with pungent humor. Jane Young and Thomas Keith take us on an inventive roller-coaster ride that dips into low slapstick and with startling speed propels us to the upper limits.

Gladys is Every Man and Every Woman, and the mirror is held up to the audience to show that each one of us is, in truth, *Gladys. Gladys* puts all the human foibles on display for us to examine, and then turns us inside out with caustic wit and hilarious aplomb.

Young and Keith as a composite *Gladys* are deft and beguiling and conjure up their personal brand of magic. Spend some time with *Gladys* and you too will fall under its spell.

I asked SAGE to print this in their December *Bulletin.* Inasmuch as Tom Keith was a dedicated volunteer for SAGE, they were happy to help boost the play.

Though Rupert was the soul of a caring sensitive professional, he found his patience stretched to the breaking point. In the throes of the dementia, Bruhs would pummel him with his fists, cursing him and shouting at the top of his lungs for help every time Rupert tried to bathe him. Bruhs seemed to have lost all sense of cooperating with a caregiver no matter how loving.

Throughout Bruhs's trauma I had endeavored to keep my

metaphysical beliefs uppermost in my mind. To offset his increasingly difficult behavior, I had tried to remember that he was a prisoner of the dementia that possessed him. But his health deteriorated so steadily it became a gargantuan struggle to maintain my beliefs and translate them into a restrained compassion. Furthermore, as 1990 wore on, I gradually was losing the ability to be objective.

I finally realized we had reached the end of this road when, after a particularly violent and exhausting episode in a matter-of-fact but chilling tone, Bruhs said, "I guess I am going to have to kill you, because you side with all those people who come in and push me around."

I tried not to let him see how shaken I was, but for the first time I felt fear. He could get at the kitchen knives, and who was to say what he might do. I realized with sickening surety that even with Rupert's exemplary efforts, it had become a losing battle. Placing Bruhs under institutional professional care was his only option still open to us.

It was an agonizing decision for me, and one that grew more painful by the day, particularly when I began to search for the "best" place. When I looked at this man in repose, the man with whom I had shared my life for sixty years, I was overwhelmed by the enormity of removing him from his home to a new, unfamiliar environment where his frustrations could be compounded. It was too painful to contemplate, yet I had no other choice, and an effort to find the most satisfactory solution had to become my top priority. I had the valuable support of Arlene Kochman at SAGE, who could draw on her expert knowledge of nursing homes to steer me in the right direction. She finally chose Amsterdam House as the one we should concentrate on. I went to Marilyn Graubert at Bellevue, and she prepared all the necessary papers.

I recalled her words to me when Bruhs had first enrolled for treatment there. She had summed up the devastating impact of Alzheimer's on the other partner in one sentence: "Gean, you have to reconcile yourself to the fact that Bruhs is leaving you, bit by bit." Those words had reverberated as I began to live the nightmare. I realized that she had uttered the ultimate, inescapable truth.

All through these months I had been assailed with doubts about the wisdom of my caring for him. Maybe I had done both of us a disservice by keeping him in this halfway station between ordinary life and the life of the institutionalized. The nutrients I had insisted on trying had not cured him, and each tentative semblance of restoration was a tantalizing straw to cling to before the downward spiral resumed its inexorable progress. It is frightening to realize that one is responsible for another too impaired to think for himself. It is like playing God; my reluctance to play this role had mounted daily. So, I constantly questioned myself, my attitudes, my methods, my decisions, until I was forced to acknowledge that, as inadequate or ineffectual as I felt myself to be at times, no one else would do this for Bruhs. Whatever my shortcomings, it has been up to me to carry on, and in the final analysis, this is what love is all about.

36

Toward a New Life

Now that the die had been cast, the wait began for Amsterdam House to notify us that they had accepted Bruhs. The final wrenching ordeal of transferring him was on hold. As the tearful, sleepless nights finally passed, I tried to adopt a stoic attitude for the time that was left. I had to let go of the past and deal with the present. Putting my loved one in a nursing home was devastating. I had to let go of the past and deal with the present.

One day during that long, difficult period an advertisement in the *New York Times* caught my eye. For a limited time Steinway & Sons offered a trade-in on other makes of pianos at their full cost. My heart began to pound. I had always wanted to own a Steinway grand piano. Why shouldn't I realize my dream? Once back in the 1940s we had had a Steinway, an antique, square piano with a lovely mellow tone. But in no way did it compare to the modern Steinway grand's superb resonance. The offer was more than I could resist.

I got on the phone with Lenny and told him about the ad. I asked him if he could spare the time to meet me at Steinway Hall. Lenny was almost as excited as I was and quickly agreed. I could not leave Bruhs alone, so I hustled him into some clothes and together we boarded a bus for uptown.

Once in Steinway Hall I must have tried ten or twelve different instruments of varying sizes. I tried to include Bruhs by having him sing songs as I played. Lenny's congenial presence made Bruhs willing to go along, even if he didn't understand it.

After playing a glorious seven-foot grand, I was hooked. If Steinway had not allowed me what I had paid for the Yamaha piano, I could never have met the purchase price. It was going to be great to have a real Steinway! Bruhs's care kept me confined to the house every day. What a joy it would be to have this magnificent instrument to play for us both; it would transport us to another world.

Finally, again thanks to Arlene, Amsterdam House called me to announce that a room was available for Bruhs. Rupert helped pack Bruhs's clothing and took us to the nursing home in his car. Tom Keith also accompanied us on the long ride from the Lower East Side to West 112th Street and diverted Bruhs by getting him to sing. Bruhs had no inkling of what this trip meant or the change it would make in our lives.

At Amsterdam House we were joined by Cathy Shugrue, a sweet young intern with SAGE Social Service. As we took Bruhs up to his room, he was totally unaware that this would be his final home. I left him with Rupert, Tom, and Cathy while I went to the intake office and the comptroller's to sign some admission papers. I was glad to get away—the longer I stayed with Bruhs the more I felt my self-control slipping. If I had spent any more time with him, I would have broken down. As it was, I had to fight back tears while talking with the officials, and I did not trust myself to go back to the room to see Bruhs. The others spared me the torture of goodbye. They stayed until he was busy eating lunch, then quietly bowed out. When I got back to our apartment and turned the key in the lock, I felt I was entering a tomb. I was engulfed in abject, desolate grief and loneliness. The feeling overwhelmed me for days and it abated only slowly. The realization that I no longer had Bruhs to care for was disorienting, instead of liberating, and filled me with guilt.

Caring for Bruhs had brought about a complete role reversal. In the past I had leaned heavily on him and had willingly let him assume control of our lives. Bruhs had been capable of home decorating, repairs, and all the rest of managing our apartments. I had always taken the easy way out—"let Bruhs do it." But when his dependence on me increased, like it or not, I had to take charge. I began to realize that I was entirely on my own; what I did with my life from this point on was totally my choice.

I had never adjusted to life on the Lower East Side. And even though I was emotionally and physically exhausted, I knew I would eventually relocate. I had often thought of a return to our old Third Avenue home, but when we left in 1987, the building had gone co-op, and our apartment had been purchased for $150,000, a figure that was totally beyond my reach. When our former Third Avenue neighbor Edith Tanzer phoned to tell me that the old apartment had been vacated and was being offered for sale at a lower figure, my hopes began to grow about "going home again." The demand for co-ops had shrunk drastically. By 1991 real estate in New York City had reached bottom. As part of my awakening independence, I purchased my first home at the age of eighty-three.

Bruhs's nephew Richard had endeared himself to me over the years by his watchful and loving care. I really needed someone to be a part of me—a child. I realized he was the perfect choice. When I broached with Richard my wish to adopt him, he seemed touched. I told him it would be a privilege to have him as my son. What at first appeared to be hesitation on his part was only a wish to think things through, and I was thrilled when this rare and beautiful man consented to my proposal.

Of course the idea of adopting Richard did not come to me overnight. I had known him since he was a child of six. With Bruhs, I had attended his bar mitzvah at thirteen, and probably embarrassed him by hugging and kissing him. Upon his bar mitzvah the thirteen-year-old Jewish boy is recognized as having achieved manhood. Except in the exuberance of winning at sports, American men just don't hug and kiss each other! I had watched Richard grow into a fine youth and move on to college. When he married in 1969, neither Bruhs nor I could attend the wedding because Bruhs was suffering from a severe case of shingles. I was aware of Richard's service in the air force, stationed in England. The next opportunity I had to see him was at the wedding of a cousin, and I remembered feeling, as I watched him dance with his wife, how fortunate she was to have this man as a mate.

Richard's biological father was Bruhs's brother Lee. When Lee died in 1976, we went to the cemetery with his family. After the services Richard found us and offered to drive us to the train. He waited with us for the train, then, with a warm embrace, said tenderly, "Take good care of each other." Such depth of caring in his tone communicated his feeling for us; I had not forgotten that moment. Nor had I forgotten that Richard had visited us in 1981 to tell us that his marriage of twelve years was being amicably dissolved.

His sharing his innermost feelings with us struck a deeply responsive chord in me and heightened my wish to be closer to him. Perhaps the idea of adoption had its beginning then.

Richard Harwood Brown officially became my son on February 27, 1991, before New York's surrogate judge Eve Preminger. We celebrated the event at (where else?) Fedora's Restaurant. Close friends—Rupert Blearie, Tom Keith, Howard Sosnicki, John Harbster, Hal Gomeau, and Mary Jean Sanford—shared the occasion and the happiness it brought Richard and me.

Thomas Wolfe once said, "You can't go home again!" Yet in 1991 that is precisely what I managed to do. By returning to the Third Avenue apartment that I had occupied with Bruhs for twenty-three years, I had my old Gramercy Park neighbors back. My exile in the no-man's-land of the Lower East Side was ended. Once again I was back in civilized territory where I could bask in a heightened quality of life and shop to my heart's content in my favorite stores, all open on Saturdays.

Moving my household involved thousands of details, but with the support of my new son, I had a different outlook. No problem seemed insurmountable, and eventually all the pieces fell into place. My "homecoming" had been blessed in all sorts of ways. Rupert's attention to and sensitive nursing care for Bruhs had made Rupert a vital and essential part of our family, and now my needs became his primary concern. The weekly visits to Bruhs in the nursing home were made easier when either Rupert or Tom accompanied me.

Mr. Stern, a gentleman in his late nineties, occupied the room with Bruhs. He was extremely deaf, but very alert. He occupied himself with a daily perusal of the *New York Times* and was writing a book about the inadequacy of the building's safety regulations. He and Bruhs seemed to hit it off rather well. On one occasion my visit coincided with a visit by Mr. Stern's son and granddaughter. When I came into the room, the young woman turned to me and asked Bruhs, "Is this your brother?" Bruhs's surprising reply was swift and to the point: "No, he's my husband." Perhaps the girl was unprepared for this statement, but I was enormously pleased that Bruhs was still aware of our relationship, and that he had every intention of declaring it.

Bruhs gradually adjusted to life in the nursing home. Although he had limited cognitive ability, his first reaction when he saw me was to cry. This upset me. I attributed his tears to his recognition of our relationship and his frustration at being unable to voice his feelings and his fears. He was unable to formulate his earlier entreaties "Can't we be together, somewhere?" or "I only want to be with you."

The nursing home had several pianos, and I would take Bruhs by the hand to one and play for him. But he no longer recognized our songs. He had long since stopped trying to sing along, and he often fell asleep while I was playing. I hoped that the monotony of Bruhs's existence did not oppress him as it did me.

When I learned that SAGE had formed a Caretakers and Bereavement Support Group, I signed up. With a great sense of expectation I attended my first session in early 1991. It was comforting to be welcomed warmly by a group of gay men and have their sympathetic ear as I related my problems. They conveyed a genuine sense of caring.

At the next visit, taking turns in the circle, each repeated for another time his previous account. Everyone seemed trapped in his grief. By the third visit I began to question what sort of goal the group had for improving their outlook. I tried to suggest that we strive for lifting and brightening our spirits. My suggestions were met with instant rejection. One of the men, who had been attending since the death of his partner two years before, took pains to remind me that they all came to grieve. I became aware that most of the group were quite content to flounder in a pool of self-pity. Week after week I was more and more oppressed by their outlook. They seemed to prefer sitting in a darkened room in sackcloth and ashes, not permitting a bit of warm sunlight to enter their lives.

Because of the demands of Rupert's nursing career and Tom Keith's theatrical activities, they became unable to accompany me on my visits to see Bruhs. I found it increasingly difficult to handle these visits. At the entrance to the nursing home, my eyes would fill with tears and I did not want to approach Bruhs if I could not be cheerful and upbeat.

It was a serious dilemma for me. Then an acquaintance casually, but pointedly, remarked, "Well, after sixty years with someone, you can't just put them in a nursing home and abandon them." Abandonment was the furthest thing from my mind. But I did feel guilt. I needed to resolve the situation. My internist at Bellevue Hospital, Dr. Thomas McRae, with his usual sympathetic interest referred me to a staff psychotherapist, Dr. Lucia Kellar.

From the first, Dr. Kellar seemed open to the details of my relationship with Bruhs, and I felt comfortable discussing any problem with her. She demonstrated that she respected me as a person, listening carefully to my views and opinions. Something about her facial structure reminded me of Martina Navratilova, for whom I have had a great admiration both as a highly accomplished athlete and as a gay activist. This was definitely a plus in my visits with Dr. Kellar.

I saw her each week for over a year to sort out my feelings and establish a sense of direction. By talking about it, I was able to handle the stress of the nursing home visits a little more easily. Dr. Kellar helped me address my growing despair at how negligible the benefits of the visits were, given Bruhs's ever-fading ability to recognize me. The damage from each visit devastated me for days afterward. I finally did stop visiting him, remaining in close touch with the staff. Dr. Kellar reduced my appointments to once a month. I will always be grateful for the sensitive and dedicated therapy she provided. Her help was sent to me in the most trying period of my life.

37

The Music of the Two Oldest Gay Men in America

In January of 1995, my son Richard informed me that his partner Matthew had secured three days at the Troy Savings Bank Music Hall, in his capacity as its business manager, to record my music. This hall has legendary acoustical qualities. Musicians come from all over to record there. I was unnerved by the short notice, but launched into feverish practice sessions. Because I was required to do the program from memory, since there was little written music, I needed to recollect many pieces I had not played in a very long time.

On a cold January night, we assembled in the Music Hall for the first of the recording sessions. As I sat at the nine-foot concert Steinway, I took a deep breath and let the Spirit move through me. It was sheer magic; the music just flowed. I never felt nervous; I never became flustered. Only one song out of the four classical instrumentals and thirty-eight song melodies presented any problems, and after several days and some laughter, it was all recorded. The expertise of the sound engineer, Danny Toma, helped a great deal, due not only to his ability but also to the sensitivity of one gay man for another.

With no written music, I kept Bruhs's lyrics in front of me so that I would not embellish them, as I sometimes do. On the second night, Danny announced that there would be space to fill on the two-CD set and we should consider adding a few medleys. This was relatively uncharted territory for me. As I played, I selected songs for each medley, without repeating them, and provided improvised segues from one song to another. Even this impromptu demand seemed natural. When it was all finished, I went up to the recording room three floors above to receive a warm hug from Danny and compliments for my performance. When he played back some of what he had recorded, I could not believe the quality of the sound. Listening to the compact disc, I am sure that on those three nights in January 1995, while I appeared to be completely alone in the hall, I had an angel on my shoulder.

Early in 1995, Tom Wilson Weinberg approached me about a project of his. He had been commissioned by the New York City Gay Men's Chorus to write an approximately fifteen-minute mini-musical, which they would perform at their June concert at Carnegie Hall. He had briefly considered President Buchanan as the subject since Buchanan never married, had a gentleman-friend, and might well have been gay. But Tom decided against Buchanan because there was no interesting peg on which to fashion his music. Instead, having had a chance to look at my manuscript, he asked permission to use our story. This was totally unexpected recognition, and I realized immediately the honor of being chosen to be one of the subjects of a NYC Gay Men's Chorus piece. Tom Wilson Weinberg's *Sixty Years With Bruhs and Gean* began rehearsals in May and I was invited to attend. Tom had divided the action between three different sets of men. Two youngsters were the youthful Bruhs and Gean first meeting as lovers. Two more mature men did the mid-portion of our lives; an older pair portrayed Bruhs and Gean late in life. Tom's score is tender, bright, and touching by turns as he skillfully condenses sixty years into twelve minutes of full-bodied sound.

I got to know several of the members of the NYCGMC, particularly Dr. William Brown Jr., who played the eldest of the three Geans. He has been a gracious figure in my life from the first meeting. After he was assigned the role of the oldest Gean with NYCGMC in Tom Wilson Weinberg's composition, he lost no time in contacting me to learn about my life. He wished to strengthen his characterization by knowing everything about me. A deep and lasting friendship has developed between us. Ever attentive, I welcome his almost daily "phone hugs" and treasure the card he once sent that read, "A hug is something that warms and charms. Maybe the reason God gave us arms."

Again, as with the recording, Richard took matters in hand and completed all the details of a stunning cocktail hour and CD release party on June 22, 1995, at the Russian Tea Room. Over one hundred people attended. The *Music of the Two Oldest Gay Men in America* was then released.

Afterward, everyone went next door to Carnegie Hall for Tom Wilson Weinberg's premiere of *Sixty Years with Bruhs and Gean*. I sat with Tom, his mother, and his partner, Dr. John Whyte. In the second half of the program, as the chorus stood poised to perform Tom's work, the chorus director, Gary Miller, spoke to the audience. He first introduced Tom, who took a bow. Then he said that in the audience that evening was one of the "Two oldest gay men in America," and asked me to stand. I received a standing ovation. It was totally unexpected, and it probably will be the most unforgettable experience of my life. To have this kind of recognition at age eighty-six is unbelievably sweet.

I still create and compose. The release of the CD means that my music was at last published, and my long dreamed-for membership in the American Society of Composers, Authors, and Publishers was established.

Bruhs Mero, my lifelong partner, died on August 10, 1995, but my grieving had started much earlier when I learned that his illness was irreversible and our life together had ended. At his death, I actually experienced relief that he was at last released from the prison of Alzheimer's. I have a comforting belief about what we term death. I choose to view it not as an ending but as a doorway to another dimension. The loved one is separated from us but is not lost. There is a continuity of Spirit.

Less than a week after Bruhs died I began to have dream visits from him. There never seemed to be an opportunity for a dialogue between us, but what he had to say was both inspiring and illuminating. Everything he said deserved great respect because he had a much wider vantage point. On his first visit his tone was reassuring. He encouraged me to live my life to its fullest. "Life on earth is meant to be enjoyed," he said, "and should be lived with love for every living thing on its surface." His closing thought, "There is no sin except not loving enough," will always be with me.

When I mentioned this dream to some of my friends, they were highly skeptical of my opinion that it was a "visit." They felt I had only given voice to my own ideas by ascribing them to Bruhs to give them more authority.

I had an even greater feeling that the second dream was a "visit." Bruhs spoke of the many hours of study we had done together, poring over first the Bible, then volumes of Rosicrucian philosophy. He recalled how troubled we both were by the chapter and verse of Leviticus that condemns homosexual acts as an abomination. His words from then on were as if an adult were patiently explaining something to a child, "The Bible is God's word, but not every word in the Bible is sacrosanct. It has gone through many translations, interpretations, and misinterpretations. Many parts of the Old Testament are historical, but it contains great truth and lessons, if we can recognize them. The teachings of Jesus changed the face of God from the vengeful Jehovah of the Old Testament to a loving Father and taught us to love others as we love ourselves."

The dream ended, but I felt I had corroboration for the historical aspect of the Old Testament. I had long held the view that because the ancient Jewish people were in virtual bondage, they needed to increase by multiplying. Anything that interfered with that had to be strongly condemned, as was done in Leviticus. A favorite song from Tom Wilson Weinberg's musical review *Get Used to It* is entitled "My Leviticus." Tom's clever use of satire refreshingly sets this issue to lyric and music. As Tom pointedly expresses in his song, what was expedient for biblical times and had a purpose then has been distorted into a moralistic issue. Today, in an overpopulated world, much of Leviticus is not relevant. I suppose we should be grateful that Moses did not bring it down from the mountain as the Eleventh Commandment. We should welcome the forward movement throughout the United States to remove sodomy from the law books. The term is again a throwback to the ancient city of Sodom and is a blanket indictment of a variety of sexual offenses, covering consensual as well as coercive acts, and should be retired.

I had experienced unconditional love with Bruhs and had been singularly blessed to have had over sixty years with a beautiful, creative, courageous man. I was surely as fulfilled as one could be. I felt it was not realistic, at age eighty-six, to expect a romantic alliance with anyone, but I knew I must get on with my life. I am grateful to Bruhs for preparing me to accept love in whatever manner it is expressed and wherever I find it. I have, therefore, developed warm and rewarding friendships.

In March of 1996, we traveled to Asheville, North Carolina, for the spring concert of their Gay Men's Chorus. Austin Probst, the director, had arranged a program that provided a beautiful showcase for the *Music of the Two Oldest Gay Men in America.* He performed "I Want to Be Bad" as a solo, followed by "I'll Learn to Dream Again" sung by Andy Reed. I was then given the opportunity to perform five of my songs as a soloist. The program concluded, with a performance of two of my favorites sung by the Asheville Gay Men's Chorus, "It's Only My Heart" and "Come and Take My Hand," which Austin Probst had skillfully arranged. The audience for each performance was warmly appreciative and it gave me a great lift to finally hear my songs done by a group that obviously loved the material.

I have compassion for all who are separated from loved ones and am especially mindful of those who shared but a brief measure of life together. I am convinced that, as there are many faces of love, love will manifest itself in some form if we open ourselves to it. We must think of love, and believe. In the words of Rod McKuen, "It matters not who we love or how we love, only that we love."

"Thoughts" are "things." Before any creation became tangible, it was a thought. So it is important to watch our thoughts and to make them positive. Shakespeare said, "There is no good or bad, but thinking makes it so." We must not let fear rule our lives. We may bear different labels that we attach to ourselves and each other by early programming, but we are all traveling the same path. And we are all connected. I believe that we are all here to learn, and those lessons we fail to recognize will be repeated until we do.

At times, as I listen to the media, I am overwhelmed by the feeling that everyone is consumed by greed, motivated by chicanery, and inured to mindless violence. But I am unwilling to accept this negative portrayal of humanity because I firmly believe there is a groundswell of people all over the world who are foregoing materialism and are beginning to search for answers from spiritual sources. In line with this thinking, there is a growing emphasis on how we view our relationships, and a recognition that bodily joys and sensations do not make the person complete.

A friend recently said to me, "You appear to have a firm belief in God. I have never been a church-going or religious-minded person. Yet when I see the peace that your belief brings to your life, I want to believe. How does one find God?"

As simply as I can say it, this is how I feel about God. He is a personal Father figure that I know loves me and to whom I can turn whenever I feel the need. He also is a part of every living thing. If He is everywhere, then of course, He is in the church, the synagogue, the mosque, and the pages of the Bible. But you can find Him as well in the heart of a flower, the wings of a butterfly, the waves that caress the shore, the glory of a sunset, or the softness of the moonlight. It is possible to communicate with Him in a centered meditative state and His answers will always come to you in "the still small voice" that speaks within. It would be wonderful if everyone realized that as God is a part of us, so are we a part of Him, and nothing can separate us from His love.

On October 22, 1995, there was a memorial service for Bruhs, attended by more than sixty of his friends and family. I particularly chose Congregation Beth Simchat Torah, the gay synagogue, for the ceremony, because of the happy association with SAGE socials there that Bruhs had enjoyed so much. I was determined to keep the event as a celebration of our life together with no sad overtones. Richard had a program printed that listed opening remarks by me, followed by the deeply moving Jewish prayer for the dead, the kaddish. One of Bruhs's nieces, Jean Shulman, gave a warm and loving testimonial to the importance of Bruhs in her life. After her remarks, "Come and Take My Hand," written by us in 1933, was beautifully sung by Matthew Moross. I accompanied him on the piano. Joan Schwartz, another niece, gave a touching account of how deeply Bruhs had affected her life. Tom Keith followed with an eloquent reading from Walt Whitman's "Song of My Self." Tom Wilson Weinberg performed excerpts from his musical, *Sixty Years with Bruhs and Gean*, which had premiered recently at Carnegie Hall.

A responsive reading from 1 Corinthians was led by Richard, my son and Bruhs's nephew. The closing lines particularly underlined the theme of the day: "So—faith, hope, love—abide these three; but the greatest of these is love."

After a beautiful tribute to Bruhs and to our relationship by Adrian Mayer, president emeritus of the SAGE board, Matthew Moross sang the Mero/Harwood song featured in the documentary *Silent Pioneers*, "It's Only My Heart." My final remarks brought to a close what had been a tender, loving, but happy tribute to the man I will always love.

In silence I composed this prayer to him:

To Bruhs, my partner, my beloved—
You were never closer than you are this moment.
Each day I breathe your name to morning skies.
At eventide your name is on my lips
To ask God's blessing.
One day, when it is time,
We will meet in joyous reunion.
With the sound of strings and muted trumpets
A heavenly choir will join us in singing
Our song—"I Have You Back Again."
Till then, know that we are one,
That you are eternally loved.

The Tom Wilson Weinberg opus *Sixty Years With Bruhs and Gean* was repeated by NYCGMC in June 1996 at Alice Tully Hall and Dr. Bill Brown again reprised his role, which he so enjoys, as the eldest Gean. Later, in July, the piece was performed in Tampa, Florida, as part of a week-long GALA Choruses Festival. The Asheville, North Carolina Gay Men's Chorus repeated several of the Mero/Harwood songs that they had done the previous March. It would appear that our life story and our music was being told and heard.

In October 1995, I composed the music for a poem of mine, "Assignment for Today." The final message I wish to leave is this. In whatever way you can, and as soon as you can, put aside attitudes of mourning. Lift your spirits by the knowledge that we are not alone and that we are loved. As soon as possible, let go of the past. Calmly position yourselves in the now, and move on.

Epilogue

Because music has filled so much of my life, I have always thought of life in terms of music: it is a symphony in process. It has a beginning, development quietly building toward crescendo, followed by diminuendo. The mood evolves, from bright allegro to steadier allegretto, then to sober andante and at last to somber adagio. And so my relationship with Bruhs, spanning six decades, I think of in musical terms—the throaty sonority of a cello, the gentle purity of the flute, an oboe's insistently seductive voice, the mellow sweetness of violins, or the thunderous clamor of the timpani, all the instruments together describe the musical fabric that our life with each other has woven. The orchestra is poised to perform and the symphony begins. The notes come in their proper places, with their harmonies and dissonances, and we move through a rhythmic series of progressions of chords and melodies that are alternately tender, bittersweet, maudlin, or majestic, to the inevitable finale. I have tried to gather all the golden threads and make them shine for others as they have for us.

I have never questioned my own homosexuality or asked, "Why was I created this way?" Scientists have studied the brains of gay and straight men and noted differences in their hypothalamuses. Other studies have concluded that there is indeed a genetic basis to sexual preferences. If these findings improve the attitude of society toward gay people, that is fine. I am content to be what God created, and going about my Father's business, I will continue to view myself as healthy and normal. Scripture often calls for "multiplying," but never prescribes "dividing," which is what society does in separating gays and straights. God is love and expresses only love through every living thing. Unless we learn that lesson, we are doomed to repeat our mistakes over and over.

Throughout my professional life, such as it was, I had always felt I stood in Bruhs's shadow. He held center stage and I was only a prop to his performance. Whatever musical potential I may have possessed, at best modest, was only partially realized, forced out of me by Bruhs's persistent persuasion and insistence and love. In all the years of performing I really never had approval of my playing. I never knew the satisfaction that comes with solo accomplishment.

Metaphysical philosophy has carried me through trouble and has given me knowledge of why we are here and where we go when we leave. I have an idea of this life as a class in which we struggle with lessons to be learned to better prepare ourselves. I have known the tension that comes from feeling that I am being constantly tested. I have sensed the value of commitment and love declared openly and honestly. My love for Bruhs is the only possession of which I can truly claim ownership, the only thing of any permanence in my life. Everything else has merely been loaned me for use in this life. Even my homes were temporary, to accommodate the body, not places in which the spirit feels tranquil residence.

Now as I come down to the end, I am ready to accept the role of a transient. I am more at peace with myself than I have been before in this tenure on earth. Perhaps now I am prepared to welcome other worlds and other challenges. My overriding wish is that my future may behold a blessed continuity of spirit with Bruhs and an even greater measure of mutual fulfillment for both of us.

The two people about whom I have written—Bruhs and myself—no longer fully exist in an earthly sense, and I wait for the spiritual to fully assert itself and move onward. I had never envisioned the relationship that Bruhs and I had in this life ending in this fashion. But my early study of metaphysics had taught me that the laws of karma must be acknowledged. To effect a balance, it has been a source of deep encouragement to know that the soul profits from seeming adversity as we move along the difficult path.

We all travel the same path. But some learn to walk in the light and others stay in the darkness. Lessons are constantly being offered to us, and the choice to accept or reject them is ours. What we fail to recognize as a lesson will be repeated until we do.

Negative forces are constantly at work in an unceasing effort to separate all of us. NYNEX adopted "We are all connected" as an advertising slogan some time ago. Repetition has made it a cliché, but it still carries the germ of truth: we are all connected. But we must strive to be aware that this is indeed so.

Today I am no longer the person who began this book more than ten years ago. I am aware that everything is always changing. I have released my grip on the past and choose not to be concerned with the future. I try to keep my focus on making the most of today.

I intend to shun comparisons, forgo judgment, strive to be forgiving, motivated by the unity and guidance of Spirit in the place of Ego. I leave the reader with the thoughts best expressed by this recent poem:

Assignment For Today

by Gean Harwood

We only have today.
Graven images of yesterday
that claimed us as their own
have crumbled into dust.
The glittering Chimera
that calls itself tomorrow
may never show its face.
We only have today—
to make the silent journey
deep within ourselves
to know the source of strength
through peace and love
to claim the birthright of serenity
to hear the music of the spheres.
We only have today—
to nurture every needy soul
to comfort the disconsolate
to give the fallen hope for their discouragement
to embrace all men as brothers
for, in truth, we are all one.

Index